BLACKSTONE'S GUIDE TO

The Fraud Act 200

BLACKSTONE'S GUIDE TO

The Fraud Act 2006

Simon Farrell QC, Nicholas Yeo,
and Guy Ladenburg

OXFORD
UNIVERSITY PRESS

OXFORD
UNIVERSITY PRESS

Great Clarendon Street, Oxford OX2 6DP
United Kingdom

Oxford University Press is a department of the University of Oxford.
It furthers the University's objective of excellence in research, scholarship,
and education by publishing worldwide.

Oxford is a registered trade mark of Oxford University Press in the UK
and in certain other countries

© Simon Farrell QC, Nicholas Yeo, Guy Ladenburg 2007

British Library Cataloguing in Publication Data
Data available

Library of Congress Cataloging in Publication Data
Data available

ISBN 978-0-19-929624-8

Contents—Summary

Contents—Detailed

Foreword

One might think it self-evident that every criminal statute should be comprehensible to the general public, but these days how often can this be said? The Fraud Act 2006, due to come into force on 15 January 2007, may, however, prove to be a welcome exception, for its stated purpose is to make the law relating to offences of fraud easier to understand and apply. Nevertheless, this important new Act, with its abolition of the 'deception offences' contained in the Theft Acts 1968 and 1978, and with its philosophy that fraud should now be in essence a 'dishonesty-based' offence, still requires careful elucidation and exposition.

I am pleased to say that this book provides just the assistance that is needed. Its three authors are highly experienced and respected criminal lawyers, much of whose courtroom work is in the field of fraud. They have an enviable theoretical and practical understanding of the 'old' law, and they have made a close study of the new Act from its early beginnings in the office of the Law Commission to its appearance as a parliamentary Bill. They have followed the passage of the Bill through all of its stages, and have observed, sometimes at first hand, how the new law has been shaped by consultation and debate. Their research and insights into the thinking behind the provisions of the Act are a valuable bonus, making the text all the more fascinating and informative.

The authors have sought to place the Act in context. They have examined the new offences not merely against the background of the old, but in the context of the law of fraud as a whole. To this end they have helpfully included in the book those offences of fraud not covered by the Act, but which have been preserved, including a penetrating analysis of the retained and controversial offence of conspiracy to defraud. This is illustrated with examples of how the law may be expected to work in practice and with specimen forms of indictments. The result of their efforts and expertise is to be seen in the following pages, and I am confident that this Guide will quickly establish itself as a leading work on the Act—an indispensable aid to the practitioner and judge alike.

Having followed through the provisions of the Act, in Chapter 9 the authors go on to deal with 'case management' and 'sentencing'. Here they include in accessible form much of the reference material trial lawyers will need, and this Foreword would not be complete without reference to these valuable passages.

I have mentioned the work of the judge. When the Fraud Bill was introduced, one of its aims was said 'to encompass most forms of fraudulent conduct within a law that is flexible enough to deal with developing technology. That could prove to be particularly beneficial in complex and serious fraud cases, and could shorten the time taken by each trial and lead to more efficient prosecutions'. It is to be hoped that the Act will advance these important aims, but the objective of judicial trial management is not just to make the case shorter; it is to ensure that the evidence is concentrated upon the central allegations of dishonesty, and that the trial will be bearable for judge, jury, witnesses and, by no means least, defendants. To this end the judge must inspire confidence that he understands the case, and is resolved to ensure that the trial process will focus upon the issues, at the same time respecting within these limits the needs of the parties to present their cases fully and fairly. Given that our trials are conducted in an adversarial system, how this can be achieved in a judge-alone trial is a matter for legitimate concern. The Fraud (Trials without a Jury) Bill sets out to implement s 43 of the Criminal Justice Act 2003. Quite apart from the deep wound that this would inflict upon the principle that indictable crimes should be tried by judge and jury, it must surely be a matter for disquiet that judges may well be called upon to decide whether the prosecution should be entitled to withhold information from the defence under the law relating to Public Interest Immunity or even stayed on the grounds of abuse of process of the court, how the case should be 'trial managed', which charges to try, what material should be disclosed to the defence as being relevant to the issues in the case, which evidence to admit in the trial and which to exclude as being irrelevant or unduly prejudicial, whom should be believed, whether the defendant is proved to be guilty, and, if so, what sentence he should serve.

The maximum sentence for crimes under the Act is 10 years' imprisonment. When it comes to crimes of fraud and money laundering, the scope of illegal transactions is now so great (ranging from hundreds or thousands of pounds to very many millions) that it will be interesting to see what the Sentencing Guidelines Council recommends. The authors do rightly concentrate upon the important subject of plea-bargaining, and its future development. In this regard they make timely reference to the little known but intriguing provisions of the Serious Crime and Police Act 2005 which enable a defendant who pleads guilty having given assistance to the authorities investigating crime, and who offers more (for example, by agreeing to give evidence), to receive specified additional credit for this, on pain of his sentence being increased later if he fails to fulfil his promises.

The Fraud Advisory Panel booklet, *The Human Cost of Fraud*, begins with the words: 'The victims of fraud tend to attract little attention and limited sympathy. The reasons are obvious. The tendency is to think of fraud as a crime without pain; as a crime that afflicts the well-off; or, quite simply, as one that people suffer because of their own greed or stupidity'. It goes on to explain how in many cases nothing could be further from the truth, and how fraud can have a devastating effect upon its victims, some of whom may be unknown to, or not even in the contemplation of, the fraudsters at the time they commit their offences. As vast sums, running into many billions of pounds, are dishonestly obtained each year from the public purse, corporate institutions, and private individuals, there is certainly a need to alter any distorted perception of the seriousness of fraud. It is hoped that the Fraud Act 2006, served so well by this excellent guide, will play a central role in doing so.

H H J Geoffrey Rivlin QC
Southwark Crown Court
London

5 January 2007

Table of Cases

References are to Paragraph Numbers

Table of Legislation

References are to Paragraph Numbers

UK Statutory Instruments

1

INTRODUCTION

A. THE MAIN PROVISIONS OF THE FRAUD ACT 2006

The Fraud Act 2006 represents the most radical change in the law of criminal fraud   1.01
since 1968. The Act came into force on 15 January 2007 (SI 2006/3200). As with
all criminal statutes its provisions apply to conduct after that date. The old law will
continue to apply to earlier conduct. Although it is a short Act it will have the effect
of significantly altering the way in which the criminal courts deal with fraud. Its
main provisions are:

(a) The abolition of all the deception offences in the Theft Acts 1968 and 1978.

(b) The creation of a new offence of fraud which can be committed in three ways:
  (i)   fraud by false representation,
  (ii) fraud by abuse of position, or
  (iii) fraud by failure to disclose,

  carrying a maximum sentence of ten years' imprisonment. The new offence
  relies heavily on dishonesty and does away with any requirement for the Crown
  to prove operative deception.

(c) The introduction of wide offences of possessing or making or supplying any
  articles for use in fraud.

(d) The creation of a new offence of fraudulent trading which can be committed by
  any person (individual or sole trader) who carries on any 'business' fraudulently
  or with intent to defraud creditors.

(e) The replacement of the offence of dishonestly obtaining services by deception in the Theft Act with an offence of dishonestly obtaining services, with no need for the Crown to prove that any deception took place.

(f) The retention of the common law offence of conspiracy to defraud, despite a strong recommendation from the Law Commission that it should be abolished and attempts to achieve this as the Bill passed through Parliament.

B. DRIVERS BEHIND THE NEW FRAUD LAW

1.02   In certain respects the law has been simplified through a return to many aspects of pre-1968 jurisprudence, but the 2006 Act also represents a new era in the law of fraud. Although the Theft Act 1968 was heralded as a new dawn, a modern law for modern times, it has since received much judicial and academic criticism. Many of its provisions led to technical arguments and practical difficulties in its application. The new fraud law sweeps away technicalities but has been criticized for creating offences which rely too heavily on dishonesty. The danger is that one jury might find conduct dishonest while another will not. There are also 'certainty of law' issues which arise under Article 7 ECHR where offences are not adequately defined.

1.03   The aim of the 2006 Act is to widen the law of fraud so that prosecuting fraudsters is made easier. It arises out of the Law Commission's Report of July 2002,[1] whose stated aim was to broaden the law of fraud, while at the same time eliminating problems, and to allow for the abolition of the common law offence of conspiracy to defraud. The Law Commission hoped that the new law would offer 'a single, comprehensive definition of criminal fraud, which can be used to make fraud indictments simpler and more self explanatory'.[2]

1.04   In the event, conspiracy to defraud was not abolished despite a number of amendments being tabled during the passage of the Bill through Parliament. The Attorney General Lord Goldsmith said that there were some circumstances in which the offence of conspiracy to defraud would still be necessary. There would be cases where such a charge would still be appropriate and an easier way of prosecuting fraud cases. The Attorney General announced[3] that new guidance would be published on when the use of conspiracy to defraud was the proper charge. He identified two sorts of case: firstly, where the interests of justice can be served only by presenting to a court an overall picture that cannot be achieved by charging a series of substantive offences or statutory conspiracy and, secondly, cases where the conduct is such that it can only be prosecuted as conspiracy to defraud.

---

[1] Law Commission, *Fraud* (Law Com No 276, 2002), available at <http://www.lawcom.gov.uk/docs/lc276.pdf> and Law Commission *Legislating the Criminal Code: Fraud and Deception* (Consultation Paper No 155, 1999) available at <http://www.lawcom.gov.uk/docs/cp155.pdf>.

[2] 'News from the Law Commission', 30 July 2002; available at <http://www.lawcom.gov.uk/docs/lc276sum.pdf>.

[3] *Hansard*, HL 14 March 2006 col 1115.

1. The Fraud Review of July 2006

A driving force behind the new law has been the Government's strategy to combat **1.05**
fraud. The new fraud law is part of the Government's wider plan expressed in the
Fraud Review of 24 July 2006. On that date the Attorney General announced a
package of measures designed to make prosecuting fraudsters easier. These included:

(a) the establishment of a Financial Court jurisdiction so that different proceedings
arising out of serious fraud cases can be brought together;

(b) the extension of sentencing options;

(c) allowing plea bargaining as an alternative to a full trial;

(d) the establishment of a National Fraud Strategic Authority;

(e) forming a national lead police force based in the City of London Fraud Squad;
and

(f) establishing a National Fraud Reporting Centre.

At the same time the Attorney General announced that the Government intended **1.06**
to bring forward a stand-alone bill to permit non-jury trials in a limited range of
serious and complex fraud cases. Such a bill was announced in the Queen's
Speech in November 2006. Section 43 of the Criminal Justice Act 2003, which
makes provision for non-jury trials in serious fraud cases, cannot be brought into
force without a resolution of both Houses of Parliament. The intention of the
Government is to bring serious fraud cases under the umbrella of a new fraud court
jurisdiction without the need, in the event of trials, for there to be a jury trying
the case.

2. UK International Obligations

The 2006 Act is consistent with the UK's anti-fraud international obligations **1.07**
reflected in the EU's Convention on the Protection of the European Community's
Financial Interests of 1995 and also its Framework Decision of 28 May 2001
on combating fraud. It is also in line with the Third EC Money Laundering
Directive published in November 2005. Within two years the UK, along with
other Member States, will be required to bring into force stricter money laundering
laws to ensure, for example, that new and stricter verification, identification, and
reporting procedures are put in place. In addition, increased customer due diligence
requirements, new sanctions, and a 'risk based' approach will be introduced.[4]

3. Extent of the Fraud Problem

Fraud has been on the increase. The number of reported offences of fraud and **1.08**
forgery rose from 174,742 in 1991 to 317,900 in 2003–04.[5] The cost of fraud in

---

[4] Ie, special attention to be given to certain high-risk individuals and accounts.
[5] DCA, *A Fairer Deal for Legal Aid* (Cm 6591, 2005).

2000 was estimated to be around £14 billion per year (equivalent to about £230 per head of the population), taking no account of undetected fraud.[6] The Government lost £11.9 billion in VAT revenue in 2002–03 and benefit fraud costs £2 billion per year.[7] According to some estimates the figure had risen to £340 per head in 2004 (the equivalent of £16 billion per year)[8] or the equivalent to 1.4% of gross domestic product. Over half of all businesses report that they have been defrauded and 49% of people are either victims or know victims of a credit card fraud.[9]

4. Pre-1968 Jurisprudence Reflected in the Fraud Act 2006

1.09 The 2006 Act returns to the pre-1968 Theft Act idea that it is not so much what the victim of a fraud thought but rather what was the intention of the fraudster. In this sense the 2006 Act moves away from operative deception on the mind of the victim being important and back towards the idea of dishonest false pretence being the basis of criminal liability. The reason for this is so that a move can be made towards simplicity and away from technicality. The new fraud law criminalizes the conduct of the defendant rather than focusing on the effect or result of what he has done.

1.10 It would be wrong though to suggest that the 2006 Act is merely a return to the days of the old larceny laws which existed before the 1968 Theft Act. The old law of fraud was complex, illogical, and often obscure. The Larceny Acts of 1861 and 1916 had never represented a new beginning: rather, they sought to consolidate a number of other statutes and common law rules which had been created over hundreds of years.

1.11 The difficulties prior to the Theft Act 1968 stemmed from the basic definition of the crime of larceny, which was limited to the taking of a thing from the possession of another without consent. This meant, for example, that a servant could not steal his master's goods as he already had possession of them. Such difficulties were solved by a series of illogical and ingenious interventions by the judiciary and by piecemeal statutory reform.

1.12 For example, it was held that a servant did not possess his master's goods even though he held them in his hands. Thus the servant could be convicted of larceny. Problems arose when another stole property which belonged to the master but which was in the possession of the servant. In the prosecution of the thief it was necessary for the law to hold that the servant did possess his master's property. It followed from this that the servant in the eyes of the criminal law was both in possession and not in possession of his master's goods at the same time, depending on who stole them.

1.13 To solve the numerous difficulties which had arisen as a result of the basic law of larceny statutory offences were created. These included obtaining property by

---

[6] National Economic Research Associates, *Economic Cost of Fraud: a report for the Home Office and the Serious Fraud Office* (July 2000).

[7] DCA, *A Fairer Deal for Legal Aid* (Cm 6591, 2005) para 5.37.

[8] Report by Norwich Union, November 2005, available at <http://www.aviva.com/index.asp?pageid =317> and also quoted at <http://www.thisismoney.co.uk>.

[9] DCA, *A Fairer Deal for Legal Aid* (Cm 6591, 2005) para 5.36.

false pretences, embezzlement, fraudulent conversion, larceny by a bailee, obtaining credit by fraud, and false accounting.

5. Problems with the Theft Act 1968

The aim of the Theft Act 1968 was to sweep away all the earlier difficulties. 1.14 However, it failed to have this effect. Since its introduction the deception offences, in particular, have been bedevilled by technical argument. The post-1968 problems had been foreshadowed in the minority view of the Law Commission in its Eighth Report which led to the Theft Act of 1968 in the first place. The minority expressed the view that it was undesirable to have a fraud offence too reliant on operative deception. The reason given was that such an offence would lead to technical distinctions and submissions which would cause hours of semantic argument divorced from the true merits of the case. The minority recommended an offence of dishonestly using deception for the purpose of gain. This proposal was rejected at the time but now we have come full circle and the minority view has prevailed in the Fraud Act 2006.

Lord Goff in *Preddy*,[10] a case which epitomized the technical difficulties of the 1.15 Theft Act 1968, said that the minority view of the Law Commission in its Eighth Report had been 'prescient' and that they had been correct in deciding that the nature of the loss and the relationship between the loss and the illegitimate gain ought to be irrelevant to the definition of fraud.

The Theft Act 1968 and subsequent legislation produced a large number of 1.16 technical attacks. *Preddy* was not alone. There were a number of other cases involving the deception offences: *Duru*,[11] *Halai*,[12] *King*,[13] *Mitchell*,[14] and *Manjdadria*.[15] All argued that the consequences that they had brought about by deception did not amount to a deception offence.

One other criticism of the post-1968 fraud law was that there were too many 1.17 different offences, which led to prosecutors frequently choosing the wrong ones and making mistakes. In cases such as *Gomez*,[16] in which the House of Lords had to decide the issue of appropriation, there would have been no argument if the defendant had been charged with obtaining by deception rather than theft. In addition, many of the offences, although distinct, overlapped with each other, causing confusion.

C. CHRONOLOGY OF THE PASSAGE OF THE FRAUD BILL THROUGH PARLIAMENT

The Fraud Bill was published on 25 May 2005 in the House of Lords and received 1.18 its first reading then with the second reading taking place on 22 June. The Bill

---

[10] [1996] AC 815.   [11] [1974] 1 WLR 2.   [12] [1983] Crim LR 624.
[13] [1992] 1 QB 20.   [14] [1993] Crim LR 788.   [15] [1993] Crim LR 73.
[16] [1993] AC 442.

went into committee in the Lords on 19 July 2005 and had its Report Stage there on 14 March 2006. It was published in the House of Commons on 29 March 2006 having received its third reading in the Lords on that date. The Bill received its second reading in the Commons on 12 June 2006 and committee stage took place between 20 and 22 June 2006. Report stage and third reading took place on 26 October 2006 and Royal Assent was given on 8 November 2006. Appendix 2 of this book sets out the legislative progress of the Bill with detailed references to *Hansard*.

D. POSSIBLE WAYS OF CRIMINALIZING FRAUDULENT CONDUCT

1.19   In broad terms, there are three models of criminalizing fraudulent conduct:

(a) deception-based models which require proof of a deception that operated on the mind of the victim;

(b) models based on the conduct of the accused which imperils the economic interest of another; and

(c) where false representations are made by a person without proof of their having the potential to imperil economic interests or cause the victim to believe them.

1.20   English law currently recognizes (a) and (b), but (c) is a new concept which has been put at the heart of the Fraud Act 2006. It has been suggested[17] that a safeguard should have been inserted into the new fraud law requiring the prosecution to prove not only that the defendant behaved dishonestly and with intent to gain or cause loss but also that there were in fact economic interests imperilled by the conduct. The new offence of fraud by false representation can be committed whether or not the conduct of the accused had any effect or even when the victim knew that the representations were false.

1.21   The Law Commission of Canada in 1987 proposed a fraud law which required that the victim either suffered economic loss or the risk thereof. Although the offence was not introduced, the proposal sought to capture all or most forms of fraudulent behaviour by reference to other elements than mere dishonesty. The Canadian Commission proposed two alternatives:

(a) everyone commits a crime who dishonestly by false representation or by non-disclosure induces another person to suffer economic loss or risk thereof; *or*

(b) everyone commits a crime who, without any right to do so, by dishonest representation or dishonest non-disclosure induces another person to suffer an economic loss or risk thereof.

---

[17] By the CBA: *Fraud Law Reform Consultation on Proposals for Legislation: Response from the Criminal Bar Association July 2004*, available at <http://www.criminalbar.com>.

E. THE NEW OFFENCES INTRODUCED BY THE
FRAUD ACT 2006

The Fraud Act abolishes all the deception offences in the Theft Acts 1968 and 1978   1.22
including those created by the Theft (Amendment) Act 1996. It creates an offence
of criminal fraud[18] which can be committed in three basic ways: fraud by false
representation,[19] fraud by failure to disclose information when a person is under
a legal duty to do so,[20] and fraud by abuse of position when one is expected to
safeguard, or not to act against, the financial interests of another person.[21] The
maximum sentence upon conviction on indictment is ten years' imprisonment.

The new law of fraud is wide in scope. For example, the false representation   1.23
offence can be committed without any necessity of proof of the defendant having
in fact put at risk any economic interests or even causing a victim to believe the
representations.

The *actus reus* of the new offence of fraud by false representation is widely   1.24
expressed. The defendant must make a representation. Originally the Fraud Bill
defined a representation by reference to 'words or conduct'. These words were taken
out in the House of Lords, mainly to ensure that representations made to machines
were caught by the new offence.[22] This is also made clear by s 2(5) which states that
a representation 'may be regarded as made if it or anything implying it is submitted
in any form to any system or device designed to receive, convey or respond to
communications (with or without human intervention)'. In certain circumstances a
representation may even be made by an omission. For example, where D knows that
there has been a material change of circumstances and V does not, if D continues
to deal with V that, coupled with his failure to put right the latter's misconception,
may amount to a representation.

The offence is further widened by the fact that a representation is defined as   1.25
false if 'it is untrue or misleading'.[23] Many representations may be misleading.
The Home Office in its response to consultees expressed the view that misleading
meant 'less than wholly true and capable of an interpretation to the detriment of
the victim'.[24] The new offence is aimed at any situation where a person dishonestly
makes false or misleading statements including those made to machines or over the
Internet (such as phishing).

A representation is false if it is untrue or misleading and the person making it   1.26
knows that it is, or might be, untrue or misleading.[25] Thus a person would have
to know either that the representation is misleading or that it might be. Although
knowledge is a higher form of *mens rea* than recklessness, belief or suspicion, proving

---

[18] Section 1(1).   [19] Section 2.   [20] Section 3.   [21] Section 4.
[22] *Hansard*, HL 14 March 2006 col 1107.   [23] Section 2(2).
[24] *Fraud Law Reform*, Government response to consultation, para 19. Available at <http://www.
home office.gov.uk/documents/cons-fraud-law-reform/Government_response.pdf?view=Binary>.
[25] Section 2(2)(a) and (b).

that a person knows that a representation 'might be misleading' in many cases would not be difficult. This phrase was inserted so that it would be easier for the Crown to prove falsity in respect of future facts. Moreover, 'shutting one's eyes to the obvious' has in certain circumstances been held to amount to 'knowledge'.

1.27   In all three ways that the new offence of fraud can be committed the *mens rea* is 'intending to make a gain for himself or another or to cause loss to another or to expose another to risk of loss'. Gain and loss extend only to gain or loss in money or other property. This is the same definition as used in s 34(2)(a) of the Theft Act 1968.

1. Dishonestly Obtaining Services

1.28   Another key change is that the offence of dishonestly obtaining services by deception contained in s 1 of the Theft Act 1978 is replaced by an offence of obtaining services dishonestly. The new offence, in line with the thinking behind the new fraud law, does not require the prosecution to prove that any deception was operative or had any effect on a victim. There must be an obtaining of services for which payment is or will become due and a failure to pay in whole or in part. A person is guilty if he acts dishonestly with intent to avoid payment in whole or in part and he knows that the services are to be paid for or knows that they might have to be paid for.

2. Possessing, Making, or Supplying Articles for Use in Frauds

1.29   The 2006 Act also creates offences of possessing, making, or supplying articles for use in frauds.[26] The offence of possession of articles for use in fraud again is very wide. A person is guilty of an offence if 'he has in his possession or under his control any article for use in the course of or in connection with any fraud'. It is likely that the phrase 'for use in' means that the defendant was in possession of the article and intended the article to be used in the course of or in connection with some future fraud. The Home Office Explanatory Notes state that 'a general intention to commit fraud will suffice'. The *mens rea* for this offence is likely to be the same as that which has been established for the offence of 'going equipped' in s 25(1) of the Theft Act 1968 (ie, possession of the article and an intention that it will be used in the course of or in connection with some future burglary).[27]

3. Fraudulent Trading by Sole Trader

1.30   Section 9 makes it an offence for a person knowingly to be a party to the carrying on of a fraudulent business where the business is not carried on by a company. The offence mirrors the current offence under s 458 of the Companies Act 1985, which is retained. The maximum sentence for the new offence is ten years' imprisonment and the sentence under s 458 is increased to the same level.

---

[26] Fraud Act 2006, s 6.   [27] *Ellames* [1974] 3 All ER 130.

The new offence of fraudulent trading can be committed by any individual 1.31
without the need for there to be any corporate structure in place. Non-corporate
traders include sole traders, partnerships, trusts, and companies registered overseas.
The new offence is committed where any 'business' is carried on by a person with
intent to defraud creditors of any person or for any other fraudulent purpose. This
change is likely to be significant as it will allow prosecutions of substantive fraud in
a wide range of situations where prosecution was not easy before.

4. The Controversial Decision to Retain the Common Law Offence of Conspiracy to Defraud

One major bone of contention during the Fraud Bill's passage through Parliament 1.32
was the Government's desire to preserve the common law offence of conspiracy to
defraud. After consultation and despite severe criticism the Government decided
to retain the common law offence and at the same time broaden the criminal
law of fraud. This in a sense drove a coach and horses through the logic of
the Law Commission's position. Successive Law Commissions have argued that
the offence of conspiracy to defraud should be abolished and at the same time
that the law of fraud should be widened. To leave the one and to widen the
law on the other hand is both illogical and unfair. In its 2002 report the Law
Commission wrote:

The advantages of abolishing it [ie, conspiracy to defraud], in our view, greatly outweigh
any possible advantage that might accrue from retaining it alongside the new offences we
recommend. We believe that those offences cover enough of the ground presently covered
by conspiracy to defraud to make it unnecessary to retain that offence any longer.[28]

One major criticism of conspiracy to defraud is that is depends too much on what 1.33
an individual jury might find to be dishonest. This raises questions of breaching
the certainty of law test contained in Article 7 of the ECHR. Another criticism
was what the Law Commission in 2002 called the 'indefensible anomaly' by which
the continuing survival of conspiracy to defraud meant that it may be a crime for
two people to agree to do something which in the absence of agreement either of
them could lawfully do.[29] The reason for the anomaly is that prior to the Criminal
Law Act 1977 a criminal conspiracy could be based on an agreement to commit an
unlawful but non-criminal act, such as a tort or a breach of contract.

Successive Law Commissions have reached the conclusion that the offence of 1.34
conspiracy to defraud should be abolished. The Law Commission in 2002 included
an abolition clause in their draft Bill and expressed the view that:

either conspiracy to defraud is too wide in its scope (in that it catches agreements to do
things which are rightly not criminal) or the statutory offences are too narrow (in that they
fail to catch certain conduct which should be criminal) or which is our view, the problem is

---

[28] Law Commission, *Fraud* (see n 1 for reference) para 9.4.
[29] For example, *Attorney General's Reference (No 1 of 1985)* [1986] QB 491; cf *Cooke* [1986] AC 909.

a combination of the two. On any view the present position is anomalous and has no place in a coherent criminal law.[30]

1.35   The justification by Lord Goldsmith for keeping the offence of conspiracy to defraud is unconvincing. He said on 22 June 2005:

We recognised, in the light of the consultation, that the common law offence has advantages and works well in cases involving multiple offenders and offences, where there can be hundreds of possible counts [31] ... conspiracy to defraud allows the agreement that is the essence of the conspiracy to be reduced to one short, well drafted count that reflects the totality of the enterprise.[32]

1.36   The position of the Government in retaining the common law offence of conspiracy to defraud met with robust criticism at the second reading and in committee. Lord Lloyd said: 'There is a flaw, and the flaw is ... the failure to abolish the common law offence of conspiracy to defraud—as strongly recommended by the Law Commission'.[33]

1.37   This criticism would seem to be justified, particularly so when it is borne in mind that conspiracies to commit the new fraud offences can be charged. In particular, the new offence of fraudulent trading contained in s 9 applies to any person or persons who are party to the dishonest carrying on of any 'business'. In addition, the careful analysis of the Law Commission demonstrates that the offence of conspiracy to defraud is too wide as it is only the element of dishonesty which renders the agreement criminal.

1.38   It was argued by those seeking the abolition of conspiracy to defraud that the broadening of the current law of fraud in the Fraud Act 2006 could not be justified without abolishing the offence of conspiracy to defraud. Further, the Domestic Violence, Crime and Victims Act 2004 contained provisions allowing for a judge to try a defendant without a jury on multiple charges.

1.39   The new single fraud offence replacing the deception offences in the current Theft Acts is a sensible rationalization of an area which had become dogged by technical argument. The refusal to repeal the common law offence of conspiracy to defraud has been the subject of criticism as it may be that prosecutors continue to use that offence which has been severely criticized by successive Law Commissions.

1.40   Considering reform of the law of theft was not within the Law Commission's remit in 2002. However theft, in the light of cases such as *Hinks*[34] and *Gomez*,[35] has now become defined purely by dishonesty. The effect of these decisions is that theft is now an offence of dishonestly receiving property belonging to another by any means lawful or unlawful. It may be that in future the law of theft will have to be examined as it relies on the question of dishonesty.

---

[30] Law Commission, *Fraud* (see n 1 for reference) p 13.
[31] *Hansard*, HL 22 June 2005 col 1654.   [32] Ibid, col 1655.
[33] *Hansard*, HL 22 June 2005 col 1665, although Lord Lloyd of Berwick 'changed' his mind at report stage (see *Hansard*, HL 14 March 2006 col 1112).
[34] [2001] 2 AC 442.   [35] [1993] AC 442.

F. CONCLUSION

The stated objective of the Fraud Act 2006 is to make the law of fraud more simple   1.41
and readily understandable. As Judge Alan Wilkie QC, the Law Commissioner with
responsibility for criminal law, said on 30 July 2002 when the Law Commission
report was published:

Our aim, by these technical changes to the law, is to make the law of fraud clearer and
simpler. We believe that as a result all concerned whether jurors, police, victims, defendants
or lawyers, will be better placed to understand who has committed a crime and who has not.[36]

The aim of the new law is also to improve justice and in particular to reduce   1.42
the amount of time and money wasted in dealing with the current 'complexity and
vagueness of the law'.[37]

The new fraud law is also part of the wider Government strategy of combating   1.43
fraud, most recently set out in the July 2006 Fraud Review. Extra resources have
been made available to the Serious Fraud Office and the City of London Police.
The other proposed measures are set out earlier in this chapter. The Proceeds of
Crime Act 2002 introduced tough new money laundering laws and civil recovery.
It also established the Assets Recovery Agency. The aim of the Fraud Act 2006 is to
get away from the difficulties of the existing over-specific statutory offences based
on operative deception in the Theft Acts 1968 and 1978.

Although the Fraud Act 2006 will be a major change in the law many of the   1.44
current legal weapons for prosecuting fraud remain. These include:[38]

(a) tax evasion offences such as the common law offence of cheating the Revenue
    under s 72 of the Value Added Tax Act 1994;

(b) fraudulent trading in s 458 of the Companies Act 1985;[39]

(c) insider dealing in s 52 of the Criminal Justice Act 1993;

(d) forgery and counterfeiting offences under ss 1 to 5 and 14 to 19 of the Forgery
    and Counterfeiting Act 1981;

(e) false accounting under s 17 of the Theft Act 1968;

(f) misleading market practices under s 397 of the Financial Services and Markets
    Act 2000;

(g) the intellectual property offences under s 107 of the Copyright, Designs and
    Patents Act 1988 and s 92 of the Trade Marks Act 1994; and

(h) theft.

---

[36] *News from the Law Commission* 30 July 2002, available at <http://www.lawcom.gov.uk/docs/
lc276sum.pdf>.
    [37] Ibid.   [38] See Appendix 6 for relevant statutory materials.
    [39] Section 458 of the Companies Act 1985 has been repealed and replaced by an identical offence in
s 993 of the Companies Act 2006 which received Royal Assent on 8 November 2006, although s 993
has not yet been brought into force.

2

FRAUD

A. OVERVIEW

The fraud offence, contrary to s 1 of the Fraud Act 2006, may be committed in   2.01
three broad ways:[1]

(a) Fraud by false representation.[2]
(b) Fraud by failing to disclose information that one is under a legal duty to
    disclose.[3]
(c) Fraud by abuse of a position in which one is expected to safeguard, or not to
    act against, the financial interests of another person.[4]

Each of ss 2 to 4 defines a different way of committing the s 1 offence, rather than
defining a further offence. Section 1 of the Fraud Act 2006 states:

1 Fraud

(1) A person is guilty of fraud if he is in breach of any of the sections listed in subsection
    (2) (which provide for different ways of committing the offence).
(2) The sections are—
    (a) section 2 (fraud by false representation),
    (b) section 3 (fraud by failing to disclose information), and
    (c) section 4 (fraud by abuse of position).
(3) A person who is guilty of fraud is liable—
    (a) on summary conviction, to imprisonment for a term not exceeding 12 months or to
        a fine not exceeding the statutory maximum (or to both);

---

[1] Sample counts of the new fraud offences are contained in Appendix 9 of this book.
[2] Section 2.   [3] Section 3.   [4] Section 4.

13

(b) on conviction on indictment, to imprisonment for a term not exceeding 10 years or to a fine (or to both).

(4) Subsection (3)(a) applies in relation to Northern Ireland as if the reference to 12 months were a reference to 6 months.

2.02   Each of ss 2 to 4 is expressed in a similar way, eg, s 2 states:

2 Fraud by false representation

(1) A person is in breach of this section if he—
   (a) dishonestly makes a false representation, and
   (b) intends, by making the representation—
       (i)   to make a gain for himself or another, or
       (ii) to cause loss to another or to expose another to a risk of loss ...

Two elements are common to each limb: the person must be dishonest, and must[5] act with the required intention. That is, he must intend by his conduct to make a gain for himself, or another, or to cause loss to another or to expose another to a risk of loss. For ease of reference, we refer to this intention as the fraudulent intention.

2.03   In contrast to the old deception offences, where it was necessary to prove that the victim had in fact been deceived, the focus of the fraud offence is upon the acts and state of mind of the offender: eg, the making of the false representation with a fraudulent intention, rather than its effect. Ancillary to this shift is the fact that most conduct, which would have amounted to an attempt at a deception offence, constitutes a completed fraud offence.[6] There is no need for anything actually to be obtained: the offence is completed when the conduct is performed with the required state of mind. The old deception offences might be referred to as result crimes—defined by an outcome; the new offences might be referred to as conduct crimes—defined irrespective of the outcome.

B. COMMON ELEMENTS

1. Dishonesty

(a) *The Ghosh Test*

2.04   Dishonesty is for the jury to determine—whether on the ordinary meaning of the word they consider that the defendant acted dishonestly. Where the circumstances of the case require elaboration, the judge will direct the jury along the following lines:

The prosecution must make you sure that the defendant was acting dishonestly. In this case you must decide two questions:

1. Was what the defendant did dishonest by the ordinary standards of reasonable and honest people?

---

[5] Or omit to act, where appropriate.   [6] See Chapter 4.

14

In this regard, you the jury must form your own judgment of what those standards are.
2. Must the defendant himself have realized that what he was doing would be regarded as dishonest by those standards?
In deciding this you must consider the defendant's own state of mind at the time.
If, after taking into account all of the evidence, you are sure that the answers to both of these questions are YES, the element of dishonesty is proved. If you are not sure of that, the element of dishonesty is not proved and the defendant is 'Not Guilty' of the offence.[7]

So the standard of honesty is that of reasonable and honest people, and the defendant is only to be held to be dishonest if he realizes he is acting contrary to that standard. The direction is known as the *Ghosh* direction after the case in which it was formulated by the Court of Appeal.[8] 2.05

The test is partly in the minds of reasonable and honest people and partly in the mind of the defendant. It is to be contrasted, firstly, with a purely subjective test in which the jury look into the mind of the defendant and determine whether he felt he was acting dishonestly, by his standards. If the purely subjective test were applied, Dickens's Artful Dodger could argue that, on the basis of the moral education he received from Fagin, he sees nothing wrong or dishonest in picking pockets, and he should thereby be exonerated. Secondly, the *Ghosh* test is to be contrasted with a purely objective test, in which the jury apply a fixed standard of decent behaviour: 'in our society we regard acting in such a manner as dishonest'. By that test, a defendant who comes from a country where public transport is free and travels by bus in England without paying would be judged dishonest. His mind might not be regarded as culpable because he has no idea that payment is required, but judged objectively travelling for free on public transport is, in our society, dishonest.[9] 2.06

In *Ghosh*[10] the Court of Appeal reconciled these tests in favour of the hybrid of objective and subjective elements in the formula above.[11] The subjective element in dishonesty in an offence gives juries the flexibility to do justice. 2.07

(b) *Ghosh and the Fraud Act*
Besides the fraud offence, dishonesty is also a necessary element in two other offences in the Fraud Act: fraudulent trading (see Chapter 5), and obtaining services dishonestly (see Chapter 6). In the Lords' committee stage, the cross-bench Lord Lloyd of Berwick sought an assurance that the Bill used the term *dishonesty* in the *Ghosh* sense, saying: 2.08

I certainly would not support a Bill in which the test of dishonesty was to revert to the old-fashioned objective test. I hope that the noble and learned Lord the Attorney-General will be able to say, 'We are enacting this Bill on the basis that *Ghosh* is the law as we understand it'.[12]

---

[7] Judicial Studies Board specimen direction (December 2004).   [8] 75 Cr App R 154.
[9] See the discussion in *Ghosh* at 161.   [10] *Ghosh* at 162–3.   [11] Paragraph 2.04, above.
[12] *Hansard*, HL 22 June 2005 col 1666.

2.09   The Attorney General refused to give such an assurance, stating:

I can say that that is the current definition of dishonesty; it is referred to in the Explanatory Notes; no other definition is offered in the Bill. I cannot preclude your Lordships from in due course taking a different view and saying that *Ghosh* was wrong all along, but I have no reason to think that it is. That is the most assurance that I can give to the noble and learned Lord.[13]

The Attorney General thereby left the definition of dishonesty in the hands of the common law.

2.10   However, the Solicitor General did go further in referring to *Ghosh*:

The judgment sets out a two-stage test … the first question is whether the defendant's behaviour would be regarded as dishonest by the ordinary standards of reasonable and honest people. If the answer is positive, the second question is whether the defendant was aware that his conduct was dishonest and would be regarded as dishonest by reasonable and honest people. That is the approach to dishonesty that we want to see the Bill take.[14]

(c) *Claim of Right*

2.11   In theft, the test for dishonesty is tailored by four partial definitions:[15]

(a) 'claim of right': the defendant is not dishonest where he has a genuine belief[16] that he is entitled in law to the property;

(b) 'belief in consent': the defendant is not dishonest where he believes that the owner would have consented to the taking;

(c) the defendant is not dishonest where he believes the owner cannot be found;[17]

(d) a defendant may be held to be dishonest notwithstanding that he intended to pay for the property.

The most significant of these is (a) the 'claim of right'. Where a defendant genuinely believed (however erroneously) that he was entitled, under the civil law, to the property that forms the subject of a theft charge, he is deemed not to have been dishonest. Hence he is entitled to be acquitted. Rather than apply the *Ghosh* test, the jury would be directed to acquit if they accept that he so believed (or think he may have so believed).

2.12   These partial definitions of dishonesty do not apply to the Fraud Act 2006[18] so the jury are left with the *Ghosh* direction. If the jury apply the unfettered *Ghosh* test strictly to a claim of right under a fraud charge, they are free to find a person to be dishonest notwithstanding that they accept he had a genuine claim of right. There is an argument for saying that the jury should be specifically directed that claim of right negates dishonesty in non-theft offences, just as it does in theft, as there is no rationale for a distinction to be drawn between theft and the fraud offences.[19]

---

[13] *Hansard*, HL 22 June 2005 col 1674.
[14] *Hansard*, HC Standing Committee B 20 June 2006 col 8.   [15] Theft Act 1968, s 2.
[16] Whether reasonable or otherwise.   [17] Except in the case of trusts.
[18] Or indeed to any offence other than theft.
[19] See Smith and Hogan, *Criminal Law* (11th edn, 2005) 756.

2. Fraudulent Intention

To be guilty of the fraud offence under each of ss 2 to 4, in making the 2.13
false representation, failing to disclose information, or abusing the position, the
defendant must intend, by so doing:

(a) to make a gain for himself, or for another, *or*
(b) to cause loss to another, or to expose another to a risk of loss.

The offence requires only that there be an intention with respect to gain and 2.14
loss. There need not be proof of actual gain or loss. So, for example, in the case
of fraud by false representation, the offence is complete when the representation is
made with the necessary intention.

(a) *Gain and Loss*

The Law Commission stated that 'fraud is essentially an economic crime, and we 2.15
do not think the new offence should extend to conduct which has no financial
dimension'.[20] This was also the intention of Parliament.[21] The Act seeks to
achieve this result by defining the offence in terms of 'gain' and 'loss' in the same
way as in the Theft Act 1968,[22] which defines them as extending only to gain
or loss 'in money or other property'. Section 5 of the Fraud Act defines gain
and loss:

5 "Gain" and "loss"

(1) The references to gain and loss in sections 2 to 4 are to be read in accordance with this
    section.
(2) "Gain" and "loss" —
    (a) extend only to gain or loss in money or other property;
    (b) include any such gain or loss whether temporary or permanent; and "property"
        means any property whether real or personal (including things in action and other
        intangible property).
(3) "Gain" includes a gain by keeping what one has, as well as a gain by getting what one
    does not have.
(4) "Loss" includes a loss by not getting what one might get, as well as a loss by parting with
    what one has.

The definition of gain and loss extends to a temporary gain or loss. So, unlike theft 2.16
and the old offence of obtaining property by deception,[23] there is no requirement
for an intention to permanently deprive.

Blackmail is defined in terms of gain and loss.[24] In relation to that offence it has 2.17
been suggested that *gain* and *loss* are to be interpreted to include the case where
the defendant does not intend the victim to 'lose out', as he intends to return an

---

[20] Law Commission, *Fraud* (see Chapter 1, n 1, above for reference) para 7.53.
[21] *Hansard*, HL 19 July 2004 col 1435.   [22] Theft Act 1968, s 34(2)(a).
[23] Theft Act 1968, s 15.   [24] Theft Act 1968, s 21.

economic equivalent. If the defendant intends the loser to be deprived of particular money or property, he intends to cause loss to another, even if he intends that the loser be fully compensated in economic terms.[25]

(b) *Property*

2.18 Property includes real or personal property (including things in action and other intangible property).[26] Again, this is modelled on the Theft Act definition.[27] In Parliament, the Attorney General said 'We would think it highly desirable that the definitions of "property" for the purposes of theft and fraud should be the same'.[28] However, this is not quite the practical effect of the Act. The Theft Act 1968 limits what can be stolen by the operation of s 4. Generally, a person cannot steal land, but as it is real property it can be the subject of a fraudulent intention. Things growing wild on any land may be property, but they are specifically exempted from being the subject of an offence of theft. In the fraud offence there is no such exemption—nor is there for wild creatures.

2.19 The definition of property does not extend to confidential information. In *Oxford and Moss*[29] the defendant, whilst an undergraduate at the University of Liverpool, dishonestly took a question paper for an examination, which was shortly due to be held. The prosecutor accepted that there was no theft of the paper (as the defendant intended to return it), but contended that there was a theft of confidential information, namely the meaning of the words printed upon the paper—a form of intangible property. The magistrate held that this was not a form of intangible property, and the divisional court agreed.

2.20 It follows that trade secrets cannot be stolen, nor can they be the subject of a charge of fraud. It has been remarked, 'it is not too much to say that we live in a country where ... the theft of the boardroom table is punished far more severely than the theft of the boardroom secrets'.[30] The Law Commission has separately consulted on the subject of trade secrets,[31] and excluded confidential information from their definition of property in the draft Fraud Bill.

2.21 In Parliament it was suggested that the definition of property within the Act should be extended to include confidential information, but the idea was rejected:

A person who commits a fraud is not interested in obtaining information for its own sake. He obtains credit card details, for example, with a view to financial gain. If his only intention lies in obtaining the information then fraud is not the right charge.[32]

---

[25] *Smith on Theft* (8th edn, 1997) para 10–18.   [26] Fraud Act 2006, s 5(2).
[27] Theft Act 1968, s 4(1).   [28] *Hansard*, HL 19 July 2004 col 1435.
[29] (1979) 68 Cr App R 183.
[30] Rt Hon Sir Edward Boyle MP (later Lord Boyle) (*Hansard*, HC 13 December 1968, vol 775, col 806).
[31] Law Commission, Legislating the Criminal Code: Misuse of Trade Secrets (LCCP150, 1997), available at <http://www.lawcom.gov.uk/docs/cp150.pdf>.
[32] *Hansard*, HL 19 July 2004 col 1435.

Anyone who has in his possession information, such as credit card details, for use in a fraud, having obtained that information in whatever way, would commit an offence under [section 6[33]]. That provides for an offence if a person has in his possession an article, 'for use in the course of or in connection with any fraud'.[34]

The obtaining of confidential information is also covered by offences out- 2.22
side the Fraud Act 2006. Where confidential information is obtained by means of unauthorized access to computer data, an offence under the Computer Misuse Act 1990[35] is committed. Furthermore, where confidential information is obtained pursuant to an agreement with another, it may be a conspiracy to defraud.

(c) *The Intention*

The fraudulent intention is manifested in two ways. Firstly, the intent to gain for 2.23
self, or another. This is the stock in trade of a fraudster. It is rare that the fraudster acts other than with the intention to gain for self, or at least on behalf of another. Secondly, the intent to cause loss to another, or to expose another to a risk of loss. Outside malice, it is rare that someone acts with the purpose of causing loss to another, far less the risk of economic loss. In part, this limb is directed at resolving evidential difficulties for cases where it is difficult to prove exactly what the benefit to the defendant would be, but the loss to others is plain.

'Intention' is ordinarily a straightforward concept: a person intends something if 2.24
he acts with the purpose of causing that result. Juries are usually directed simply upon the subject: 'You must be sure that, when the defendant did the act, he intended [X]'. However, a person may also be said to intend a result if he knew that it was a highly probable result of his act. This was considered by the House of Lords in the case of *Woolin*[36] with the result that, according to Smith and Hogan, *Criminal Law*, the law stands as:[37]

(a) A result is intended when it is the actor's purpose to cause it
(b) A jury may also find that a result is intended, though it is not the actor's purpose to cause it, when—
   (i)   the result is a virtually certain consequence of the act, and
   (ii) the actor knows that it is a virtually certain consequence.

In the past, where statutes have referred to *gain* and *loss*,[38] in a similar context, 2.25
the expression used has been 'with a view to gain for himself or another or with intent to cause loss to another'. In the draft Bill for the Fraud Act 2006 the Law Commission abandoned the distinction between 'with a view to ... ', and 'an intent to ... ', believing it to be of little consequence.[39] It considered that 'view' is a kind of purpose, whereas 'intent' includes that which the defendant knew to be an inevitable side-effect of the making of the desired gain. The phrase 'gain and loss' has been the

---

[33] See Chapter 4 below.   [34] *Hansard*, HL 19 July 2004 col 1435.
[35] Section 1.   [36] [1999] AC 82.   [37] 10th edn (1997) 71.
[38] For example, s 34(2)(a) of the Theft Act 1968 or s 92 of the Trade Marks Act 1994.
[39] Law Commission, *Fraud* (see Chapter 1, n 1, above for reference) p 71, footnote.

subject of judicial scrutiny in cases of false accounting contrary to s 17 of the Theft Act 1968. The court has held that although gain and loss must relate to money or other property it is not necessary for the Crown to prove that the defendant had no legal entitlement to the property.[40] However in another[41] case the Court of Appeal held that where a company director created two false invoices to improve the apparent financial status of a recently obtained company for the purpose of placating fellow directors he did not act with a view to a gain within the meaning of s 34(2). A desire to improve relations with business partners did not involve monetary gain and an intent to retain his own resources was not sufficient in the circumstances.

2.26   An example of a conspiracy to defraud case in which the defendant was held to be guilty notwithstanding a lack of intention to make a gain for himself, or to cause a loss to another, is *Wai Yu-Tsang*.[42] In that case the defendant acted in what he thought were the best interests of the bank at which he worked (and the interests of its shareholders and its creditors), by covering up bad payments in order to keep the bank afloat. He did not seek to gain for himself, or to cause loss to anyone. However, by improperly attempting to cover up difficulties at the bank, he was clearly exposing creditors and shareholders to the *risk* of loss notwithstanding any good intentions.

2.27   In another case[43] the Privy Council gave a wide definition to the phrase 'with a view to a gain'. The defendants were charged with false accounting. They were employed by a company dealing in futures contracts. They opened accounts in the names of friends, which was not permitted by their employers. The allegation of false accounting was in respect of the falsification of withdrawal slips to authorize the release of funds. Although the defendants accepted that they had been dishonest in falsifying the withdrawal slips they argued that it had not been done with a view to a gain as no gain resulted from this, only from the sale of the futures contracts themselves, and the company suffered no loss because the money had always been that of the appellants. It was held that as the defendants as employees had used their position to make a personal profit, regardless of whether their employer had made a loss, they were liable to account for this to their employers. The falsification of the withdrawal slips enabled them to recover an unauthorized profit and was done 'with a view to a gain'.

C. FRAUD BY FALSE REPRESENTATION (SECTION 2)

1. Introduction

2.28   A person commits fraud if he dishonestly makes a false representation, intending thereby to make a gain for himself or another, or to cause loss to another or to

---

[40] *Attorney General's Reference (No 1 of 2001)* [2002] 3 All ER 840.
[41] *Masterson* (unreported) 30 April 1996, CA 94 02221 X5.   [42] [1992] 1 AC 269.
[43] *Lee Cheung Wing v R* 94 Cr App R 355.

expose another to a risk of loss. A representation may be made by conduct as well as by words, and may relate to fact (including as to a person's state of mind) or law. A representation is false if it is untrue or misleading, and the person making it knows that it is, or might be, untrue or misleading.[44] The section reads:

2 Fraud by false representation

(1) A person is in breach of this section if he—
    (a) dishonestly makes a false representation, and
    (b) intends, by making the representation—
        (i) to make a gain for himself or another, or
        (ii) to cause loss to another or to expose another to a risk of loss.
(2) A representation is false if—
    (a) it is untrue or misleading, and
    (b) the person making it knows that it is, or might be, untrue or misleading.
(3) "Representation" means any representation as to fact or law, including a representation as to the state of mind of—
    (a) the person making the representation, or
    (b) any other person.
(4) A representation may be express or implied.
(5) For the purposes of this section a representation may be regarded as made if it (or anything implying it) is submitted in any form to any system or device designed to receive, convey or respond to communications (with or without human intervention).

The section relates to the obtaining, and the attempting to obtain, property (and   2.29 other pecuniary advantage) by deceit. The Fraud Act repeals[45] the offences of:

(a) obtaining property by deception (Theft Act 1968, s 15);
(b) obtaining a money transfer by deception (Theft Act 1968, s 15A);
(c) obtaining a pecuniary advantage by deception (Theft Act 1968, s 16); and
(d) procuring the execution of a valuable security by deception (Theft Act 1968, s 20(2)).

It is intended that this section will cover all conduct that was previously covered by those sections. The law no longer defines different offences dependent upon the form in which a gain is obtained, or sought to be obtained.

In many cases it was difficult to determine the correct charge dependent upon   2.30 the form in which the gain was obtained. For example, in the case of *Duru*[46] the deception resulted in a bank making out a cheque by way of mortgage advance. The defendant was charged with obtaining property (the cheque) by deception, and convicted. He appealed on the basis that the cheque, in the ordinary course of events, would be returned to the drawer and hence there was no intention to permanently deprive. The Court of Appeal upheld the conviction on the basis that there was an intention to permanently deprive the drawer of the cheque in its substance—as a thing in action. The decision by the House of Lords in *Preddy*[47] overruled that decision and it is apparent, now, that such a charge was unsustainable. However,

---

[44] Section 2.   [45] Section 14(1) and Sch 1.   [46] [1974] 1 WLR 2.   [47] [1996] AC 815.

had the defendant been charged with procuring the execution of a valuable security by deception, contrary to s 20(2) of the Theft Act 1968, no such difficulty would have arisen.

2.31 The problem is illustrated starkly where there is an attempt to obtain money, where the defendant does not care whether it is paid in cash, money transfer, or cheque. This would have been an attempt at obtaining property by deception,[48] or obtaining a money transfer by deception,[49] or obtaining the execution of a valuable security by deception,[50] but it could not be said for certain that it was one specific offence. Under the Fraud Act 2006 such technical issues no longer arise, as the form of that which is sought to be obtained does not matter.

2. The Representation

(a) Contrasted with Deception

2.32 The basis of the new offence is misrepresentation rather than deception. The focus is shifted to the making of the representation by the offender, rather than the effect it has upon the mind of the person to whom the representation is made. In the majority of cases the change makes no practical difference. However there are three significant areas:

(a) the use of payment cards;
(b) representations made to a machine; and
(c) representations made where the victim has been pre-warned of the fraud.

2.33 Where payment cards are used to purchase goods in a shop, the act of using the card is an implied representation that the person using the card has authority to so use it. Generally, the agreement between the merchant and the card issuer is such that if the card is used by someone in breach of their authorization the merchant will nevertheless be paid the sum by the issuer. For this reason the merchant may well not rely upon the implied representation of the person using the card that they have the necessary authority, as in fact it matters little to them one way or the other—they get the money in any event. The House of Lords held in *Charles*,[51] and then in *Lambie*,[52] that it may be *inferred* that the merchant would not have accepted the card but for the representation, and hence there was a deception. These cases have been much criticized[53] and give practical difficulties where, for instance, the merchant accepts in cross-examination that he did not rely upon the representation. These difficulties are overcome by the fraud offence as it is simply the making of the implied representation by the purchaser with the intention of gaining the goods which constitutes the offence—it is irrelevant whether the merchant relies upon it or not. There remains a difficulty under the Act. The prosecution will have to prove an intended causation: that the defendant intended to get the desired property *by*

[48] Theft Act 1968, s 15.   [49] Theft Act 1968, s 15A.
[50] Theft Act 1968, s 20(2).   [51] [1977] AC 177.   [52] [1982] AC 449.
[53] For example, Professor J C Smith, *The Law of Theft* (8th edn, 1997) para 4–09.

means of the misrepresentation.[54] A defendant, who was over his credit limit, might perhaps deny this on the ground that he knew that the retailer would be indifferent whether the representation was true. So he did not intend to gain *by means of* the misrepresentation. The Law Commission expressed itself to be 'not especially concerned at the possibility of an acquittal in such circumstances'.[55]

The concept of deception arguably implies a belief on the part of the recipient of the representation. For this reason it has been widely considered that a machine cannot be deceived.[56] Where cigarettes are bought with fake coins from a person, a deception offence is committed, but where they are bought from a vending machine, it is not. With the growth of the use of the Internet as a marketplace the issue becomes more significant. The use of a credit card without authority to buy an item from an Internet shopping site, without any human intervention, was not a deception offence under the Theft Act, but to do likewise in a bookshop, would, of course, have been. The fraud offence overcomes this problem. At the time of entering card details into the website the person is making a representation that they have authority to use the card. It no longer matters that the representation never reaches a human mind. This is made clear by subsection (5)—if it were not clear otherwise. 2.34

The final contrast with deception is demonstrated by cases in which the police are watching a defendant and have set up a sting operation. If the victim is pre-warned of the pending fraud he inevitably does not believe the assertions made by the defendant. The deception is not operative. The victim nevertheless goes along with them for the sake of the operation. Strangely the defendant's conduct, which would have been the full deception offence but for the sting operation, becomes an attempt by virtue solely of that fact. Under the Fraud Act the defendant's conduct and state of mind are not affected by the victim's knowledge and, in either case, the full offence is committed. The anomaly is cured. 2.35

(b) *Nature of the Representation*

The Law Commission modelled fraud by false representation upon misrepresenta- 2.36 tion in contract law. 'The assertion may be express, implicit in written or spoken words, or implicit from non-verbal conduct'.[57] For example, by using a credit card a person makes the implied representation that they have authority to use the card for the transaction.

The representation may be as to fact or law.[58] This mirrors the position in civil law with respect to misrepresentation—although the practical effect of the inclusion of representations as to law may be limited. 2.37

---

[54] For example, in s 2: 'a person is in breach of this section if he dishonestly makes a false representation, and intends *by* making the representation to make a gain for himself ... '.

[55] Law Commission, *Fraud* (see Chapter 1, n 1, above for reference) para 7.57.

[56] See Professor J C Smith, *The Law of Theft* (8th edn, 1997) para 4–12 and Professor E Griew's *The Theft Acts* (7th edn, 1995) para 8–12, and *Holmes v The Governor of Brixton Prison and another* [2004] EWHC 2020.

[57] Law Commission, *Fraud* (see Chapter 1, n 1, above for reference) para 7.17.

[58] Fraud Act 2006, s 2(3).

2.38   This section includes representations[58] as to the state of mind of the maker or of another person. For example, by ordering a meal in a restaurant a person thereby impliedly claims to have, not only the means of payment, but also the intention to pay. If, in fact, the person does not have the intention to pay this would be a false representation. The fact that the drafters felt it necessary to explicitly include representations as to a state of mind is due to decisions under the Larceny Act 1916 law of false pretences. In *Dent*[59] a man took fees from farmers to keep their land free from pests for a period, without ever intending to actually undertake any pest control—it was held that this did not amount to a false pretence for the purposes of that Act, as it related only to his own state of mind at the time.

(c) *Silence as a Representation*

2.39   In *Firth*[60] the defendant was a consultant gynaecologist who omitted to inform a hospital that certain patients referred by him for treatment were private patients. Had the hospital known this, either he or the patients would have been charged for the services provided. It was held that he had evaded a liability by deception. The deception lay in the act of referring private patients plus the failure to correct the hospital's natural assumption that they were NHS patients. The courts will usually find that a deception has taken place if the defendant has formed a dishonest intent, and then subsequently entered into or continued his dealings with the victim in an apparently honest manner. However, each case involving silence or non-disclosure must be judged on its merits. In *Rai*[61] the Court of Appeal pointed out that *Firth* should not be taken as general authority for the proposition that mere silence can constitute deception.

2.40   Generally, mere silence is not enough for fraud by false representation. Section 2 is silent on the subject, unlike s 4(2) which specifically includes omissions in the case of fraud by abuse of position. The Law Commission did not intend fraud by false representation to apply to mere silence, and specifically enacted the following sections: fraud by failure to disclose, and fraud by abuse of position, to deal with cases where failings rather than acts would be sufficient to constitute fraud.

2.41   The Solicitor General's remarks tended to support the view that there must be some positive act, when he said:

> The types of representation covered by the clause may be of fact or law, including a representation as to a person's state of mind. They can be stated in written or spoken words, or in non-verbal communication.[62]

2.42   It may be that the courts will need to look at contract law precedents in determining the extent of fraud by false representation. In contract law, silence may be taken to amount to a misrepresentation in three ways:

---

[59] [1955] 2 QB 590.   [60] (1990) 91 Cr App R 217.   [61] [2000] 1 Cr App R 242.
[62] *Hansard*, HC Standing Committee B 20 June 2006 col 7.

(a) Half-truths—where the maker of the representation tells part of the truth but is silent upon part of the truth.[63]

(b) Statements which become false—where a statement was true when made, but due to a change of circumstances has become false by the time it is acted upon, there is a duty to disclose the truth.[64] In criminal law, where a person orders a restaurant meal intending to pay for it, but in the course of the meal determines not to pay, he is impliedly making a continuing representation that he will pay.[65]

(c) In contracts of utmost good faith such as contracts of insurance, which impose a duty of disclosure of all material facts, a failure to mention such a fact may be held to be a misrepresentation. In the Fraud Act 2006 such failures to disclose are better considered under s 3—fraud by failure to disclose.

(d) *False Representation*

A representation is false if it is objectively untrue or misleading and, subjectively, 2.43 the person knows that it is, or might be, untrue or misleading. The Home Office took the view that misleading means 'less than wholly true and capable of an interpretation to the detriment of the victim'.[66]

If the representation happens to be objectively true, but the person makes it 2.44 believing it to be false, they may be guilty of an attempt to commit the fraud offence, but not the full offence.

The fact that a person may be guilty of the offence by making an untrue statement 2.45 without knowing it to be untrue, eg, where the defendant knows that it might be misleading, broadens the offence to include statements which are unintentionally false.

3. Unintentional Falsity

Under the old law deception was defined in terms of recklessness. 'Deception' meant 2.46 'any deception (whether deliberate or *reckless*) by words or conduct as to fact or as to law, including a deception as to the present intentions of the person using the deception or any other person'.[67] Recklessness in this context meant 'an indifference to or disregard of the feature of whether a statement be true or false'.[68] In considering the draft Fraud Bill, the Law Commission was concerned that recklessness was an uncertain concept.[69] At the time it meant different things in different contexts.[70] Its draft Bill adopted the formula 'knows that it is untrue or misleading, or is aware that it might be'.[71] After consultation, the Home Office settled upon the current

---

[63] For example, *Nottingham Brick & Tile Co v Butler* (1889) 16 QBD 778.
[64] For example, *With v O'Flanagan* [1936] Ch 575.   [65] See *DPP v Ray* [1974] AC 370.
[66] *Fraud Law Reform*, Government response to consultation, para 19. Available at<http://www.homeoffice.gov.uk/documents/cons-fraud-law-reform/Government_response.pdf?view=Binary>.
[67] Theft Act 1968, s 15(4).   [68] *Staines* 60 Cr App R 160.
[69] Law Commission, *Fraud* (see Chapter 1, n 1, above for reference) para 7.17.
[70] *Caldwell* [1982] AC 341—though in this context it could only have been *Cunningham* recklessness—that is to say actual foresight of the risk that it might be untrue or misleading.
[71] Clause 2 of the draft Bill in Law Commission, *Fraud* (see Chapter 1, n 1, above for reference).

formula 'person making it knows that it is, or might be, untrue or misleading'[72] as being better precedented and less likely to give rise to technical arguments.

2.47   The Home Office gives the example of a fraudster claiming in a brochure that a particular scheme involved a 'High Yield Investment'. It may be difficult to show that he knows in advance that this is untrue, but he would be aware that it might be misleading.[73]

2.48   By the time the Bill was debated in Parliament any confusion that there may have been in respect of the legal meaning of *recklessness* had been resolved in the case of *G*.[74] At the House of Lords committee stage it was sought to amend the Bill to return to a definition based on recklessness.[75] The following example was given: where an auction house has good reason to believe a painting to be a genuine Renoir, and sells it as such, but it turns out to be incorrectly attributed, are they not guilty of the offence as drafted? They must know, given the inevitable uncertainties in the area, that their attribution might be untrue. To be safe they would have to state 'we honestly believe this to be a Renoir' rather than 'this is a painting by Renoir'.[76] Only where such an auction house could be said to be reckless, in the sense of not caring to make sufficient checks, should they be held culpable. The Attorney General's response was that the definition would remain the way it was, and that the element of dishonesty would draw the line in such marginal cases.[77]

2.49   Another common example of conduct which may be caught was given by Lord Kingsland:

> For example, advertisers may make representations knowing that they might be misleading. As they clearly act with the intention of making a gain, their only protection from criminal liability is the question of dishonesty. It is too uncertain to leave culpability in these circumstances to the subjective view of the jury.[78]

Nevertheless, the Act was passed in the terms of the Bill. Section 2(3) makes the offence wide. The Law Commission's antipathy to 'letting dishonesty do all the work'[79] failed to determine the wording of this part of the Act.

D. FRAUD BY FAILING TO DISCLOSE INFORMATION (SECTION 3)

1. Introduction

2.50   A person commits fraud if he dishonestly fails to disclose to another person information which he is under a legal duty to disclose, intending thereby to make

---

[72] *Fraud Law Reform*, Government response to consultation, para 17. (See n 66, above, for reference).
[73] Ibid, para 16.   [74] [2003] UKHL 53.
[75] Lord Kingsland proposed retaining the requirement for knowledge that it might be untrue or misleading but replacing 'or might be untrue ...' with recklessness.
[76] *Fraud Law Reform*, Government response to consultation, para 18. (See n 66, above, for reference).
[77] *Hansard*, HL 19 July 2005 col 1416.   [78] Ibid.
[79] For example, Law Commission, *Fraud* (see Chapter 1, n 1, above for reference) para 7.3.

a gain for himself or another, or to cause loss to another or to expose another to a risk of loss.[80] Section 3 reads:

3 Fraud by failing to disclose information

A person is in breach of this section if he—

    (a) dishonestly fails to disclose to another person information which he is under a legal duty to disclose, and

    (b) intends, by failing to disclose the information—

        (i) to make a gain for himself or another, or

        (ii) to cause loss to another or to expose another to a risk of loss.

The section extends the offence of fraud from the making of a positive false representation to include non-disclosure in cases where there is a legal duty to make a disclosure. It thereby seeks to remove the need artificially to imply a positive representation for the purposes of fraud by false representation, where the true dishonesty lies in the failure to provide crucial information, rather than the making of a specific representation. The Attorney General explained in the House of Lords that the section applies: **2.51**

when something that most of us naturally might think of as a non-disclosure is transformed by a fiction of the law into an implicit misrepresentation. But it is a fiction; it is not how people think about it. People will frequently say, 'I was not misled because I understand that he was implicitly making this representation to me. He just did not disclose something; he was dishonest in not disclosing it; and the purpose of that was to make a gain or to do something else'. One can think of many other examples where that would be the true basis on which a charge would be laid.

There are many occasions in the law where there is a duty of disclosure: in contracts of insurance, under certain market customs or certain contractual arrangements. In those circumstances, people may well be under a duty to make a disclosure and fail to make it. That will have consequences in law. The noble Lord may imagine, for example, the ability to set aside contracts on the grounds of non-disclosure and that sort of thing. Furthermore, those may have given rise to an economic loss to the person to whom the disclosure was not made or a benefit to the person who failed to make the disclosure. The Government believe, as did the Commission, that it was right, fairly and squarely, to identify that as a form of unlawful conduct.[81]

There is an overlap between s 3 and fraud by false representation cases where it is possible to infer a positive representation from silence of the person with a legal duty to disclose. The Home Office recognized that s 3 is the clearer charge as it is helpful to juries to have the point made clear on the face of the law.[82]   **2.52**

2. Examples

In the case of *Firth*[83] described at para 2.39 above it may well have been that the doctor had a contractual duty to disclose to the hospital whether his patients were   **2.53**

---

[80] Sample counts of the new fraud offences are contained in Appendix 9 of this book.

[81] *Hansard*, HL 19 July 2005 col 1411.

[82] *Fraud Law Reform*, Government response to consultation, para 21. (See n 66, above, for reference).

[83] (1990) 91 Cr App R 217.

referred under the National Health Service or privately, in which case his failure so to disclose would be fraud under the s 3 limb. However, in the absence of a clear legal duty, it would presumably remain necessary to stretch the effect of his silence to amount to a positive misrepresentation as under the existing law.

2.54　　In the case of *Williams (Jean Jacques)*[84] the defendant took obsolete Yugoslavian banknotes to a bureau de change and said words to the effect of 'will you change these notes?' The cashier paid him over £100 for notes that were worth £7. The Court of Appeal upheld his conviction for theft and went on to remark that a deception charge could have been made out: the defendant had impliedly represented that he believed the notes to be valid currency in Yugoslavia. Arguably it was for the bureau de change to make such enquiry as they wished before buying the notes—the defendant having been silent on the matter. Under the new law, such a defendant is not under a legal duty to disclose so would not be caught by s 3 (nor is he in a position of trust for the purposes of s 4 below). If the courts are to find that such conduct amounts to fraud the same sort of reasoning as was used under the old law will be necessary in order to bring the conduct under the fraud by false representation limb.

2.55　　In light of these examples it may be that s 3 will be of relatively narrow application, confined, as it is, to cases in which a clear legal duty can be readily discerned.

3. The Legal Duty

2.56　In the words of the Attorney General:

although the expression 'legal duty' is not commonly used in statutory law, it clearly distinguishes the kinds of duty which should be considered, so that the offence does not encroach on civil or moral duties. I suggest that there will be no difficulty in distinguishing a legal duty from what is not a legal duty.[85]

2.57　　The Law Commission explained the extent of the legal duty to which it intended to give effect:

LEGAL DUTY OF DISCLOSURE

7.28 First, non-disclosure of information should suffice if there is a legal duty to disclose it. Such a duty may derive from statute (such as the provisions governing company prospectuses [Financial Services and Markets Act 2000 section 90]), from the fact that the transaction in question is one of the utmost good faith (such as a contract of insurance), from the express or implied terms of a contract, from the custom of a particular trade or market, or from the existence of a fiduciary relationship between the parties (such as that of agent and principal).

7.29 For this purpose there is a legal duty to disclose information not only if the defendant's failure to disclose it gives the victim a cause of action for damages, but also if the law gives the victim a right to set aside any change in his or her legal position

---

[84] [1980] Crim LR 589.　　[85] The Attorney General, *Hansard*, HL 19 July 2005 col 1427.

to which he or she may consent as a result of the non-disclosure. For example, a person in a fiduciary position has a duty to disclose material information when entering into a contract with his or her beneficiary, in the sense that a failure to make such disclosure will entitle the beneficiary to rescind the contract and to reclaim any property transferred under it.[86]

The draft Bill used the expression 'is under a duty under any enactment, instrument or rule of law to disclose the information'.[87] This was replaced by the undefined *legal duty* in the Bill passed by Parliament. The Attorney General explained that this 'would cover all forms of legal duty, such as duties arising under the express terms of an oral contract'.[88] 2.58

(a) *Two Examples*

The Solicitor General outlined two possible examples that are intended to be caught by the Act: 2.59

An example would be where a solicitor fails to tell a client relevant information about the law or case that would result in the solicitor gaining financial benefit personally and the client losing. There is a clear relationship between the solicitor and the client. There is a duty to disclose that information. He has failed to disclose that information. He has done so knowing that he has the duty and, therefore, he has acted dishonestly. The result of that should be that he has failed to disclose information and therefore committed an act of fraud.

Another question might arise in a more difficult case, when a person is applying for insurance and has a heart condition, which they failed to disclose. That is a civil matter; to some extent, it involves a breach of an *uberrima fides* duty to disclose information in particular types of contract. Obviously, insurance companies may well take the view that they would deal with that through the civil procedures and that would be the normal way. However it is possible for someone who was deliberately intending to obtain insurance coverage and, in due course, to make a claim on it to be in a position where they were failing to disclose relevant information where they had a legal duty to do so, with the intention of benefiting, either by insurance coverage or by undertaking a medical procedure using that insurance. The result might be that they are in breach of the clause.[89]

(b) *Dependence upon Civil Law*

It is apparent that an analysis of whether or not a person is under a legal duty to make a particular disclosure will necessitate a consideration of the civil law. It is likely that it will be considered a matter of mixed fact and law. It will be for the judge to direct the jury that, if they find a certain set of facts in the case to be made out, then there is a legal duty. 2.60

The criminal law need not, in principle, exactly follow civil law.[90] 2.61

---

[86] Law Commission, *Fraud* (see Chapter 1, n 1, above for reference) paras 7.28–7.29.
[87] Clause 3(3) of the draft Bill in ibid.   [88] *Hansard*, HL 19 July 2005 col 1427.
[89] *Hansard*, HC Standing Committee B 20 June 2006 col 10.
[90] See para 2.72, below.

(c) *Knowledge of Circumstances which Give Rise to the Duty*

2.62 There is no explicit requirement in the Act that the person who makes the non-disclosure is aware of their duty to make the disclosure, or even the circumstances that give rise to it. In the Law Commission's draft Bill it was required that 'D knows that the circumstances which give rise to the duty to disclose the information to P exist or is aware that they might exist'.[91] It stated:

> It is perhaps unlikely that a person might be under a legal duty to disclose information despite being ignorant of the circumstances giving rise to the duty. On principle, however, we believe that the offence should require knowledge that such circumstances exist, or at least awareness that they might exist.[92]

The Act omits any such requirement, but it is unlikely that a person who does not make a disclosure could be held to be dishonest if they are unaware of the circumstances which give rise to a duty to disclose.

2.63 The knowledge of the circumstances is certainly a requirement in the case of a conspiracy to commit fraud—see Chapter 3.

(d) *Moral Duty to Disclose*

2.64 Originally, the Law Commission sought to criminalize non-disclosure in circumstances where the person is under a moral duty to disclose, that is to say where:

(a) the information is the kind of information that P trusts D to disclose to him;
(b) D knows that P is trusting him in this way or is aware that he might be; and
(c) any reasonable person would expect D to disclose the information to P.[93]

They had in mind, for instance, the conduct of an antiques dealer who preys upon vulnerable persons by building a relationship of trust, and appearing to offer value for antiques, but in fact offering substantial under-value.[94]

2.65 After consultation the Government decided that it was inappropriate to include such conduct:[95]

(a) It would intrude upon the principle of *caveat emptor* (buyer beware: it is for the buyer to make such enquiry as is necessary of the seller of goods), so that it would become criminal not to provide information which it is legitimate to withhold under civil law. As the Solicitor General confirmed, this was not the intention of the Bill:

> When people are engaged in commercial relationships, there is the principle of *caveat emptor*, which has been restricted by various pieces of legislation over the years by Parliament. Let the buyer beware. That will still be the case. When people engage in normal commercial

---

[91] Clause 3(3)(b) of the draft Bill in Law Commission, *Fraud* (see Chapter 1, n 1, above for reference).
[92] Law Commission, *Fraud* para 7.30.
[93] Clause 3(4) of the draft Bill in Law Commission, *Fraud* (see Chapter 1, n 1, above for reference).
[94] Law Commission, *Fraud* para 7.33.
[95] *Fraud Law Reform*, Government response to consultation, para 22. (See n 66, above, for reference).

relationships, the buyer will need to be beware, to be aware of what the person who is selling the product says.[96]

(b) It would be too uncertain, as it would be necessary, in each case, to make a subjective analysis as to whether the victim is trusting the person withholding the information, and as to what a reasonable person would expect to be disclosed.

It is clear that Parliament intended to confine the fraud offence to cases where there is a clear legal duty to disclose, as opposed to a moral one. An example was given by the shadow Solicitor General:

Clearly, there are numerous instances in which individuals might elect not to tell somebody something because they think that it is to their financial advantage. The classic example is the person being offered an object for sale at £50 who knows very well from his greater expertise that the item is worth £50,000 and chooses not to tell the vendor. He is under no legal duty to give him that information and, therefore, he would not be caught by the provisions of clause 3.[97]

E. FRAUD BY ABUSE OF POSITION (SECTION 4)

1. Introduction

A person is guilty of fraud if he occupies a position in which he is expected to 2.66 safeguard, or not to act against, the financial interests of another person and he dishonestly abuses that position, intending thereby to make a gain for himself or another, or to cause loss to another, or to expose another to a risk of loss.[98] A person may be regarded as having abused his position even though his conduct consisted of an omission rather than an act. The section states:

4 Fraud by abuse of position

(1) A person is in breach of this section if he—
    (a) occupies a position in which he is expected to safeguard, or not to act against, the financial interests of another person,
    (b) dishonestly abuses that position, and
    (c) intends, by means of the abuse of that position—
        (i) to make a gain for himself or another, or
        (ii) to cause loss to another, or to expose another to a risk of loss.
(2) A person may be regarded as having abused his position even though his conduct consisted of an omission rather than an act.

The section extends the fraud offence to cover fraud by act or omission by those in a position of trust.

    Where a person is in a position of trust they may be able to commit fraud 2.67 with considerably more ease than those who are not in such a position. Whilst

---

[96] *Hansard*, HC Standing Committee B 20 June 2006 col 10.
[97] *Hansard*, HC Standing Committee B 20 June 2006 col 9.　　[98] Section 4.

the ordinary person may need to enlist another person's cooperation, through a false representation, to achieve their desired purpose, those in a position of trust already have access to everything they need to commit fraud. For this reason fraud by those in a position of trust must be handled separately within the legislation.

2.68   An employee is given access to his employer's premises, equipment, and customers and is trusted to use them for his employer's benefit, not his own. Often, if he wishes to use them to his own benefit there may be nothing to stop him doing so. The section is intended to bring those who make use of their employer's premises and equipment for their own purposes within the ambit of the fraud offence.

2. The Position of Trust

2.69   The position in which a person is expected to safeguard, or not to act against, the financial interests of another person may present some problems of interpretation. The principal difficulty is who is expected to so safeguard? It is clear that those in a fiduciary relationship are intended to be included in the section. Beyond that, matters become less clear. It is not immediately apparent whose expectation is determinative—is it the victim's subjective expectation or a wider objective expectation? Does the expectation need to be a reasonable one? The Government appears to anticipate it being a straight question of fact for the jury to determine according to their own standards, like dishonesty:

> We see no problem in a jury determining when one person is in a position to safeguard the interests of another. Furthermore, in most cases the crucial issue will not be the relationship between the defendant and the victim, but whether the defendant's actions were, in its sum, dishonest.[99]

2.70   Alternatively it may be a question of mixed fact and law. The judge would determine whether or not the particular relationship is capable of falling within the definition, before the jury determine that this is as a matter of fact within the definition.

2.71   The Law Commission explained the intended scope of the section:

> 7.38 The necessary relationship will be present between trustee and beneficiary, director and company, professional person and client, agent and principal, employee and employer, or between partners. It may arise otherwise, for example within a family, or in the context of voluntary work, or in any context where the parties are not at arm's length. In nearly all cases where it arises, it will be recognised by the civil law as importing fiduciary duties, and any relationship that is so recognised will suffice. We see no reason, however, why the existence of such duties should be essential. This does not of course mean that it would be entirely a matter for the fact-finders whether the necessary relationship exists. The question whether the particular facts alleged can properly be described as giving rise to that relationship will be

---

[99] *Hansard*, HC Standing Committee B 20 June 2006 col 21.

an issue capable of being ruled upon by the judge and, if the case goes to the jury, of being the subject of directions.[100]

In civil law those in a position of trust are said to have fiduciary duties towards the person who trusts them. It is likely that any relationship recognized by the civil law as importing fiduciary duties will fall within the definition of the section. In *Bristol and West Building Society v Mothew*,[101] Lord Justice Millet said:

A fiduciary is someone who has undertaken to act for or on behalf of another in a particular matter in circumstances which give rise to a relationship of trust and confidence. The distinguishing obligation of a fiduciary is the obligation of loyalty. The principal is entitled to the single-minded loyalty of his fiduciary. This core liability has several facets. A fiduciary must act in good faith; he must not make a profit out of his trust; he must not place himself in a position where his duty and his interest may conflict; he may not act for his own benefit or the benefit of a third person without the informed consent of his principal. This is not intended to be an exhaustive list, but it is sufficient to indicate the nature of fiduciary obligations. They are the defining characteristics of the fiduciary. As Dr. Finn pointed out in his classic work *Fiduciary Obligations* (1977), p. 2, he is not subject to fiduciary obligations because he is a fiduciary; it is because he is subject to them that he is a fiduciary.[102]

However, the determination of whether a particular position falls within the scope of section 4 need not be bound by a strict analysis of the civil law. As can be seen from the case of *Hinks*, the purposes of the civil law and the criminal law are somewhat different. In theory the two systems should be in perfect harmony. In a practical world there will sometimes be some disharmony between the two.[103] It is the intention of the section to go beyond fiduciary relationships:

It would be difficult in some circumstances for prosecutors to argue that a particular relationship, which members of the public may well see as a relationship where someone is expected to safeguard the interests of another, was necessarily a fiduciary relationship. While in most cases the measure would apply to circumstances where a duty clearly exists, there would be some cases where a formal legal duty may not exist. Those cases will arise particularly in personal and family relationships.[104]

3. The Abuse of Position

With the trust to act in accordance with someone's financial interests comes the power to damage those interests. If a person in a position of trust acts against the financial interests of the person who trusts them, they abuse that position.

The abuse of position may be by omission as well as a positive act. So an employee passing off the opportunity of a lucrative contract so that an associate can take

[100] Law Commission, *Fraud* para 7.37 (see Chapter 1, n 1, above for reference).
[101] [1998] 1 Ch 1.   [102] Ibid, at 18.
[103] *Per* Lord Steyn in *Hinks* [2001] 2 AC 241 at 252 (Lord Slynn of Hadley and Lord Jauncey of Tullichettle agreeing).
[104] *Hansard*, HC Standing Committee B, Solicitor General 20 June 2005 cols 20–21.

advantage of it is caught by the section, just as a person entering into a poor contract to advantage an associate would be.

2.76 The wording of the Act means that theoretically the person to whom it is intended to cause loss or expose to risk of financial loss need not be the same person as the person whose financial interests are expected to be protected.

4. Examples

2.77 Two examples of conduct likely to be within the scope of the section are:

(a) A public house manager, employed by a brewery, secretly bought and sold his own supply of beer at the premises, in order to make a secret profit. As an employee he is in a position in which the brewery company expects him to safeguard their financial interests (amongst other things, by selling as much of their beer as possible). He has abused that position by using the brewer's facilities to make his own profit. He did so with the intent of making a gain for himself, so (provided the jury consider him to be dishonest) he is guilty of fraud by abuse of position.

Note that he is not guilty of stealing the secret profit as this was not property belonging the brewery.[105] However, where two or more people are involved in the scheme it would be a conspiracy to defraud.[106]

(b) The operators of a residential care home for the elderly are entrusted by a lady in their care with her financial affairs. They conduct her affairs so as to benefit themselves. They are not obviously within the types of formal relationship listed above in para 2.69, but, nevertheless, they are in a position in which they are expected to safeguard her financial affairs, and they have dishonestly abused that position with intent to make a gain for themselves. So (provided the jury consider them to be dishonest) they are guilty of fraud by abuse of position.

Note that they are also likely to be guilty of a conspiracy to steal.[107]

2.78 A technically possible use of the literal application of the section is:

The compliance officer of a large bank ceases to monitor the bank's risk and exposure but instead spends his day playing card games on his computer. He is in a position of trust and by his omission he is abusing his position and exposing the bank to the risk of financial loss. Provided the jury find that he is dishonest, he is in breach of the section and guilty of fraud. Are all employees who fail to dedicate their whole working time to their employer's interests guilty of fraud? Perhaps companies could choose to privately prosecute indolent staff rather than go through the trouble of dismissing them by other means!

---

[105] *Attorney General's Reference (No 1 of 1985)* [1986] QB 491.
[106] *Cooke* [1986] 1 AC 909.
[107] *Hopkins and Kendrick* [1997] 2 Cr App R 524.

5. Abuse of a Public Office

Many public officials are in a position in which they are expected to safeguard or 2.79
not to act against the financial interests of another person (ie, the public at large
or, perhaps, the monarch). So the section would catch fraud by local or central
government officials.

If a public officer wilfully neglects to perform his duty and/or wilfully misconducts 2.80
himself to such a degree as to amount to an abuse of the public's trust in the office-
holder, without reasonable excuse or justification, he is also guilty of the common
law offence of misfeasance in public office.[108]

6. Secrecy

It was originally thought that secrecy should be an essential ingredient of this 2.81
offence.[109] There is no requirement in the Act for the abuse of position to be done
secretly in the sense that the perpetrator believes the victim is ignorant of the abuse.

The Law Commission included a requirement for secrecy in their draft Bill, but 2.82
it was removed from the Government Bill before Parliament. The Government
believed that it would be difficult to define and would risk giving rise to technical
arguments. It believed that secrecy would always be present in practice, and is
embodied in the value-laden concepts of *abuse* and *dishonesty*.[110] It is certainly
difficult to conceive of an abuse of position, which was done in the full knowledge
of the 'victim' being held to be dishonest.

---

[108] *Attorney General's Reference (No 3 of 2003)* [2004] 2 Cr App R 23 (CA).
[109] Law Commission, *Fraud* (see Chapter 1, n 1, above for reference) para 7.18 *et seq.*
[110] *Fraud Law Reform*, Government response to consultation, para 28. (See n 66, above, for
reference).

3

AGREEMENTS TO COMMIT FRAUD

A. OVERVIEW

Agreements to commit fraud are dealt with in three ways by the criminal law: 3.01

(a) A statutory conspiracy to commit the fraud offence contrary to the Fraud Act 2006, s 1.
(b) A statutory conspiracy to commit an offence contrary to some other act, eg, conspiracy to steal,[1] or conspiracy to perform unauthorized modifications to a computer.[2]
(c) The common law offence of conspiracy to defraud.

   The Government intends to abolish conspiracy to defraud, if it is shown that the   3.02 statutory offences effectively cover all the conduct which ought to be covered. The Law Commission believes that this has been achieved. In the meantime, the use of the common law offence is restricted in a number of ways, with the emphasis upon finding an appropriate statutory alternative wherever possible.

---

[1] Theft Act 1968, s 1.   [2] Computer Misuse Act 1990.

B. STATUTORY CONSPIRACY TO COMMIT FRAUD

3.03   If a person agrees with any other person or persons that a course of conduct shall be pursued which, if the agreement is carried out in accordance with their intentions will necessarily amount to, or involve the commission of, a fraud offence contrary to the Fraud Act 2006, s 1 he is guilty of conspiracy to commit fraud under the Criminal Law Act 1977, s 1.

1. Criminal Law Act 1977

3.04   The Criminal Law Act 1977 creates the statutory offence of conspiracy:

1 The offence of conspiracy

(1) Subject to the following provisions of this part of this Act, if a person agrees with any other person or persons that a course of conduct shall be pursued which, if the agreement is carried out in accordance with their intentions, either—
- (a) will necessarily amount to or involve the commission of any offence or offences by one or more of the parties to the agreement, or
- (b) would do so but for the existence of facts which render the commission of the offence or any of the offences impossible,

he is guilty of conspiracy to commit the offence or offences in question.

(2) Where liability for any offence may be incurred without knowledge on the part of the person committing it of any particular fact or circumstance necessary for the commission of the offence, a person shall nevertheless not be guilty of conspiracy to commit that offence by virtue of subsection (1) above unless he and at least one other party to the agreement intend or know that that fact or circumstance shall or will exist at the time when the conduct constituting the offence is to take place.

    ...

(4) In this Part of this Act "offence" means an offence triable in England and Wales ...

3.05   In a case of a conspiracy the jury will usually be directed as follows:[3]

Just as it is a criminal offence to ... so is it a criminal offence for two or more persons to agree with one another to commit that offence. An agreement to commit an offence is called a conspiracy; and that is the offence which is charged here.

Before you can convict either/any of these defendants of this offence, you must be sure:

1. That there was in fact an agreement between two or more persons to commit (the crime in question); and
2. That the defendant whose case you are considering was a party to that agreement in the sense that:
   - (i) he agreed with one or more of the other persons referred to in the count that the crime should be committed; and
   - (ii) at the time of agreeing to this, he intended that they [he/X] should carry it out.

---

[3] Judicial Studies Board specimen direction August 2005.

You may think that it is only in a rare case that a jury would receive direct evidence of a criminal conspiracy (e.g. eye witness/documentary evidence). When people make agreements to commit crimes you would expect them to do so in private. You would not expect them to agree to commit crime in front of others or to put their agreement into writing. But people may act together to bring about a particular result in such a way as to leave no doubt that they are carrying out an earlier agreement.

Accordingly, in deciding whether there was a criminal conspiracy, and if so whether the defendant whose case you are considering was a party to it, look at all the evidence as to what occurred during the relevant period (this is usually but not necessarily the period covered by the count), including the behaviour of each of the defendants/alleged conspirators. If having done that you are sure that there was a conspiracy and that he was a party to it, you must convict. If you are not sure, you must acquit.

When criminal conspiracies are formed it may well happen that one or more of the conspirators is more deeply involved in and has a greater knowledge of the overall plan than the others. Also, a person may agree to join in the conspiracy after it has been formed or he may drop out of it before the crime has been fully carried out. Providing you are sure in the case of any defendant that he did at some stage agree [with a named co-conspirator] that the crime [in question] should be committed and at that time intended that it should be carried out, it does not matter precisely where his involvement appears on the scale of seriousness or precisely when he became involved, he is guilty as charged.

2. Actus Reus

The *actus reus* of the offence is the forming of the agreement that a course of 3.06
conduct be pursued. The course of conduct must necessarily amount to or involve the commission of any offence or offences by one or more of the parties to the agreement. It is not necessary to prove that the carrying out of the agreement will necessarily result in the commission of a *specific* offence, provided that it can be shown that it would result in the commission of an offence or offences.

(a) For example, an agreement to launder either drug money (an offence under the Drug Trafficking Act 1994) or the proceeds of other crime (an offence under the separate regime contained in the Criminal Justice Act 1988, as amended) may be charged as a single conspiracy to commit one offence *or* the other.[4]

(b) An agreement to commit one offence or another may be a conditional agreement to commit each of them.[5]

In the offence of conspiracy to commit fraud the underlying offence-creating 3.07
section is s 1 of the Fraud Act 2006. This creates a single offence that may be committed in three ways.[6] So the conspiracy offence is a conspiracy to commit the s 1 offence, albeit that the particulars of the offence would describe one (or more) of the three branches. If it were to be uncertain which branch of the fraud offence the course of conduct would amount to, there would be no problem as the s 1 offence covers all of the branches. The Fraud Act is an improvement over the

---

[4] *El-Kurd* [2001] Crim LR 234; *Hussain* [2002] 2 Cr App R 26.
[5] *Attorney General's Reference (No 4 of 2003)* [2005] 1 Cr App R 2.   [6] Sections 2–4.

Theft Act deception offence where conspiracies would be difficult to prove if it were uncertain in what form the benefit would be received, eg, cash, money transfer or cheque.[7]

3. Agreements to Assist Fraud

3.08 The agreement must relate to offences that would be committed by one or more of the parties to the agreement, so an agreement to enable third parties to inflict loss would not amount to a statutory conspiracy. This is a significant difference between the statutory offence and common law conspiracy to defraud—see para 3.31 below.

4. The *Mens Rea* in Conspiracy

3.09 In *Yip Chiu-Cheung v R*[8] (a Privy Council case concerning the Hong Kong common law) Lord Griffiths said:

The crime of conspiracy requires an agreement between two or more persons to commit an unlawful act with the intention of carrying it out. It is the intention to carry out the crime that constitutes the necessary *mens rea* for the offence.

Hence, in that case, an undercover officer who agreed to export drugs but did not intend to carry out the operation did not have the necessary *mens rea* for conspiracy.

3.10 However, where the existence of a specific circumstance is part of the definition of an offence, the position is more complicated. In the Law Commission report underlying the Criminal Law Act 1977[9] the Commission said:[10]

What the prosecution ought to have to prove is that the defendant agreed with another person that a course of conduct should be pursued which would result, if completed, in the commission of a criminal offence, and further that they both knew any facts they would need to know to make them aware that the agreed course of conduct would result in the commission of the offence.

3.11 Section 1(2) provides for the latter requirement of *mens rea*. A person shall not be guilty of a conspiracy to commit an offence unless he and at least one other party to the agreement intend or know that the facts necessary to the commission of the offence shall or will exist at the time of the conduct. The subsection applies to all offences. Whenever an ingredient of an offence is the existence of a particular fact or circumstance, the subsection applies to that ingredient.[11] 'The provision is intended to ensure that strict liability and recklessness have no place in conspiracy.'[12]

---

[7] See the remarks in relation to attempts in Chapter 4 below (para 4.02).
[8] 99 Cr App R 406.
[9] Law Commission, *Conspiracy and Criminal Law Reform* (Law Com No 76, 1976).
[10] Ibid, para 1.39.   [11] *Saik* [2006] UKHL 18 para 21, per Lord Nicholls of Birkenhead.
[12] Per Professor Smith [1977] Crim LR 598.

(a) *Strict Liability Example*

It is an offence for an adult to engage in sexual activity with a child.[13] There is no 3.12
need for knowledge, on the part of the defendant, that the person is a child.[14] So
the offence is of strict liability in this respect; if A does not know that V is a child,
it provides him no defence to the substantive charge. If A and B agree to engage in
sexual activity with V, *without knowing or intending* that V is a child, common sense
dictates that they are not party to a conspiracy to engage in sexual activity with a child.

The age of the victim is a fact or circumstance necessary to the commission of 3.13
the offence. So A and B can only be guilty if they knew or intended the victim to
be a child.[15]

(b) *Recklessness Example*

The Criminal Damage Act 1971 states: 3.14

1 Destroying or damaging property

(1) A person who without lawful excuse destroys or damages any property belonging to
another intending to destroy or damage any such property or being reckless as to whether
any such property would be destroyed or damaged shall be guilty of an offence.

That the property is property that belongs to another is a particular fact or 3.15
circumstance necessary for the commission of the offence. Liability for the offence
may be incurred without knowledge on the part of the person committing it of that
fact: eg, where a person is reckless as to whether the property is property belonging
to another. However, 'recklessness has no place in a conspiracy', and s 1(2) requires
an additional *mens rea*: the defendant and at least one other party to the agreement
intend or know that the property is or will be property belonging to another at the
time when the conduct constituting the offence is to take place.

Professor David Ormerod has given an example of this in the *Criminal Law* 3.16
Review:[16]

As an illustration of the way the statute is designed to operate, suppose that D1 agrees to
help D2 move out of his flat. D2 is unsure whether the cabling he has installed for his
hi-fi now belongs to him or to his landlord. D1 and D2 confer together and are uncertain,
but agree, nevertheless, to remove it knowing their actions will result in damage to the
cabling in the process. They therefore have an intention to cause damage, and are reckless
as to whether the property belongs to another. The substantive offence of criminal damage
requires that D intends or is reckless as to the causing of damage (the result), and that D
knows or is reckless as to whether the property belongs to another (circumstance). If D1
and D2 went ahead, they would have sufficient *mens rea* to be convicted of the substantive
offence. As for the conspiracy, in the actual circumstances that exist, the carrying out of the

---

[13] Sexual Offences Act 2003, s 13.
[14] Subject to a reasonable belief defence where the child is 13 or over.
[15] Criminal Law Act 1977, s 1(2).   [16] *Sakavickas* Crim LR [2005] 293.

agreement 'will necessarily amount' to criminal damage; but on an orthodox reading of s 1(2), it is not a conspiracy to commit criminal damage. It would not be criminal damage in the circumstances which the parties intend, or know, or believe, shall or will exist. Ds are reckless as to the circumstance. Recklessness as to the circumstance of the *actus reus* (property belonging to another) is not a sufficient *mens rea* on a charge of conspiracy to commit a crime (criminal damage) even where it is a sufficient *mens rea* for the crime itself.

(c) *Lesser States of Knowledge Example: Suspicion*

3.17   Section 93C(2) of the Criminal Justice Act 1988 provided:

A person is guilty of an offence if, knowing or having reasonable grounds to suspect that any property is, or in whole or in part directly or indirectly represents, another person's proceeds of criminal conduct, he—

(a) conceals or disguises that property; or
(b) converts or transfers that property or removes it from the jurisdiction,

for the purpose of assisting any person to avoid prosecution for an offence to which this Part of this Act applies or the making or enforcement in his case of a confiscation order.

3.18   The acts prohibited by this offence include concealing property for the purpose of assisting any person to avoid prosecution for a relevant offence. It has been held that the property in question must as a matter of fact emanate from a crime.[17] This is a fact or circumstance falling within s 1(2). So, applying s 1(2) to that fact, the prosecution must prove that the conspirator intended or knew that fact would exist when the conspiracy was carried out. Hence, where the property has not been identified when the conspiracy agreement is reached, the prosecution must prove that the conspirator intended that the property would be the proceeds of criminal conduct.[18]

5. *Mens Rea* in Fraud Conspiracies

3.19   Applying these principles to conspiracies to commit fraud under the Fraud Act 2006, it appears that s 1(2) is of some effect in relation to conspiracies to commit a s 1 offence.

(a) *False Representation (section 2)*

3.20   Fraud by false representation requires the prosecution to prove the following elements:

(a) that the representation is made;
(b) the representation is false or misleading;
(c) that D knows that it is, or might be, untrue or misleading;
(d) dishonesty; and
(e) with fraudulent intent.

3.21   That the representation is false or misleading is a fact or circumstance necessary for the commission of the offence. For the substantive offence, the *mens rea* requirement

---

[17] *Montila* [2004] 1 WLR 3141.   [18] *Saik* [2006] UKHL 18.

in (c) is met even if the defendant did not *know* that the representation *was* untrue (or misleading), merely that *it might be* untrue (or misleading). This is different for the conspiracy offence. If s 1(2) is applied to the offence, in accordance with *Saik*, the prosecution need to prove that the defendant *knew* that the representation was false or misleading, or *intended* that it would be.

(b) *Failure to Disclose (section 3)*

Fraud by failing to disclose requires the prosecution to prove the following elements: 3.22

(a) D was under a legal duty to disclose information;
(b) D failed to disclose;
(c) dishonesty; and
(d) with fraudulent intention.

The draft Bill contained a specific requirement that D have knowledge of the   3.23
circumstances which give rise to the duty to disclose the information—this was left out of the government Bill (see Chapter 2 above). It is clear that the defendant does not need to know of the existence of the duty or of the circumstances giving rise to it, provided only that he was dishonest.

As the substantive offence may be committed without D being aware of the   3.24
circumstances giving rise to the duty, and that fact is necessary to the commission of the offence, the conspiracy charge requires the Crown to prove that D knew of the circumstances or intended that they would exist.

It is submitted that the Crown must prove that D was aware that the duty   3.25
existed (as opposed to being aware of the circumstances giving rise to it) as that is a matter of law rather than a fact or circumstance necessary to the commission of the offence.

(c) *Abuse of Position (section 4)*

Fraud by abuse of position requires the Crown to prove that: 3.26

(a) D occupied a position of trust;
(b) he abused that position by act or omission;
(c) dishonestly; and
(d) with fraudulent intention.

Again applying s 1(2) as above, D does not need to know of the circumstances   3.27
giving rise to the position of trust to be guilty of the substantive offence, but would need to do so for the conspiracy offence.

6. Use of Conspiracies

Generally, all substantive offences committed by more that one person acting in   3.28
concert necessarily also involve the commission of the corresponding conspiracy offence—the offenders agreed to commit the offence before committing it. To charge both the substantive and the conspiracy is unnecessarily burdensome, and is

to be avoided as a matter of practice. The *Practice Direction (Criminal Proceedings: Consolidation)*[19] states:

IV.34.3 ... Where an indictment contains substantive counts and one or more related conspiracy counts the judge should require the prosecution to justify the joinder. Failing justification the Crown should be required to elect whether to proceed on the substantive counts or the conspiracy counts. A joinder is justified for this purpose if the judge considers that the interests of justice demand it.

3.29　The Legal Guidance prepared by the Crown Prosecution Service states:

Where substantive counts meet the justice of the case, a conspiracy count will rarely need to be added but may be added where the substantive counts do not represent the overall criminality of the case.

One of the reasons care must be taken when deciding whether or not to charge conspiracy is the question of confiscation on conviction.[20]

7. Sentence

3.30　The maximum sentence applicable to a charge of conspiracy is that applicable to the corresponding substantive offence.

C. COMMON LAW CONSPIRACY TO DEFRAUD

1. Scope of the Common Law Offence

3.31　A partial definition of defraud is as follows:

To defraud is to deprive by deceit: it is deceit to induce a man to act to his injury.[21]

That definition is not exhaustive. A conspiracy to defraud at common law includes cases with or without economic loss:

(a) 'An agreement by two or more by dishonesty to deprive a person of something which is his or to which he is or would be or might be entitled and an agreement by two or more by dishonesty to injure some proprietary right [of the victim's]' is a conspiracy to defraud at common law.[22] The risk of possible prejudice to the victim's right is sufficient for the offence.

(b) An agreement to deceive a public official into doing something that he would not have done but for the deceit (or not doing something that but for it he would have done) is also a conspiracy to defraud. It is enough that anyone may be prejudiced in any way by the fraud.[23]

---

[19] [2002] 1 WLR 2870.
[20] Available at <http://www.cps.gov.uk/legal/section12/chapter_h.html#_toc44653352>.
[21] *Re London Globe Finance Corp* [1903] 1 Ch 728 at 732, per Buckley J.
[22] *Scott v Metropolitan Police Commissioner* [1975] AC 819 at 840F per Viscount Dilhorne.
[23] *Welham* [1961] AC 103.

In *Wai Yu-Tsang*[24] the chief accountant of a bank acted with what appears to have   3.32
been a benign motive to cover up bad cheques passing though the bank—desiring
to protect the business by preventing a run on the bank. His good intentions did
not prevent the conduct constituting the offence of conspiracy to defraud. It is the
risk of possible prejudice which is necessary to the offence:

It is however important to distinguish a conspirator's intention (or immediate purpose) ...
from his motive (or underlying purpose). The latter may be benign in that he does not wish
the victim or potential victim to suffer harm; but the mere fact that it is benign will not of
itself prevent the agreement from constituting a conspiracy to defraud.[25]

From the above it can be seen that the offence is a very broad one limited   3.33
primarily by the requirement for dishonesty. It is in the nature of ordinary business
dealings that business people try to deprive their competitors of their economic
advantage.

As conspiracy to defraud is so widely defined, it is necessary for the prosecution   3.34
to clearly identify the particulars of the allegation. The indictment for a conspiracy
to defraud must have sufficient particularity that the defence and court may know
on the face of the indictment itself the nature of the prosecution's case and that
the prosecution cannot shift its ground during the trial without leave of the judge
through an application to amend the indictment.[26]

2. Sentence

The maximum penalty for the offence has been fixed by statute to be a term not   3.35
exceeding ten years or a fine or both.[27]

3. The Debate on the Abolition of the Common Law Offence

(a) *Law Commission's Position*
The Law Commission intended that conspiracy to defraud should be abolished by   3.36
the Fraud Act 2006. In its 1976 report, *Conspiracy and Criminal Law Reform*,[28] it
said:

The object of a conspiracy should be limited to the commission of a substantive offence, and
there should be no place in a criminal code for a law of conspiracy extending beyond this
ambit. An agreement should not be criminal where that which it was agreed should be done
would not amount to a criminal offence if committed by one person.

In the 2002 report[29] it stated the underlying objectives as: 3.37

---

[24] [1992] 1 AC 269.   [25] Ibid, 280.   [26] *Landy* [1981] 1 WLR 355.
[27] Criminal Justice Act 1987, s 12.
[28] Law Commission, *Conspiracy and Criminal Law Reform* (Law Com No 76, 1976).
[29] Law Commission, *Fraud* (Law Com No 276, 2002), available at <http://www.lawcom.gov.uk/docs/lc276.pdf>.

(a) One is to ensure that the scope of the criminal law of fraud is wide enough to enable fraudsters to be successfully prosecuted and appropriately sentenced, without being so wide as to impose unacceptable restrictions on personal freedom, or so vague as to infringe the principles of the rule of law.

(b) The other is to eliminate the indefensible anomaly represented by the continuing survival of conspiracy to defraud, under which it may be a crime for two people to agree to do something which, in the absence of an agreement, either of them could lawfully do.[30]

3.38   In its latest report from 2002, which led to this Bill, the Law Commission said:[31]

This Commission has repeated its adherence to this principle in subsequent reports and we believe it commands very wide support. Either conspiracy to defraud is too wide in its scope (in that it catches agreements to do things that are rightly not criminal), or the statutory offences are too narrow (in that they fail to catch certain conduct which should be criminal), or—which is our view—the problem is a combination of the two. On any view, the present position is anomalous and has no place in a coherent criminal law.

3.39   Later in the 2002 report, the Law Commission said:[32]

If it is thought that certain torts, breaches of contract or equitable wrongs should be criminal, legislation can be framed with reference to the particular kinds of conduct involved. To retain conspiracy to defraud on the grounds that it might occasionally prove useful in certain cases would, in our view, be an excess of caution. Since it is not practicable to identify all such cases in advance, it would mean that we could never be in a position to abolish conspiracy to defraud, unless we were willing to replace it with a general dishonesty offence, an option that we rejected in Part 5, above. The advantages of abolishing it, in our view, greatly outweigh any possible advantage that might accrue from retaining it alongside the new offences we recommend. We believe that those offences cover enough of the ground presently covered by conspiracy to defraud to make it unnecessary to retain that offence any longer.

(b) *Comment in Favour of Retention*

3.40   There were various responses to consultation supporting the view that the offence should not be abolished. In particular:

Lord Justice Rose had written on behalf of senior judges:

It would be risky to repeal common law conspiracy to defraud as it can be the most effective charge in a case where multiple defendants are engaged in a fraudulent course of conduct. There are limitations on the law of statutory conspiracy, which has had something of a chequered history. All the judges present at the meeting agreed the Bill should not repeal common law conspiracy to defraud.[33]

The CPS had written in their response to consultation that they:

strongly oppose the proposal to repeal this offence ... It has a significant advantage of being an offence which can cover a whole range of activity which has allowed the courts historically to develop the offence to fit new situations ... and where facts are complex and reveal a

---

[30] Law Commission, para 1.4.   [31] Ibid, para 3.5.   [32] Ibid, para 9.4.
[33] *Hansard*, HL 14 March 2006 col 1114.

multiplicity of offences, it makes sense to encapsulate all of these in one simple statement of offence.[34]

The Serious Fraud Office had a similar view.

(c) *The Government's Position*

There was much debate in Parliament as to whether or not the offence should be 3.41 abolished. The Government refused to do so now, but intends to return to the subject in due course. The Attorney General made the following commitment at the Lords' committee stage:[35]

I shall ensure that the continuing need for the retention of the common law offence is addressed in the Home Office review of the operation of the Fraud Act, and the Government commit to review the operation of the Act three years after its implementation.

4. An Historical Note: *Ayres*

The Fraud Act 2006 is not the first time that Parliament has come close to abolishing 3.42 conspiracy to defraud. The Criminal Law Act 1977, s 5 abolished common law conspiracies other than conspiracy to defraud, and certain conspiracies to corrupt public morals or outrage public decency:

5 Abolitions, savings, transitional provisions, consequential amendment and repeals

(1) Subject to the following provisions of this section, the offence of conspiracy at common law is hereby abolished.
(2) Subsection (1) above shall not affect the offence of conspiracy at common law so far as relates to conspiracy to defraud ...

The Criminal Law Act 1977, s 5(2) as enacted, continued: 3.43

... and section 1 above shall not apply in any case where the agreement in question amounts to a conspiracy to defraud at common law.

This led the House of Lords to hold in *Ayres*[36] that the effect of the provisions was to preclude the charging of a conspiracy to defraud where the facts also revealed a statutory conspiracy. Lord Bridge said:[37]

only the exceptional fraudulent agreements will need to be charged as common law conspiracies to defraud, when either it is clear that performance of the agreement constituting the conspiracy would not have involved the commission by any conspirator of any substantive offence or it is uncertain whether or not it would do so.

In practice, *Ayres* led to difficulties in identifying whether there was in fact a statutory offence in each particular case.[38] The decision was reversed by statute under the Criminal Justice Act 1987:

---

[34] CPS response to consultation, 9 August 2004, not available on the web but can be sought from the Home Office or CPS.
[35] *Hansard*, HL 19 July 2005 col 1448.   [36] [1984] AC 447.   [37] Ibid, at 460A.
[38] *Tonner* [1985] 1 WLR 344; *Lloyd* [1985] QB 829; *Cox and Mead* The Times, 6 December 1984.

12 Charges of and penalty for conspiracy to defraud

(1) If—

(a) a person agrees with any other person or persons that a course of conduct shall be pursued; and

(b) that course of conduct will necessarily amount to or involve the commission of any offence or offences by one or more of the parties to the agreement if the agreement is carried out in accordance with their intentions,

the fact that it will do so shall not preclude a charge of conspiracy to defraud being brought against any of them in respect of the agreement.

(2) [Repeal in part of the Criminal Law Act 1977, s 5(2).]

D. LIMITATIONS ON THE USE OF CONSPIRACY TO DEFRAUD

3.44   Prior to the Fraud Act 2006, conspiracy to defraud was necessary to supplement the statutory law in a varied range of circumstances.[39] In 2003, 14,928 defendants were proceeded against in England and Wales for crimes of fraud; 1,018 (7%) of these were for the common law crime of conspiracy to defraud.[40]

3.45   The CPS guidance to prosecutors stated:[41]

… common law conspiracy is to be preferred if there is any doubt as to whether, if any, actual substantive offences have been or would be involved.

Conspiracy to defraud is a serious offence, which juries can readily understand. Consider it if:

Any substantive offences are no more than steps to achieve a wider dishonest objective.

The aim of the offending is to swindle a large number of people, and conspiracy to commit a substantive offence does not meet the justice of the case.

Don't use it if, eg, two people conspire to steal from their employer, and conspiracy to steal is more appropriate.

3.46   Other than such principles of practice, there was little restriction on the use of the offence. Whilst the Fraud Act 2006 does not abolish conspiracy to defraud (it makes no mention of it), its passage into law should greatly curtail the use of the offence.

1. General Principles of Use of Common Law Offences

3.47   As a general principle, the courts will not greatly extend the boundaries of the common law beyond its defined limits.[42]

3.48   The use of the offence of conspiracy to defraud in circumstances where a statutory alternative exists is subject to the general principles applicable to the use of common law offences in such circumstances.

---

[39] Law Com No 276, 2002 (see n 29 above for reference), paras 4.5 to 4.59 (pp 24–37).

[40] Home Office statistics.

[41] Crown Prosecution Service, *Legal Guidance*, available at <http://www.cps.gov.uk/legal/index. html>.

[42] *DPP v Withers* [1975] AC 842.

Some have long had an aversion to common law offences. In *Truth versus Ashurst*, 3.49
written in 1792 and published in 1823, Jeremy Bentham referred to judge-made
law as 'dog-law':

It is the judges (as we have seen) that make the common law. Do you know how they make
it? Just as a man makes laws for his dog. When your dog does anything you want to break
him of, you wait till he does it, and then beat him for it. This is the way you make laws for
your dog: and this is the way the judges make law for you and me. They won't tell a man
beforehand what it is he should not do—they won't so much as allow of his being told: they
lie by till he has done something which they say he should not have done, and then they
hang him for it.[43]

The European Convention for the Protection of Human Rights and Fundamental 3.50
Freedoms has been used to control the growth of common law offences outside
their established bounds. Article 7 of the Convention states:

Article 7—No punishment without law

1 No one shall be held guilty of any criminal offence on account of any act or omission
which did not constitute a criminal offence under national or international law at the time
when it was committed. Nor shall a heavier penalty be imposed than the one that was
applicable at the time the criminal offence was committed.

2 This article shall not prejudice the trial and punishment of any person for any act or
omission which, at the time when it was committed, was criminal according to the general
principles of law recognized by civilized nations.

It reflects the principle of domestic law, that conduct which did not contravene the
criminal law at the time when it took place should not retrospectively be stigmatized
as criminal, or expose the perpetrator to punishment. Article 7 represents the
operation of 'the principle of legal certainty'.[44] A vague law impermissibly delegates
basic policy matters to policemen, judges, and juries for resolution on an ad hoc
and subjective basis, with the attendant dangers of arbitrary and discriminatory
application.[45]

More recently, the House of Lords considered in *Rimmington & Goldstein* 3.51
whether it is appropriate to charge the common law offence of public nuisance in
circumstances in which a statutory offence may be applicable.[46] Lord Bingham of
Cornhill said:

30. ... Where Parliament has defined the ingredients of an offence, perhaps stipulating
what shall and shall not be a defence, and has prescribed a mode of trial and a maximum
penalty, it must ordinarily be proper that conduct falling within that definition should be
prosecuted for the statutory offence and not for a common law offence which may or may not
provide the same defences and for which the potential penalty is unlimited [in the case of the
offence of public nuisance] ... It cannot in the ordinary way be a reason for resorting to the

---

[43] See *Rimmington & Goldstein* [2006] 1 AC 459.
[44] *Brumarescu v Romania* (2001) 33 EHRR 35, para 61 and *Kokkinakis v Greece* (1993) 17 EHRR
397, para 52.
[45] *Rimmington & Goldstein* [2006] 1 AC 459.   [46] Ibid.

common law offence that the prosecutor is freed from mandatory time limits or restrictions on penalty. It must rather be assumed that Parliament imposed the restrictions which it did having considered and weighed up what the protection of the public reasonably demanded. I would not go to the length of holding that conduct may never be lawfully prosecuted as a generally-expressed common law crime where it falls within the terms of a specific statutory provision, but *good practice and respect for the primacy of statute do in my judgment require that conduct falling within the terms of a specific statutory provision should be prosecuted under that provision unless there is good reason for doing otherwise.* [Emphasis added.]

Lord Rodger of Earlsferry said:

52. ... a charge could not have been regarded as bad simply because it was framed in terms of the common law rather than in terms of the statute. To put the matter more generally, where Parliament has not abolished the relevant area of the common law when it enacts a statutory offence, it cannot be said that the Crown can never properly frame a common law charge to cover conduct which is covered by the statutory offence. Where nothing would have prevented the Crown from charging the defendant under the statute and where the sentence imposed would also have been competent in proceedings under the statute, the defendant is not prejudiced by being prosecuted at common law and can have no legitimate complaint.

53. Here, ... the Crown had deliberately chosen the common law offence in order to avoid the time-bar which Parliament had enacted and to allow the judge, if he thought fit, to impose a heavier sentence than the one permitted under statute ... There is no suggestion, of course, that the Crown acted in bad faith. On the contrary, it is easy to understand why they did what they did. In a particular case, such as this, a time-limit which prevents prosecution once a certain time has passed since the act was committed can appear to be arbitrary and to reward an offender for concealing his offences. The sentence available under the statute may also seem inadequate to reflect the gravity of the defendant's conduct. But Parliament has deliberately chosen to intervene and to prescribe a period within which conduct of this kind can be prosecuted summarily under statute. This must be taken to reflect Parliament's judgment that, if the conduct has not been prosecuted within that time, the public interest is now against proceeding ... Similarly, in the matter of sentence, Parliament has reached a view that certain conduct is appropriately covered by an offence which can be tried only summarily and which should attract no more than a particular level of sentence. Parliament has also fixed the maximum sentence to be imposed in summary proceedings, even where the defendant is convicted of more than one charge. Again, in any particular case, the sentence available under statute may appear to the prosecutor to be inadequate. But Parliament is entitled to place an offence in what it regards as the appropriate level in the hierarchy of offences and to limit the sentencing power of a court ...

54. It is not for the Crown to second-guess Parliament's judgment as to any of these matters by deliberately setting out to reject the applicable statutory offences and to charge the conduct in question under common law in order to avoid the time-limits or limits on sentence which Parliament has thought appropriate. It may be that, in the light of experience, Parliament's judgment can be seen to have been flawed or to have been superseded by events. Doubtless, the prosecuting authorities have channels through which they can—and perhaps should—draw any such perceived deficiencies to the attention of the Home Secretary. It is then up to ministers and, ultimately, Parliament to decide whether the law should be changed. But, unless and until it is changed, its provisions should be respected and the Crown should not devise a strategy to avoid them.

Their lordships' judgment is thought to be of wide application.[47] There is no reason in principle for it not to affect the use of conspiracy to defraud.

Two main principles arise: 3.52

(a) Conduct falling within the terms of a specific statutory provision should be prosecuted under that provision unless there is good reason for doing otherwise.

(b) It is not a good reason to use the common law offence where there is a procedural bar to the use of the corresponding statutory offence (eg, a time bar), or that there is a perception that the sentencing power is deficient for the statutory offence.

2. The Attorney General's Guidance

On 9 January 2007 the Attorney General issued 'Guidance on the use of the 3.53 common law offence of conspiracy to defraud'[48] to the prosecuting authorities in England and Wales. In the view of the Attorney General, the common law charge may still be appropriate in the following types of cases:

(a) Conduct that can more effectively be prosecuted as conspiracy to defraud.
(b) Conduct that can only be prosecuted as conspiracy to defraud.

The former category includes those cases where various kinds of criminality are 3.54 involved (possibly with a wide range of victims). Prosecuting such cases under statutory provisions might lead to indictments with an unwieldy number of separate counts, and possibly separate trials for separate parts of the conspiracy.[49] Cases falling within this category are considered at section E below (para 3.63 ff).

The latter category includes those types of conduct which are not covered by 3.55 any statutory provision, but would amount to conspiracy to defraud.[50] Cases falling within this category are considered at sections F and G below (paras 3.67 ff and 3.76 ff).

In selecting charges in fraud cases, the prosecutor should first consider:[51] 3.56

(a) Whether the behaviour could be prosecuted under statute—whether under the Fraud Act 2006 or another Act, or as a statutory conspiracy.
(b) Whether the available statutory charges adequately reflect the gravity of the offence.[52]

Whenever a conspiracy to defraud charge is proposed, the prosecutor must set 3.57 out in writing the reason for using that charge including, in particular, how that charge will add to the evidence likely to be called by the prosecution and defence, and the justification for using the charge. The reason for this is to ensure that the

---

[47] See the comments of Professor Ormerod in relation to acts outraging public decency: [2006] Crim LR 993.
[48] See Appendix 5.   [49] Paragraphs 12–14.   [50] Paragraph 15.   [51] Paragraph 6.
[52] This consideration is of doubtful assistance, given the comments of Lord Earlsferry in *Rimmington and Goldstein*—see 3.51 above.

reviewing prosecutor has focused his or her mind on why the common law offence is the right one to use in that case; and to provide the Attorney General with a record which can be used to inform further deliberations as to the continued need for the common law offence.[53]

3. Statements in *Hansard*

3.58   The Guidance should be considered in the context of what was said, in the course of debates in Parliament, about the use of conspiracy to defraud. The Government made it plain that 'the conspiracy to defraud offence should be used sparingly'.[54]

3.59   The statements of ministers and other promoters of a bill can be used in the courts to assist in identifying the Parliamentary intention behind ambiguous or obscure legislation.[55] The comments in relation to the use of conspiracy to defraud made in the course of the passage of the Bill through Parliament are unlikely to fall within the scope of this principle. The Act is silent on conspiracy to defraud and hence there is no particular wording in the Act to be interpreted. However, there is a strong precedent for ministers in Parliament limiting prosecution policy by means of a statement to the House, recorded in *Hansard*. Since 1923 the Government has expressed the Inland Revenue policy in relation to tax frauds by means of a written answer in *Hansard*. Most recently, Gordon Brown explained that 'the Board will accept a money settlement and will not pursue a criminal prosecution, if the taxpayer, in response to being given a copy of this Statement by an authorized officer, makes a full and complete confession of all tax irregularities'.[56] This '*Hansard* Procedure' has worked effectively. The Government's commitment to restrict the use of conspiracy to defraud may work on the same principles.

3.60   The Attorney General explained the purpose behind the Guidance. At the report stage in the Lords he stated:[57]

> I propose to recognise the concerns that some noble Lords have expressed about the overuse of conspiracy to defraud by giving guidance to prosecutors when the new Act comes into effect, outlining the criteria to be considered before they use the common law offence. It will ask prosecutors to consider: first whether the behaviour could be prosecuted under statute, under the Fraud Act 2006, or under some other Act as a statutory conspiracy. It will also outline the cases in which the common law charge may be appropriate and … will ask prosecutors to record their reasons for using the common law charge in any case for which they do so.

---

[53] *Hansard*, HL 14 March 2006 col 1115.
[54] The Solicitor General, *Hansard*, HC 26 October 2006 col 1698.
[55] *Pepper (Inspector of Taxes) v Hart and related appeals* [1993] AC 593, [1993] 1 All ER 42: see Appendix 2.
[56] *Hansard*, HC 7 November 2002 col 784 W (Written Answers); see also the comments of Lord Hutton in *Allen* [2001] UKHL 45.
[57] *Hansard*, HL 14 March 2006 col 1115.

He made it clear that he intends the Guidance to be binding. During the third 3.61
reading of the Bill in the Lords, the Attorney General said:[58]

I propose to issue final guidance around the time of Royal Assent ... The guidance will then
be issued to the directors of the prosecuting authorities: the Crown Prosecution Service, the
Serious Fraud Office, the Revenue and Customs Prosecuting Office and what we call the
Whitehall prosecutors—other government prosecutors who do not fall into any of those
three offices. I intend the guidance to apply to all of them ... I turn to the status of the
document ... I issue guidance and guidelines, as my predecessors have done, on a number
of topics ... I would not think it at all necessary for such guidance to have the backing of
statutory authority for it to be followed by prosecutors; I know of no problem in that respect.
As it happens, I have quite a powerful weapon to enforce it myself: the ability to intervene
in any case and to stop that case using my powers of *noli prosequi* if I were not satisfied
with the way in which the prosecuting authority was acting. That is a longstop, but it is
effective.

The Solicitor General turned to the subject in the Commons committee stage. 3.62
He said:[59]

The aim of that guidance is to indicate the Attorney-General's wish that we do not use
conspiracy unless it is necessary to do so, but it accepts that there may well be circumstances
in which it is necessary.

E. CONDUCT THAT CAN MORE EFFECTIVELY
BE PROSECUTED AS CONSPIRACY TO DEFRAUD

There may be cases where the interests of justice can only be served by presenting 3.63
to a court an overall picture as a conspiracy to defraud, which cannot be achieved
by charging a series of substantive offence or statutory conspiracies.

A conspiracy to defraud charge is necessary where there are many different kinds 3.64
of underlying offences. There may be a single agreement with multiple unlawful
objectives falling under various enactments. The Guidance also suggests that where
there is a large network of conspirators whom the interests of justice dictate should
be tried together, a conspiracy to defraud charge might be necessary to prevent
severance.[60] However, it may be that, in practice, severance would be a separate
issue, whatever the charge.

Where individuals have committed a large number of substantive offences 3.65
together, consideration should also be given to trying specimen counts before the
jury, under the Domestic Violence, Crime and Victims Act 2004.

For a long time, it was thought that it was permissible to sentence someone for 3.66
the full scale of their offending, their having been convicted only upon specimen

[58] *Hansard*, HL 29 March 2006 cols 781–2.   [59] *Hansard*, HC 20 June 2006 col 71.
[60] Paragraphs 12–14.

counts representative of the overall conduct. The Court of Appeal held in *Kidd*[61] that this is not so. This decision presented the problem of reflecting the gravity of the offending where the number of offences alleged to have been committed is too large to be listed in a manageable indictment. The Domestic Violence, Crime and Victims Act 2004[62] seeks to provide a solution:[63]

17 Application by prosecution for certain counts to be tried without a jury

(1) The prosecution may apply to a judge of the Crown Court for a trial on indictment to take place on the basis that the trial of some, but not all, of the counts included in the indictment may be conducted without a jury.

(2) If such an application is made and the judge is satisfied that the following three conditions are fulfilled, he may make an order for the trial to take place on the basis that the trial of some, but not all, of the counts included in the indictment may be conducted without a jury.

(3) The first condition is that the number of counts included in the indictment is likely to mean that a trial by jury involving all of those counts would be impracticable.

(4) The second condition is that, if an order under subsection (2) were made, each count or group of counts which would accordingly be tried with a jury can be regarded as a sample of counts which could accordingly be tried without a jury.

(5) The third condition is that it is in the interests of justice for an order under subsection (2) to be made.

(6) In deciding whether or not to make an order under subsection (2), the judge must have regard to any steps which might reasonably be taken to facilitate a trial by jury.

(7) But a step is not to be regarded as reasonable if it could lead to the possibility of a defendant in the trial receiving a lesser sentence than would be the case if that step were not taken.

(8) An order under subsection (2) must specify the counts which may be tried without a jury.

(9) For the purposes of this section and sections 18 to 20, a count may not be regarded as a sample of other counts unless the defendant in respect of each count is the same person.

F. CONDUCT THAT CAN ONLY BE PROSECUTED AS CONSPIRACY TO DEFRAUD

3.67 It is the Attorney General's intention that fraudulent conduct that is not covered by specific statutory provision under the Fraud Act 2006, or other legislation, should continue to be prosecuted as conspiracy to defraud. Where there is an appropriate

---

[61] [1998] 1 WLR 604.

[62] For defendants committed to the Crown Court after 8 January 2007 (or who have been sent, and served with their evidence, after that date).

[63] No date has been given for the implementation of this section at the time of writing although it is anticipated that it will be in force at the time of publication of this book.

statutory alternative, that charge should be used in the absence of a good reason not to do so.

In the Law Commission 1994 report on Conspiracy to Defraud,[64] and their 2002 report on Fraud,[65] the Commissioners listed specific types of conduct which would, at that time, cease to be criminal if conspiracy to defraud were abolished. It was their view that the new Fraud Act would cover in its provisions all of the conduct which ought to be criminal, and hence conspiracy to defraud could safely be abolished.[66] To this overall view, they identified two main exceptions: dishonestly failing to fulfil a contractual obligation, and dishonestly infringing a legal right. These, they suggested, were rarely prosecuted as conspiracies to defraud, and could be left for any future legislation required. The following paragraphs deal with those two, and other, types of conduct which it is thought may only be prosecuted as conspiracy to defraud. 3.68

1. Conduct Not Covered by the Fraud Offence nor the Theft Act

In cases where there is no false representation, abuse of trust, or failure to disclose within the terms of the Fraud Act 2006, there can be no fraud offence. If there is nevertheless a dishonest appropriation of property the conduct will be theft, except in a number of narrow circumstances. These circumstances are of little practical consequence and are dealt with in section G below (para 3.76 ff). 3.69

2. Dishonestly Infringing Another's Right

The Attorney General cites the dishonest exploitation of another's patent, in the absence of a legal duty to disclose information about its existence,[67] as a type of conduct which can only be prosecuted as conspiracy to defraud.[68] 3.70

3. Assisting Fraud by Third Parties

Statutory conspiracies require that the course of conduct will necessarily involve the commission of an offence *by one or more of the parties* to the agreement. This limitation does not apply to a conspiracy to defraud. Where it is intended that the final offence be committed by someone outside the conspiracy, or the accused cannot be proved to have had the necessary degree of knowledge intended for the offence, a conspiracy to defraud charge may be necessary. 3.71

So in *Hollinshead*[69] the defendants made and sold devices which affected the proper functioning of electricity meters so as to reduce the reading. The House of Lords held that this was a conspiracy to defraud, notwithstanding that the contemplated fraud was to be committed by strangers to the agreement: the people who would buy them. Notably, that case itself would in fact now be covered by the supplying of articles for use in fraud offence. 3.72

---

[64] Law Com No 228, 1994 (Part IV).   [65] Law Com No 276 (Part IV) (see n 29 above for reference).
[66] Ibid, para 9.3.   [67] Paragraph 15.
[68] See para 3.81 below in relation to confidential information.   [69] [1985] AC 975.

4. A General False Impression

3.73 In a 'long firm fraud' the defendants build up what appears to be an ordinary trading concern, so as to achieve credit from suppliers, and they then vanish. Such conduct may be a fraudulent trading offence,[70] or fraudulent business.[71] Otherwise it may be difficult to establish a particular representation made by the defendants—as opposed to general false impression.

5. Gambling Swindles

3.74 The Gaming Act 1845 makes it an offence to employ a 'fraud or unlawful device or ill practice' in connection with gaming or wagering. The Law Commission felt that this section may be too narrow to cover all gambling swindles.

6. Dishonestly Failing to Fulfil a Contractual Obligation

3.75 The Law Commission stated:

> 4.53 Dishonest breach of a contractual obligation is not in itself an offence, though there will be a deception offence if the defendant intends to break the contract from the start. Even if the breach consists in a dishonest dealing with property, it will not be theft unless the property 'belongs' to someone other than the defendant at the material time. For example, if P pays in advance for goods to be supplied by D, when the money changes hands it becomes D's money. If D then fails to provide the goods, the money still belongs to D, despite the fact that P has a right to sue D for damages or restitution. P cannot assert any direct claim over the money itself. The result is that, if D breaches the contract and 'appropriates' the money, it may be impossible to show that the money 'belongs' to P at the time of the appropriation.

G. FRAUDULENT CONDUCT COVERED BY STATUTORY OFFENCES

3.76 The types of conduct listed below are mostly within the ambit of the Fraud Act 2006 or the Theft Act offences. For this reason they should be prosecuted under the relevant statutory offence, and not common law conspiracy to defraud. There are examples of narrow exceptions to this. In those exceptional cases it is intended that conspiracy to defraud may remain the applicable charge.

1. Property that Cannot be Stolen (Law Com No 228, para 4.6)

3.77 The Theft Act 1968 defines property for the purposes of that Act:

4 "Property"

(1) "Property" includes money and all other property, real or personal, including things in action and other intangible property.

---

[70] Companies Act 1985, s 458.   [71] Fraud Act 2006, s 9.

(2) A person cannot steal land, or things forming part of land and severed from it by him or by his directions, except in the following cases, that is to say—

(a) when he is a trustee or personal representative, or is authorized by power of attorney, or as liquidator of a company, or otherwise, to sell or dispose of land belonging to another, and he appropriates the land or anything forming part of it by dealing with it in breach of the confidence reposed in him; or

(b) when he is not in possession of the land and appropriates anything forming part of the land by severing it or causing it to be severed, or after it has been severed; or

(c) when, being in possession of the land under a tenancy, he appropriates the whole or part of any fixture or structure let to be used with the land.

For purposes of this subsection "land" does not include incorporeal hereditaments; "tenancy" means a tenancy for years or any less period and includes an agreement for such a tenancy, but a person who after the end of a tenancy remains in possession as statutory tenant or otherwise is to be treated as having possession under the tenancy, and "let" shall be construed accordingly.

(3) A person who picks mushrooms growing wild on any land, or who picks flowers, fruit or foliage from a plant wild on any land, does not (although not in possession of the land) steal what he picks, unless he does it for reward or for sale or other commercial purpose.

For purposes of this subsection "mushroom" includes any fungus, and "plant" includes any shrub or tree.

(4) Wild creatures, tamed or untamed, shall be regarded as property; but a person cannot steal a wild creature not tamed nor ordinarily kept in captivity, or the carcase of any such creature, unless either it has been reduced into possession by or on behalf of another person and possession of it has not since been lost or abandoned, or another person is in course of reducing it into possession.

The limitations contained in s 4 do not apply to the intended gain and loss under the Fraud Act 2006. Property simply means 'any property whether real or personal (including things in action and other intangible property)'.[72]   3.78

Where there is a false representation, abuse of position, or failure to disclose covered by the fraud offence, then the Fraud Act will apply. Alternatively, where there is a dishonest appropriation theft will apply.   3.79

Land, things growing wild on land, and game cannot be stolen, except as provided by s 4. However, if a person dishonestly intends to gain any of these things through the use of a false representation (or conduct which is otherwise within the terms of the Act) that person is guilty of fraud. Where there is no such false representation, but something is done dishonestly to appropriate those things, no offence is committed by one person acting alone. But where there is an agreement between two or more people dishonestly to prejudice someone's interest in those things it could be a conspiracy to defraud, eg, in the opinion of the Law Commission, an agreement to dishonestly move a fence, thus effectively depriving a neighbouring landowner of part of his land, would not be a conspiracy to steal, but would presumably be a conspiracy to defraud.[73]   3.80

---

[72] Fraud Act 2006, s 5.   [73] Law Com No 228, para 4.6.

2. Confidential Information (Law Com No 228, para 4.7)

3.81 When information is imparted from one person to another the latter receives it, but the former cannot really be said to have deprived himself of it. This characteristic makes it difficult to regard information as property. Furthermore, it is impossible to apply to information, in a meaningful way, the requirement in theft for an intention to permanently deprive the victim of the property. So taking an exam paper, reading it, and returning it cannot be theft.[74] Likewise, taking oil exploration research worth £50,000–£100,000.[75] Where, in such circumstances, a false representation is involved, the defendant will generally have an intention to gain or cause loss in financial terms within the meaning of the Fraud Act, so the fraud charge may be used. If the terms of the fraud offence do not apply, then no offence is committed. But if there is a dishonest agreement to obtain information conspiracy to defraud will apply.

3. Temporary Deprivation of Property (Law Com No 228, para 4.10)

3.82 Unauthorized borrowing does not generally amount to theft, as there is no intention to permanently deprive. There is deemed to be intention to permanently deprive if the person's intention is to 'treat the thing as his own to dispose of regardless of the other's rights; and a borrowing or lending of it may amount to so treating it if, but only if, the borrowing or lending is for a period and in circumstances making it equivalent to an outright taking or disposal'.[76] Borrowing may also amount to an alternative offence:

(a) If the subject matter is a conveyance then Theft Act 1968, s 12 would apply.
(b) Property taken from a public display is caught by Theft Act 1968, s 11.
(c) The use of the property can be considered to be a service, where it is made available on the basis that payment is to be made, Fraud Act 2006, s 11.

3.83 Where the borrowing takes place in the context of an employee making unauthorized use of his employer's equipment, the conduct may fall within the fraud offence under s 4. For example, a projectionist borrowing cinema films to make copies.[77]

3.84 There may be cases of unauthorized borrowing for which no statutory offence exists, and conspiracy to defraud will continue to apply.

4. No Property Belonging to Another (Law Com No 228, para 4.17)

3.85 In the Guinness fraud,[78] Guinness artificially inflated its own share price thereby assisting it to gain the acquisition of the Distillers group. Their competitors, and persons buying their shares at inflated prices, had lost, but it was impossible to

---

[74] *Oxford v Moss* (1979) 68 Cr App R 183.   [75] *Absolom* The Times, 14 September 1983.
[76] Theft Act 1968, s 6(1).   [77] *Scott* [1975] AC 819.
[78] See, eg, *Saunders v UK* (1997) 23 EHRR 313.

identify a flow of property belonging to another; the gain did not correspond with the loss.

This clearly amounted to a conspiracy to defraud—although, at the time, conspiracy to defraud was not available.[79] Now the lack of a correspondence between the gain and the loss represents no problem to a fraud charge under the Act.

3.86

5. Secret Profits by Employees and Fiduciaries (Law Com No 228, para 4.20)

Where the manager of a public house sold his own beer in his company's premises he was not guilty of the theft of a secret profit,[80] but where two people acting in concert did similar conduct they were committing a conspiracy to defraud.[81] Such conduct may now be prosecuted under Fraud Act 2006, s 4 and conspiracy to defraud is no longer required.

3.87

6. Obtaining a Benefit and Causing a Loss which are Not the Same Property (Money Transfers and Loans) (Law Com No 228, para 4.25)

When money is transferred between accounts the credit to one account and the debit to the other account are directly correspondent to each other, but they are not the same property in law.[82] The Law Commission was concerned that this problem extends beyond money to other examples where assets are held in a pooled fund without any person holding a specific item, eg, they suggested, Eurobonds.[83]

3.88

If a person makes a false representation, or otherwise does the acts forbidden by Fraud Act, ss 2–4 to obtain a gain in the form of a money transfer, he will be guilty of the fraud offence. Where there is no representation then theft will not apply, and only conspiracy to defraud.

3.89

7. Obtaining Without Deception Benefits Other Than Property (Law Com No 228, para 4.34) and Deception of Computers and Other Machines (Law Com No 228, para 4.40)

Obtaining property by deception is always also theft,[84] so obtaining property by making a false representation to a machine can be charged as theft. It is now better charged as a fraud by false representation. Where services were obtained by such means theft cannot apply but it may now be charged as fraud by false representation or obtaining services dishonestly provided that the services are provided on the basis that the payment will be made (Fraud Act 2006, s 11).

3.90

The same applies to situations where the deception does not operate on the mind on the victim.

3.91

---

[79] Following *Ayres*—see paras 3.42–3.43, above.
[80] *Attorney General's Reference (No 1 of 1985)* [1986] QB 491.   [81] *Cooke* [1986] AC 909.
[82] *Preddy* [1986] QB 491.   [83] Law Com 276, para 4.12.
[84] *Gomez* [1993] AC 442.

8. Evasion of Liability Without Intent to Make Permanent Default (Law Com No 228, para 4.47)

3.92   Under the Theft Act 1968, dishonestly achieving by deception the deferral of a debt was an offence under s 16:

16. Obtaining pecuniary advantage by deception

(1) A person who by any deception dishonestly obtains for himself or another any pecuniary advantage shall on conviction on indictment be liable to imprisonment for a term not exceeding five years.

(2) The cases in which a pecuniary advantage within the meaning of this section is to be regarded as obtained for a person are cases where—
  (a) any debt or charge for which he makes himself liable or is or may become liable (including one not legally enforceable) is reduced or in whole or in part evaded *or deferred*; or ...

3.93   This was repealed by the Theft Act 1978 and replaced by an offence where such conduct was not criminal unless it was accompanied by an intent to make permanent default:

2. Evasion of liability by deception.

(1) Subject to subsection (2) below, where a person by any deception—
  (a) dishonestly secures the remission of the whole or part of any existing liability to make a payment, whether his own liability or another's; or
  (b) with intent to make permanent default in whole or in part on any existing liability to make a payment, or with intent to let another do so, dishonestly induces the creditor or any person claiming payment on behalf of the creditor to wait for payment whether or not the due date for payment is deferred) or to forgo payment ...

In *Zemmel*,[85] the Court of Appeal held that conspiracy to defraud could not be used to cover the deferral of the debt otherwise it would be as if 'by a side wind the common law has suddenly re-emerged to reinstate or create as a crime that which Parliament thought it right to take off the statue book as a crime'.[86]

3.94   The wider principle to be gathered from *Zemmel* is that the common law does not apply to conduct which has formerly been the subject of specific statutory provision that has since been repealed.

---

[85] (1985) 81 Cr App R 279.   [86] Ibid, 284.

4

ACTS PREPARATORY TO FRAUD

A. OVERVIEW

As the fraud offence does not require anything actually to be obtained in the fraud, 4.01 many 'incomplete' or failed frauds constitute the full offence; the fraud offence is inchoate in character. Furthermore, where a person has taken some steps towards committing the fraud, but has not yet carried out conduct that amounts to the full offence, he may still be criminally liable:

(a) Firstly, if the person has agreed with another to carry out a course of conduct that would amount to a fraud offence, he will be guilty of common law conspiracy to defraud, or a statutory conspiracy to commit fraud under the Criminal Law Act 1977.[1]

(b) Secondly, he may be guilty of an attempt: if a person does an act, which is more than merely preparatory to the commission of a fraud offence, he will be guilty of an attempt to commit fraud under the Criminal Attempts Act 1981.[2]

(c) Thirdly, a person who has with him, when not at his place of abode, any articles for use in, or in connection with, theft[3] will be guilty of the offence of going equipped under the Theft Act 1968.[4]

(d) Fourthly, the Fraud Act further extends the law on acts preparatory to fraud: if a person has in his possession articles, which are intended to be used in fraud, or makes or supplies such articles, he is guilty of specified offences under the Fraud Act, ss 6 and 7.[5]

---

[1] See Chapter 3.   [2] See below, para 4.02.   [3] Or burglary.
[4] Theft Act 1968, s 26.   [5] See below, paras 4.15 and 4.34.

B. ATTEMPTED FRAUD

4.02　If, with intent to commit an indictable offence within the jurisdiction, a person does an act, which is more than merely preparatory to the commission of the offence, he is guilty of attempting to commit the offence.[6] The expression *more than merely preparatory* requires that the defendant has moved from the stage of planning and preparation to that of implementing his intention, and trying to commit the offence.

4.03　For example, the case of *Geddes*[7] illustrates this distinction. The defendant, a 29-year-old man, was found in a school toilet. When disturbed, he ran away, discarding, as he went, a rucksack containing a knife, string, and sealing tape. The prosecution contended that in the circumstances it was plain that the defendant was planning a kidnap. He was convicted of attempted false imprisonment. The defendant appealed and the Court of Appeal allowed his appeal. Evidence that he had the intention to commit the offence did not assist on the issue of whether he had begun to carry out the commission of the offence. He had not made any contact with pupils and had gone no further than the preparatory stages of an offence. The distinction was between putting himself in a position to commit the offence and actually trying to commit the offence.

4.04　Each of ss 2 to 4 of the Fraud Act 2006 does not create an offence, but rather a way of committing the s 1 offence. That is to say, s 1 is the offence-creating section. Therefore an attempt should be charged as an attempt to commit a s 1 offence. A consequence of this is that an attempt to commit any of the three branches of the offence is covered by the one charge of attempt to commit under s 1. This may be of assistance where the evidence points towards an attempt to commit fraud but it is equivocal as to which particular branch of the offence was contemplated. Contrast this with the previous position, under the Theft Act 1968, where an offender attempted to obtain money from a bank by a deception. If he were charged with attempted obtaining property by deception, he would be guilty provided the money he was intending to obtain was in the form of cash (within the definition of property), but not if it were in the form of an electronic transfer (not property, but a money transfer). Where the evidence as to the form in which he intended to obtain the money was equivocal, he could escape liability.

4.05　Due to the inchoate nature of the fraud offence itself, the scope of an attempt to commit fraud is extremely limited. Under the Theft Act 1968, if a fraud were discovered after the defendant had made a representation to deceive a person into giving him property but prior to his obtaining anything, he would be guilty of an attempt to obtain property by deception. So any representation made with the requisite intention, which in fact failed to deceive, was an attempt. Under the Fraud Act such conduct would amount to the full offence of fraud by false representation:[8] the false representation having been made with the intention to make a gain,

---

[6] Criminal Attempts Act 1981, s 1(1).　　[7] *Geddes* [1996] Crim LR 894, CA.

[8] Fraud Act 2006, ss 1 and 2.

notwithstanding the fact that no gain is actually made. The position is similar with ss 3 and 4. In each case, it is the conduct that makes the offence criminal rather than the result.

However, if a person makes a representation, which he intends to be false, but due to a mistake of fact on his part is in fact true, he cannot be guilty of the full offence (the requirements of s 2(2)(a) are not satisfied). He would, however, be guilty of an attempt. Also, if a person tries to make a representation but fails, eg, because of a communication failure, he would not be guilty of the full offence, but could be guilty of an attempt. | 4.06

These two examples—mistake of fact and unusual failures—appear to be the limit of the narrow scope of the offence of attempted fraud.[9] | 4.07

C. GOING EQUIPPED

Under the Theft Act 1968, having articles for use in burglary or theft is an offence, but only when not at one's place of abode: | 4.08

25 Going equipped for stealing, etc

(1) A person shall be guilty of an offence if, when not at his place of abode, he has with him any article for use in the course of or in connection with any burglary or theft.

...

(3) Where a person is charged with an offence under this section, proof that he had with him any article made or adapted for use in committing a burglary or theft shall be evidence that he had it with him for such use.

...

Prior to amendments enacted by the Fraud Act 2006, the section also applied to having any article for use in the course of, or in connection with, any 'cheat'.[10] This has been removed by the Act as a consequence of the repeal of s 15. | 4.09

In *Ellames*,[11] the defendant was charged with the s 25 offence, having admitted that he had had in his possession a bag containing guns, gloves and 'Jif' plastic lemons containing ammonia solution, which had recently been used in a robbery. However, there was no evidence that there was an intention to use the articles in any further robbery or criminal activity. Nevertheless he was convicted. The Court of Appeal allowed his appeal. 'Has with him any article for use ... ' means 'has with him for the purpose (or with the intention) that they will be used ... '. Section 25 is directed against acts preparatory to burglary and theft, and an intention to use must necessarily relate to use in the future. The Court added that it is not necessary to prove that he intended it to be used in the course of or in connection with any specific burglary, theft, or cheat. | 4.10

---

[9] See Law Commission, *Fraud* (Law Com No 276, 2002), para 7.55.
[10] Meaning obtaining property by deception contrary to Theft Act 1968, s 15 (Theft Act 1968, s 25(5)).
[11] *Ellames* [1974] 1 WLR 1391.

4.11   The requirement that the person has the article with him when not at his place of abode has limited the use of the offence. If police find incriminating articles in the course of the search of a person's home, those articles cannot form the basis of a going equipped charge. This is so even if the articles are of such a nature that they could only be intended for use in offending, eg, skimming devices for placing on the front of cash machines.

D. ARTICLES FOR USE IN FRAUD

4.12   The Fraud Act, ss 6–8 creates two new offences in relation to articles for use in fraud:

(a) Possession of articles for use in fraud (including when the offender is at his place of abode when they are in his possession).[12]

(b) Making or supplying articles for use in fraud.[13]

4.13   The European Union Council Framework Decision of 28 May 2001, *Combating fraud and counterfeiting of non-cash means of payment*,[14] places an obligation upon Member States of the European Union to take the necessary measures to criminalize the fraudulent making, receiving, obtaining, sale or transfer, or possession of instruments, articles, or computer programmes adapted for the commission of offences in relation to payment instruments.[15]

4.14   The Government intends ss 6 and 7 of the Act to strengthen the United Kingdom's compliance with the Decision.[16]

1. Possession of Articles for Use in Fraud (section 6)

4.15   The Fraud Act 2006, s 6 states:

6 Possession etc. of articles for use in frauds

(1) A person is guilty of an offence if he has in his possession or under his control any article for use in the course of or in connection with any fraud.

(2) A person guilty of an offence under this section is liable—

(a) on summary conviction, to imprisonment for a term not exceeding 12 months or to a fine not exceeding the statutory maximum (or to both);

(b) on conviction on indictment, to imprisonment for a term not exceeding 5 years or to a fine (or to both) …

4.16   A person is guilty of an offence if he has in his possession, or under his control, any article for use in the course of, or in connection with, any fraud. The section replaces

---

[12] Fraud Act 2006, s 6.   [13] Fraud Act 2006, s 7.
[14] Framework Decision 2001/413/JHA.   [15] Article 4.
[16] The White Paper (*Fraud Law Reform: Consultation on Proposals for Legislation*, Home Office, May 2004), para 44.

the offence of going equipped for cheat under the Theft Act 1968, s 25[17] with a wider definition. Unlike that section there is no requirement that the article be with the person when not at his place of abode. The section criminalizes the possession, at home, of, for example, illicit credit card skimming devices, and letters prepared to be used in a scam, such as an advance fee fraud. Prior to the Act possession of these articles would be difficult to charge, especially when found at the offender's place of abode, unless there was evidence that the possessor was a party to a conspiracy.

The Solicitor General stated in the Commons: 4.17

The requirement that a person be outside his place of abode when going equipped may have worked in 1968, but in the modern world, with computers, fraud may be perpetrated by a person sitting at his computer terminal in his home. The offence should not be limited to possession outside the home.[18]

(a) *Has in his Possession or Under his Control*

The phrase 'has with him' in the wording of the offence of going equipped to cheat   4.18 has been replaced by 'has in his possession, or under his control'. This formula is similar to those used elsewhere in the criminal law:

(a) 'to have in his possession' in the Misuse of Drugs Act 1971,[19] which is taken to include things 'subject to his control which is in the custody of another',[20] or

(b) 'to have in his custody or under his control' in the Forgery and Counterfeiting Act 1981.[21]

(b) *Article*

The Fraud Act 2006, s 8 states: 4.19

8 "Article"

(1) For the purposes of—
   (a) sections 6 and 7, and
   (b) the provisions listed in subsection (2), so far as they relate to articles for use in the course of or in connection with fraud,
      "article" includes any program or data held in electronic form.
(2) The provisions are—
   (a) section 1(7)(b) of the Police and Criminal Evidence Act 1984 (c. 60),
   (b) section 2(8)(b) of the Armed Forces Act 2001 (c. 19), and
   (c) Article 3(7)(b) of the Police and Criminal Evidence (Northern Ireland) Order 1989 (S.I. 1989/1341 (N.I. 12));

(meaning of 'prohibited articles' for the purposes of stop and search powers).

So 'article' is not defined, except to make it clear that it includes electronic   4.20 material.[22] The wording of s 8 is taken from the Computer Misuse Act 1990, s 17.

---

[17] See para 3.31 above.   [18] *Hansard*, HC 12 June 2006 col 541.
[19] Misuse of Drugs Act 1971, s 5(2).   [20] Misuse of Drugs Act 1971, s 37(3).
[21] Forgery and Counterfeiting Act 1981, s 5(2).   [22] Fraud Act 2006, s 8.

4.21 Note that the section covers both:

(a) articles which are obviously fraudulent by their very nature, such as skimming devices or faked documents; and

(b) articles which are unobjectionable of themselves but are covered because they are possessed for use in the course of or in connection with any fraud, eg, a computer that is to be used to stored stolen credit card numbers.

(c) The Mens Rea

4.22 The section lacks, on its face, any overt *mens rea*. During the Bill's committee stage in the House of Lords, the Conservative Lord Kingsland, raised this apparent lack of *mens rea* and suggested the inclusion of a requirement that the person must have the article 'without lawful excuse', and that the person must have it *intending* it to be used in connection with any fraud. The Liberal Democrat Lord Gresford, having like concerns, suggested that the clause be amended to insert the word 'knowingly'.[23] For the Government, the Attorney General stated that the intention was to import the case law that exists in relation to going equipped to cheat.

4.23 In *Ellames*[24] it was said:

In our view, to establish an offence under s 25(1) the prosecution must prove that the defendant was in possession of the article, and intended the article to be used in the course of or in connection with some future burglary, theft or cheat. But it is not necessary to prove that he intended it to be used in the course of or in connection with any specific burglary, theft or cheat; it is enough to prove a general intention to use it for some burglary, theft or cheat; we think that this view is supported by the use of the word 'any' in s 25(1). Nor, in our view, is it necessary to prove that the defendant intended to use it himself; it will be enough to prove that he had it with him with the intention that it should be used by someone else.

It made clear that the person must have the intention that it will be used in the type of offending specified in the section. Therefore there was no necessity to insert 'without lawful excuse', or an explicit *mens rea*.[25] *Ellames* also makes it clear that it is not necessary to show use in relation to any specific offence—simply, here, a general intention to use in any fraud. The fraud contemplated may be to be perpetrated by the defendant, or another.

4.24 The explanatory notes to the Fraud Act 2006 also quote the passage from *Ellames* quoted above and state:

The intention is to attract the case law on section 25, which has established that proof is required that the defendant had the article for the purpose or with the intention that it be used in the course of or in connection with the offence, and that a general intention to commit fraud will suffice.

4.25 The Solicitor General stressed that:

it needs to be shown that there was an intention that an article would be used for any involvement where someone was going equipped in connection with any burglary, theft or

---

[23] *Hansard*, HL 19 July 2005 col 1450.   [24] See para 4.10 above.
[25] *Hansard*, HL 19 July 2005 col 1450.

cheat, there is a requirement for some degree of intention. There is a *mens rea*, and case law shows that ... [26]

May I make it clear that clause 6 does not go too wide, in my view? It does not introduce a strict liability offence in any way. Its wording draws on the wording of section 25 of the 1968 Act in order to attract the case law that goes with that section—notably the case of *Ellames*, which is referred to in the explanatory notes and which established that the prosecution have to prove a general intention that the article will be used by the possessor, or by someone else, for a fraudulent purpose.[27]

and elsewhere:

The fact that the explanatory notes specifically mention *Ellames* means that the case is important.[28]

to which Mr David Heath replied:

I think that we have successfully Pepper-and-Harted *Pepper v. Hart*, which is helpful ...

(d) *In Connection with*

The phrase 'or in connection with' ensures that equipment ancillary to the actual fraud is caught by the section. Sometimes an article may not be for use in the course of a fraud, but is for use in connection with a fraud. For instance, a credit card reader is used to gather credit card numbers—not a fraud in itself, but if the intention is to use those numbers in a fraud, the credit card reader is for use in connection with a fraud.   4.26

The Solicitor General stated in Parliament: 4.27

The object and effect of the words 'in connection with' is to add something to 'in the course of'.

Whether 'in furtherance of' would carry such a wide meaning is open to question. We do not want to risk not covering any of the huge variety of acts that may be preparatory to fraud. Opposition Members may believe that 'in connection with' is too wide, but I do not agree, as the whole offence is underpinned by the requirement for a general intention to commit fraud, so no truly innocent person has, in my view, anything to fear.[29]

(e) *Two Examples*

The police raid the residence of a person and find credit card readers used to gain credit card details for use in fraud. There is insufficient evidence of any particular fraud having been committed to charge fraud. By simply possessing the devices the person has put himself in a position to commit a fraud, but has not gone beyond mere preparation, so this is insufficient for a charge of attempted fraud. However, it can be inferred from the presence of the devices at the house of a person (who has no legitimate use for them) that they are intended to be used in connection with fraud—whether by him or another. The person would be guilty of the s 6 offence.   4.28

---

[26] *Hansard*, HC 12 June 2006 col 541.   [27] *Hansard*, HC 12 June 2006 col 542.
[28] *Hansard*, HC Standing Committee B 20 June 2006 col 44.
[29] *Hansard*, HC Standing Committee B 20 June 2006 col 43.

4.29   Note that following *Ellames* if the devices may have been left over from a previous fraud, with no intention of their being used in a future fraud, the person would not be guilty of this offence.

4.30   If the police found a computer upon which was stored in electronic form data skimmed from credit cards, this would also come within the definition of 'article' and would be covered by a s 6 offence.[30]

4.31   In the case of *Doukas*[31] the defendant was a hotel wine waiter. He carried bottles of wine to work intending to sell it as his employer's wine. He admitted to the police that it was his intention to substitute for the carafe wine ordered by the hotel guests the wine he had brought with him, make out separate bills in respect of this wine, and keep the money so obtained for himself. He was convicted of going equipped to cheat under the Theft Act 1968, s 25. By serving the wine, he would be falsely, impliedly, representing to the customer that the wine was the hotel wine. He would do so with the intention of making a profit for himself, so were he to carry out his scheme, he would be guilty of the fraud offence under s 2. Alternatively, his scheme would be a dishonest abuse of his position and hence a fraud offence under s 4. Therefore, whilst the possession of wine of itself is unobjectionable, possessing it intending to use it in the fraud becomes an offence under s 6.

(f) *Contrasted with Possession of Property for the Purpose of Terrorism*

4.32   The Terrorism Act 2000 is an example of recent legislation which has taken an alternative approach to formulating an offence of the possession of property for criminal purposes:

16. Use and possession

...

(2) A person commits an offence if he -
  (a) possesses money or other property, and
  (b) intends that it should be used, or has reasonable cause to suspect that it may be used, for the purpose of terrorism.

4.33   Together with the comprehensive definitions of 'terrorism' and the 'purposes of terrorism' in s 1 and of 'property' in s 121 the section clearly presents, on its face, the forbidden acts and the *mens rea*.[32]

2. Making or Supplying Articles for Use in Fraud (section 7)

4.34   The Fraud Act 2006, s 7 states:

7 Making or supplying articles for use in frauds

(1) A person is guilty of an offence if he makes, adapts, supplies or offers to supply any article—

---

[30] See Fraud Act 2006, s 8.   [31] *Doukas* [1978] 1 WLR 372.
[32] *O'Driscoll v Secretary of State for the Home Department* [2003] ACD 35.

(a) knowing that it is designed or adapted for use in the course of or in connection with fraud, or

(b) intending it to be used to commit, or assist in the commission of, fraud.

(2) A person guilty of an offence under this section is liable—

(a) on summary conviction, to imprisonment for a term not exceeding 12 months or to a fine not exceeding the statutory maximum (or to both);

(b) on conviction on indictment, to imprisonment for a term not exceeding 10 years or to a fine (or to both) ...

The section covers such devices as credit card readers adapted to be positioned on the front of bank ATM machines for the purpose of 'skimming'. The White Paper[33] also suggests that the computer programme 'Credit Master IV' which generates (genuine) credit card numbers on request, computer templates for producing blank utility bills, and draft letters in connection with 'advance fee' frauds, are all covered by the section. Such items have no known legitimate use so dealing with them can never be legitimate. 4.35

The section also covers the making of any article, which, though innocuous of itself, is known by the maker to be intended for use in fraud. 4.36

(a) *Example*

In *Hollinshead*[34] the defendants sold devices which, when fitted to an electricity meter, reversed the flow of current so that the meter recorded fewer units of electricity than were actually consumed. The defendants were arrested when they tried to sell a unit to a person who turned out to be a police officer. The House of Lords held that this amounted to a conspiracy to defraud—on the basis that the devices were designed to cause loss to the electricity company—notwithstanding the absence of any evidence of a dishonest agreement between them and the third parties to whom they sold the devices. However, there was no substantive offence to cover the conduct, so if the conduct was done by one person acting alone (rather than agreeing with another in a conspiracy) it would not have been an offence. Assuming the users of such devices would commit a fraud offence by falsely representing to the electricity company that the reading so obtained was a true reading, the supply of such articles would be a s 7 offence (whether committed by several acting together, or one acting alone). 4.37

---

[33] *Fraud Law Reform: Consultation on Proposals for Legislation* (Home Office, May 2004), para 42.
[34] *Hollinshead* [1985] AC 975.

5

PARTICIPATING IN FRAUDULENT BUSINESS

A. Summary of the New Offence	5.01
B. History of Fraudulent Trading Offences	5.08
C. The New Offence	5.18
D. Summary	5.53

A. SUMMARY OF THE NEW OFFENCE

The new fraudulent trading offence is expressed in the following terms: 5.01

9 Participating in fraudulent business carried on by sole trader etc

(1) A person is guilty of an offence if he is knowingly a party to the carrying on of a business to which this section applies.
(2) This section applies to a business which is carried on—
    (a) by a person who is outside the reach of section 458 of the Companies Act 1985 (c. 6) or Article 451 of the Companies (Northern Ireland) Order 1986 (S.I. 1986/1032) (N.I. 6)) (offence of fraudulent trading), and
    (b) with intent to defraud creditors of any person or for any other fraudulent purpose.
(3) The following are within the reach of section 458 of the 1985 Act—
    (a) a company (within the meaning of that Act);
    (b) a person to whom that section applies (with or without adaptations or modifications) as if the person were a company;
    (c) a person exempted from the application of that section.

A person is guilty of an offence under s 9 of the Fraud Act 2006 if he is 5.02 knowingly a party to the carrying on of a fraudulent business which is 'outside the reach'[1] of s 458 of the Companies Act 1985 or Art 451 of the Companies (Northern Ireland Order) 1986, with intent to defraud creditors of any person or for any other fraudulent purpose. The offence is triable either in the Magistrates' or the Crown Court and carries in the latter a maximum sentence of ten years' imprisonment.

---

[1] The phrase used in the Fraud Act 2006, s 9.

5.03   Section 9 makes it an offence for a person knowingly to be a party to the carrying on of a fraudulent business with intent to defraud creditors or for any other fraudulent purpose, where the business is not carried on by a company or a corporate body. The new offence mirrors the existing offence that applies in the case of companies and certain other corporate bodies. It should be noted that the Companies Act 2006 which received Royal Assent on 8 November 2006 repeals and replaces s 458 of the Companies Act 1985 with an identical offence in s 993. The latter section has not yet been brought into force.

5.04   The existing offence is contained in s 458 of the Companies Act 1985 and Art 451 of the Companies (Northern Ireland Order) 1986. This extension of criminal liability to non-corporate traders was recommended by the Law Commission.[2] The non-corporate traders and others covered by the new offence include sole traders, partnerships, and trustees or any person who is a knowing party to the carrying on of any 'business'. The word 'business' is not defined in the Fraud Act but its meaning is discussed in detail below. The new offence represents a significant change in the law.

1. Fraudulent Trading Contrary to the Companies Act 1985

5.05   A person commits the offence of fraudulent trading under s 458 of the Companies Act 1985 if he is knowingly a party to the carrying on of the company's business either with intent to defraud creditors or for any other fraudulent purpose. The new section creates a similar offence. Fraudulent trading contrary to s 458 is in effect a general fraud offence similar in ambit to conspiracy to defraud, but requiring the use of a company to found criminal liability instead of the concept of a criminal agreement.

5.06   The following principles are apparent from the case law in relation to corporate fraudulent trading:

(a) dishonesty is an element of the offence;[3]

(b) the mischief aimed at is fraudulent trading generally;

(c) the offence can be committed when a business carries out one single large transaction,[4] although the section is primarily aimed at the carrying on of a business and not at individual transactions;

(d) the offence can be committed by persons who have a controlling or managerial role within the company; it is intended to cover those running the business, that is, those exercising a controlling or managing function;[5]

(e) a person must have taken some positive steps in the carrying on of the company's business; accordingly, a failure to advise the directors by a secretary and financial

---

[2] Law Com No 277, 2002.   [3] *Cox and Hodges* 75 Cr App R 291.
[4] *Gerald Cooper Chemicals Ltd* [1978] Ch 262.
[5] *Miles* [1992] Crim LR 657.

adviser that the company was insolvent and should cease trading did not amount to carrying on business within the meaning of the section.[6]

It is intended that these principles should apply to the new offence. The reason that s 9 refers to a business carried on by a person 'outside the reach' of s 458 of the Companies Act 1985 and Art 451 of the Companies (Northern Ireland Order) 1986 is because although the basic application of those sections is to companies, the offence has been applied by other statutory provisions to other corporate bodies which are not companies.[7] There are also regulations which apply these offences to limited liability partnerships and European Economic Interest Groupings.   5.07

B. HISTORY OF FRAUDULENT TRADING OFFENCES

1. The Companies Act 1928

The Companies Act 1928 created for the first time an offence of fraudulent trading by a company. The offence was introduced as a result of the recommendations of the Greene Committee, which reported in 1926.[8] The Committee's attention had been 'directed particularly to a case where the person in control of the company holds a large floating charge and, while knowing that the company was on the verge of liquidation, "fills up" his security by means of goods obtained on credit and then appoints a receiver'.[9] As a result the receiver would enforce the security against the company on the director's behalf, with the consequence that the director would be protected against losses, while the company's losses fell upon suppliers and other creditors.   5.08

The concept of a statutory offence of fraudulent trading, therefore, was originally limited to deal with the Greene Committee's isolation of a particular problem: the abuse by companies of their limited liability status. For example, a company whose directors knew very well that their creditors could never receive what they were owed would continue to operate the business on credit until liquidation. Prior to 1928, disappointed creditors would not even have had a personal claim against the directors.   5.09

2. The Companies Acts 1929 and 1948

The original provisions relating to fraudulent trading were set out in s 75 of the Companies Act 1928, which itself was substantially re-enacted in s 275 of the Companies Act 1929, and subsequently s 332 of the Companies Act 1948.   5.10

Until 1985 the fraudulent trading provisions comprised both civil and criminal liability. The civil liabilities of those found responsible for fraudulent trading were   5.11

---

[6] *Re Maidstone Building Provisions Ltd* [1971] 1 WLR 1085.
[7] Companies Act 1985, s 718 and Companies (Northern Ireland) Order 1986, Art 667.
[8] Report of the Company Law Amendment Committee, Cmd 2567.
[9] At p 28, para 61 of the report.

extensive: those parties may have been 'personally responsible, without any limit of liability, for all or any of the debts or other liabilities of the company as the court may direct'.

3. The Cork Committee and the Companies Act 1985

5.12 In 1982 the Insolvency Law and Practice Review Committee, chaired by Sir Kenneth Cork, had recommended splitting the criminal and civil liabilities for fraudulent trading. The committee found that the inter-relation of civil and criminal liabilities had, in effect, impeded litigation in respect of the civil liability of fraudulently trading directors. Liquidators in civil proceedings were inhibited by impending or current criminal proceedings. It was apparent that courts were refusing to entertain a claim for civil liability in the absence of dishonesty, and requiring an unduly stringent standard of proof in respect of the ingredient of fraud. Moreover, it was felt inappropriate to require proof of dishonesty in civil cases where creditors had unfairly lost out due to other factors, such as recklessness or incompetence.

5.13 As a consequence of the Cork Committee's recommendations, the Companies Act 1985 separated the civil and criminal liabilities for the offence. Criminal liability was re-enacted as s 458 of the Companies Act 1985 and civil liability as s 630 (prior to its re-enactment as s 213 of the Insolvency Act 1986).

5.14 Until 1947 only directors were liable for losses incurred by creditors. Section 101 of the Companies Act 1947 extended liability under s 275 of the 1929 Act to 'any parties who were knowingly party to the carrying on of the business'.

5.15 Furthermore, the offence could originally only be committed 'in the course of winding up of a company', a phrase explicit in the original provision relating to civil liability, and imported into the section creating the criminal offence by a majority decision in the House of Lords in *R v Schildkamp*.[10]

5.16 This limitation was removed by an amendment of s 332(3) of the Companies Act 1948 by the Companies Act 1981. From that time, fraudulent trading could occur regardless of the liquidity of a company, increasing the scope and variety of types of offences so charged.

4. Penalties

5.17 The original maximum penalty for fraudulent trading under the Acts of 1928 and 1929 was a term of one year's imprisonment. Section 101 of the 1947 Act increased the maximum penalty to two years' imprisonment or a fine not exceeding £200 or both. The Companies Act 1980 increased those penalties to imprisonment for a term not exceeding seven years, or a fine, or both. The penalty for fraudulent trading under s 458 of the Companies Act 1985 has been increased from seven to ten years by the Fraud Act 2006. The new s 9 fraud offence also carries a maximum sentence of ten years.

---

[10] [1971] AC 1.

C. THE NEW OFFENCE

1. The Case for Extending Liability

The Law Commission in its report on multiple offending[11] proposed that s 458   5.18
be extended to cover non-corporate traders. This recommendation was supported
by the Office of Fair Trading (OFT) in their paper *Bogus Trading*, published on 4
March 2004. The Law Commission in its report said:

Due to the limited application of this provision, there is an illogical dichotomy between the
fraudster who chooses to operate by means of a £ 10 shelf company which is no more than
his alter ego and a mechanism for fraud, and on the other hand, the fraudster whose conduct
is the same as the first but who does not either feel the need for such a device or who seeks
to give the appearance that he is trading through a company but not go through any of the
formalities of acquiring one.[12]

One reason for the extension was that the offence of fraudulent trading had   5.19
changed from its inception into a general fraud offence 'comparable to conspiracy
to defraud, but requiring the use of a company instead of a conspiracy'.[13] As the
original limitations of the corporate offence had been taken away there seemed little
logic in retaining the corporate/non-corporate distinction for the purposes of an
offence of fraudulent trading.

The Law Commission, in its report on multiple offending,[14] took the view that: 5.20

it is anomalous and illogical that fraudulent trading should be an offence where it is
done through the medium of a ... company, but not where the individual who is trading
fraudulently does not do so through the medium of such a body.[15]

The Law Commission further reasoned that the status of the fraudulent trader   5.21
made little difference to the creditor who has suffered losses. It therefore recommended that the offence of fraudulent trading should be extended to individuals
'irrespective of whether the enterprise is a company incorporated in Great Britain,
a company incorporated elsewhere, a partnership or a sole trader'. Section 9 was
drafted into the Fraud Act on the basis of this recommendation.

The Law Commission had in mind complicated 'scams' which at present could   5.22
only be charged as conspiracy to defraud (provided that more than one person was
involved) or as a multiplicity of statutory offences. An example given in the Home
Office *Consultation Document on Proposals for Legislation*[16] was of a multi-million
pound investment fraud involving a series of transactions using bank guarantees

---

[11] Law Commission, *Multiple Offending* (Law Com No 277), Part VIII: Fraudulent Trading, para
8.11.
[12] Ibid, para 8.7.
[13] *Arlidge and Parry on Fraud*, quoted in the Home Office consultation document, May 2004,
para 52.
[14] See n 11, above.   [15] Ibid, p 81.   [16] Home Office, May 2004.

and insurance whose 'fraudulent nature was only comprehensible once the whole picture of what was going on had been put together'.[17]

5.23   The attraction of a fraudulent trading offence to prosecuting authorities is that it is capable of encapsulating in one charge a number of activities and transactions. The danger of such an offence is that it is expressed in such wide terms that it becomes another crime of 'general dishonesty' and is so wide as to catch anyone who is a party to the fraudulent carrying on of any business.

5.24   During the consultation process for the Fraud Bill doubts were expressed about the need to extend fraudulent trading to sole traders. The Criminal Bar Association,[18] for example, in its response said that such an extension was not justified. The conduct intended to be criminalized by the new offence was already so by virtue of existing law and the other new fraud offences in the Fraud Act 2006. In addition the CBA agreed with the concerns expressed in the Home Office's own consultation paper that the offence should be confined to the corporate sector as a price to pay for the benefit of limited liability. This had been expressed in the Home Office's paper in the following terms:

It can be argued that it [the fraudulent trading offence] should be confined to the corporate sector on the grounds that liability to this very wide offence is part of the price that companies pay for the benefits of limited liability. It was not greatly used—only 34 people were sentenced in England and Wales for fraudulent trading.[19]

2. The Scope of the New Offence

5.25   Section 9 of the new Act sets out those to whom the new provision applies; in short, those carrying on a business 'outside the reach' of s 458. The basic application of s 458 is to companies. However, other legislative provisions apply the offence to corporate bodies which are not companies. The Companies Act 1985, s 718 applies s 458 to unregistered companies, or 'all bodies corporate incorporated in and having a principal place of business in Great Britain'. Various regulations also apply the offence to limited liability partnerships and European Economic Interest Groupings.

5.26   Those corporate bodies exempt from the provisions of s 458 will not be subject to s 9 of the Fraud Act 2006. Section 718 of the 1985 Act sets out those who are exempt: any body incorporated by or registered under any public general act of Parliament, non-profit making businesses, those specifically exempted by the Secretary of State, and open-ended investment companies.

5.27   The existing offence of fraudulent trading has often been criticized for being so widely drawn. On one view it comprises three offences expressing fraudulent trading in terms of any 'business of a company ... carried on with intent to defraud creditors of the company *or* creditors of any other person *or for any other fraudulent purpose*'. In the case of *R v Inman*[20] it was held that s 332(3) of the Companies

---

[17] Home Office, May 2004, para 53.
[18] Criminal Bar Association, *Fraud Law Reform Consultation on Proposals for Legislation: Response from the Criminal Bar Association July 2004*, available at <http://www.criminalbar.com>.
[19] Home Office, May 2004 para 56.   [20] [1967] 1 QB 140; 50 Cr App R 247.

Act 1948 (worded similarly to s 458) 'quite plainly dealt with two different types of offence, fraudulent trading with intent and fraudulent trading for the purpose of achieving certain things'.

Professor Glanville Williams described the offence as 'doubly anomalous' in that it did not extend to partnerships or individual traders, and that 'in theory it is totally unlimited as to the types of fraud, though in practice it probably adds nothing to the rest of the criminal law'.[21] In *R v Kemp*[22] the Court of Appeal referred to these comments and explained:

> While each individual transaction in this carbon paper fraud could perfectly well have been the subject of a separate count, prosecutors in order to avoid a multiplicity of counts often use this procedure without distinguishing whether the defrauded were creditors or not. Now, if this course is permissible under the section which is for decision in this case, it is clearly a much less cumbersome procedure and much easier for a jury to follow.

The new Act has dealt with the first part of the anomaly identified by Professor Williams by extending liability to non-corporate traders and anyone engaged in business. The second criticism about the scope of the offence may still hold true. The *mens rea* of the fraudulent trading offence under s 9(2)(b) is an intent 'to defraud creditors of any person or for any other fraudulent purpose'. Parliament has done nothing, therefore, to restrict the scope of the new offence.

The effect of extending the offence is to level the playing field between companies on the one hand, and partnerships and sole traders on the other. The Attorney General suggested, when introducing the second reading of the Bill in the House of Lords, that 'this "activity" offence carries procedural and evidential advantages as it is not necessarily limited to specific transactions and there is no logic in limiting its application to companies'.[23]

The logic, though, was that the offence was originally designed to prevent the abuse of limited liability status and to provide creditors with a claim against companies who had defrauded them in the course of being wound up. The procedural and evidential advantages advertised by the Attorney General are those aimed for elsewhere in the Act, which is to say that complex offending is to be combated by a single charge.

Clearly, the offence offers a good deal of flexibility. A charge of fraudulent trading would be particularly appropriate where a number of deceptions have been carried out upon a number of victims. A prosecutor might charge a single count of fraudulent trading in cases where many transactions made through many channels would otherwise result in a long and complicated indictment.

Similarly, the decision to retain the offence of conspiracy to defraud was on the basis that it provided greater flexibility in dealing with many types of fraud involving multiple transactions and defendants. As a result, the two offences (conspiracy to defraud and fraudulent trading) overlap significantly. That is a particular irony in

5.28

5.29

5.30

5.31

5.32

5.33

---

[21] Glanville Williams, *Textbook of Criminal Law* (2nd edn).
[22] [1988] 1 QB 645 (1988) 87 Cr App R 95.   [23] *Hansard*, HL 22 June 2005 col 1654.

view of the fact that the old statutory offences dealing with fraud were described by the Attorney General as 'too precise, overlapping and outmoded to give effective coverage over the breadth of frauds committed today'.[24]

5.34　　The extension of the offence to sole traders and partnerships may assist investigations and prosecutions of sophisticated frauds which employ a mixture of sole trader, partnership, and corporate forms. However, the offence of fraudulent trading is committed by a company under one section (s 458) and by a sole trader or partnership under another (s 9). It is not clear how one might indict such a fraud under the different fraudulent trading sections. If possible, a prosecutor would prefer a substantive fraud count under ss 1–4 or a count of conspiracy to defraud.

5.35　　The Attorney General made it clear during the legislative progress of the Bill that the settled principles in relation to fraudulent trading under s 458 of the Companies Act will apply equally to partnerships and sole traders under s 9.[25] The phrasing of the offence in the Fraud Act is effectively unchanged from that of the offence under s 458. The offence is committed by a person who is 'knowingly a party to the carrying on of a business … which is carried on … with intent to defraud creditors or for any other fraudulent purpose'. Section 9(5) of the Act in fact specifies that 'fraudulent purpose' has the same meaning as in s 458. The courts have construed the offence widely, and the following principles have emerged.

3. Key Concepts Relevant to the New Offence

(a) *Introduction*

5.36　As has been made clear, the case law on s 458 of the Companies Act 1985 is likely to be highly relevant when deciding the extent and scope of the new fraudulent trading offence. It was plainly the intention of the Law Commission and of Parliament that the new offence should mirror the old, with the difference being that the extension was to cover those party to carrying on a business for a fraudulent purpose or with intent to defraud creditors.

5.37　　Clearly, the financial status of a business trading fraudulently under s 9 is irrelevant. Businesses caught by the provision may be merely decoys or phantoms deployed to perpetrate or assist a fraudulent enterprise.

(b) *Is One Transaction Sufficient to Establish Fraudulent Trading?*

5.38　Can one transaction constitute the carrying on of a business? The judgment of Templeman J in the case of *In Re Cooper Chemicals Ltd*[26] was that 'it does not matter for the purposes of s 332 that only one creditor was defrauded, and by one transaction, provided that the transaction can properly be described as a fraud on a creditor perpetrated in the course of carrying on business'.[27] It is likely that a similar approach will be adopted in respect of the new offence.

---

[24] Keynote Speech, 23rd International Symposium on Economic Crime.
[25] See also the Act's explanatory notes.
[26] *In Re Gerald Cooper Chemicals Ltd (In liquidation)* [1978] Ch 262.
[27] The principle that one transaction may constitute fraudulent trading has been specifically preserved in the explanatory notes to the Act.

(c) *What Does 'carrying on business' Mean?*

The phrase 'carrying on business' is not defined in the Fraud Act 2006. Any activity 5.39
of an apparently commercial nature is plainly caught. In addition, any other activity
carried on for the requisite purposes may also be an offence, for example, someone
running a charity or a trust. The *Oxford English Dictionary* gives the following wide
definition of the word 'business':

business *noun* 1 a person's regular occupation or trade. 2 work to be done or matters to be
attended to. 3 a person's concern. 4 commercial activity. 5 a commercial organization. 6
informal a difficult or problematic matter. 7 (the business) *informal* an excellent person or
thing. 8 actions other than dialogue in a play.
—PHRASES in business *informal* operating or able to begin operation. in the business of
engaged in or prepared to engage in. like nobody's business *informal* extraordinarily. mind
one's own business avoid meddling in other people's affairs.
—ORIGIN Old English, anxiety (from BUSY + -NESS); the sense a duty, from which
other senses developed, dates from Middle English.

'Carrying on any business' has been held not to be limited to normal transactions 5.40
in the course of trade. Oliver J, giving judgment in the case of *In re Sarflax Ltd*,[28]
said that he felt:

quite unable to say that the expression 'carrying on any business' in the section is necessarily
synonymous with actively carrying on trade or that the collection of assets acquired in the
course of business and the distribution of the proceeds of those assets in the discharge of
liabilities cannot constitute 'the carrying on' of 'any business' for the purposes of the section.

Drawing on case law arising from a similar phrase in the 1914 Bankruptcy Act, he
gave the illustration that 'a bankrupt carries on business until he has performed all
the obligations that the fact of trade confers upon him'. In this case it was held that
a business may be 'carried on' where a company had ceased trading, save for the
collection of debts and the payment of creditors.

(d) *Dishonesty*

Dishonesty is an essential ingredient of the offence.[29] To this end, it is appropriate 5.41
for the judge to give a *Ghosh* direction in cases where a defendant admits the facts
upon which the prosecution rely but where dishonesty is in dispute. In *R v Smith*[30]
it was held that, in the case of fraud on creditors, evidence of dishonesty towards the
creditors was required but that this could be inferred from the dishonest conduct of
the affairs of the company by the defendant.

(e) *Knowingly a Party to the Carrying on of the Fraudulent Business*

In what circumstances is a person knowingly a party to the carrying on of a business 5.42
within the meaning of s 9? It is clear from the case law that a wide construction

---

[28] *In Re Sarflax Ltd* [1979] Ch 592.   [29] *Cox and Hodges* (1982) 75 Cr App R 291.
[30] [1996] 2 Cr App R 1.

has been put on the phrase 'knowingly a party' (to the fraudulent trading). In the judgment of Pennycuick VC in *In re Maidstone Building Supplies*,[31]

the expression 'party to' must on its natural meaning indicate no more than 'participates in,' 'takes part in' or 'concurs in'. And that, it seems to me, involves some positive steps of some nature ... so in order to bring a person within the section you must show that he is taking some positive steps in the carrying on of the company's business in a fraudulent manner.

5.43   It was held in *R v Kemp*[32] that s 458 was designed to include those who exercised a controlling or managerial function or who are 'running the business'. Those who may be 'knowingly a party' to a fraud will differ with each individual case, and a trial judge will be expected to leave the issue to the jury with clear guidance and all the appropriate and relevant facts of the case. It has been held that there must be actual knowledge of the fraudulent scheme, not merely a lack of good faith.[33]

5.44   In *Re Augustus Barnett and Sons Ltd* [1986] BCLC 170, Ch D, Hoffman J said that a person may be knowingly a 'party to the carrying on of a business' for a fraudulent purpose if he was an outsider who could not be said to have carried on the business or even assisted the carrying on of a business if he nevertheless in some way participated in the fraudulent acts.[34] It follows from this that any person who is assisting a fraudulent 'business' will be caught by the new offence of fraudulent trading.

5.45   What degree of knowledge must a person have before they are 'knowingly a party' to the carrying on of a fraudulent business? 'Knowledge' in the context of a business enterprise in civil litigation has been held to include 'blind eye knowledge', ie, a firmly grounded suspicion that relevant facts exist and a deliberate decision to avoid confirming their existence.[35] In the latter case Patten J adopted the definition of 'blind eye' knowledge used by Lord Scott of Foscote in the decision of the House of Lords in *Manifest Shipping Company Limited v Uni-Polaris Shipping Company Limited and Others*,[36] where Lord Scott at para 116 said:

In summary, blind-eye knowledge requires, in my opinion, a suspicion that the relevant facts do exist and a deliberate decision to avoid confirming that they exist. But a warning should be sounded. Suspicion is a word that can be used to describe a state-of-mind that may, at one extreme, be no more than a vague feeling of unease and, at the other extreme, reflect a firm belief in the existence of the relevant facts. In my opinion, in order for there to be blind-eye knowledge, the suspicion must be firmly grounded and targeted on specific facts. The deliberate decision must be a decision to avoid obtaining confirmation of facts in whose existence the individual has good reason to believe. To allow blind-eye knowledge to be constituted by a decision not to enquire into an untargeted or speculative suspicion would be to allow negligence, albeit gross, to be the basis of a finding of privity.

---

[31] (1971) 1 WLR 1085 at 1092.
[32] *Kemp* (1988) 1 QB 645, (1988) 87 Cr App R 95.
[33] *Rossleigh Ltd v Carlaw* [1986] SLT 204.
[34] See also *Morris v Banque Arabe et Internationale d'Investment SA (No 2)* [2001] 1 BCLC 263, Ch D.
[35] *Re Bank of Credit and Commerce International SA Morris v State Bank of India* [2004] EWHC 528, Ch D (Patten J).
[36] [2003] 1 AC 469.

The above cases concern civil disputes and will not necessarily be followed 5.46
in a criminal case. There is some authority for the proposition that in the
criminal law the word 'knowledge' includes 'wilfully shutting one's eyes to the
truth',[37] although the case law dealing with the offence of handling which requires
'knowledge or belief' makes it clear that nothing short of actual knowledge will
suffice.[38]

The offence of fraudulent trading also has a requirement that the person was 5.47
party to the carrying on of the business with intent to defraud creditors or for any
other fraudulent purpose. As the offence requires an intent it is difficult to see how
it can be committed recklessly or without knowledge of the fraudulent enterprise.
Knowledge of a risk that creditors' interests will be prejudiced will suffice. This is
discussed below in more detail.

Whatever the degree of knowledge required it must coincide with the *actus reus* 5.48
of the offence (ie, the carrying out of the business) for an offence of fraudulent
trading to have been committed. If a person knew after the event that they had been
party to the carrying on of a fraudulent enterprise then no offence would have been
committed by them.

(f) *What Does 'with intent to defraud' Mean?*
The phrases 'to defraud' and 'to act fraudulently' mean to dishonestly prejudice or 5.49
take a risk of prejudicing another's right knowing that you have no right to do so.[39]
This means that where persons carry on a business dishonestly knowing that they
are putting at risk the rights of creditors they can be said to intend to defraud the
creditors. In the context of fraudulent trading, where an intent to defraud creditors
is charged it is necessary for the Crown to prove that the persons to whom the
conduct was aimed were actual as opposed to potential creditors.[40] A person is a
creditor if he has delivered goods to a company and payment has been deferred and
whether a debt can be presently sued for is irrelevant.[41]

It has been held that where a company carries on business and incurs debts at a 5.50
time when, to the knowledge of the directors, there is no prospect of the debts being
paid it may be inferred that the business is being carried on with the intention of
defrauding creditors.[42]

(g) *For any Fraudulent Purpose*
Where this limb of the offence is charged it is not necessary for the prosecution 5.51
to prove that there were any creditors contemplated by the person accused of the
offence. In one case[43] it was argued that because s 332 (the earlier version of s 458)

---

[37] Per Lord Reid in *Sweet v Parsley* [1970] AC 132 at 149.
[38] See *Westminster CC v Croylagrange Ltd* 83 Cr App R 155 at 164 and *Harris (M)* 84 Cr App R 75.
[39] *Welham v DPP* [1961] AC 103.
[40] *Inman* [1967] 1 QB 140 and *Burgess* (unreported) 28 July 1994, CA 94/1800/X4.
[41] *Smith* [1996] 2 Cr App R 1.
[42] *Re William C Leitch Bros Ltd* [1932] 2 Ch 71 and *Grantham* [1984] Cr App R 79 at 86.
[43] *Kemp* [1988] 1 QB 645 87, Cr App R 95.

referred to creditors, it did not cover situations where a company had defrauded its customers, who were merely potential creditors. The Court of Appeal cited the judgment in *R v Seillon*[44] where it had been held that 'it is sufficient ... if the creditor is a potential creditor, because the crime relates to a time in the future'. It was also remarked that the phrase 'for any fraudulent purpose' could not have been drafted any more widely, and quoted Lord Denning's view[45] that Parliament had deliberately drafted the section in wide terms so as to bring fraudsters to book, adding that the section should be given its full width by the courts.[46]

5.52   The term 'fraudulent purpose' has been held to mean an intention to 'go beyond the bounds of what ordinary and decent people engaged in business would regard as honest'[47] or 'involving, according to the current notions of fair trading among commercial men, real moral blame'.[48] In was held in *R v Philippou* 89 Cr App R 290, CA that the dishonest concealment by a holiday company of relevant information which would have materially affected whether they were granted Civil Aviation Authority and ABTA licences was capable of amounting to the carrying on of a business for a 'fraudulent purpose'.[49]

D. SUMMARY

5.53   Section 9 maintains the width of s 458. Under that section proceedings were relatively rare. As the necessity for a corporate entity has been removed the new s 9 is likely to have a profound effect. It is so widely drawn as to be a new substantive offence of fraud with application to anyone who dishonestly engages in business. The section is broad and flexible, like conspiracy to defraud, and it may be adapted to increasingly sophisticated fraudulent mechanisms. The offence may incorporate multiple victims and transactions which may otherwise result in long and complicated indictments.

5.54   A more critical view of the section is that it is so wide that it fails to add anything distinctive to the range of fraud offences laid out in the Act, and the retained conspiracy to defraud. It relies too heavily on what an individual jury might find to be dishonest. Indeed, during consultation prior to the Bill's publication, the extended offence of fraudulent trading was envisaged to cover offences quite different to those which prompted the creation of the original offence. The Office of Fair Trading suggested extension of the offence of fraudulent trading as one of the legislative options for tackling 'bogus trading' whereby customers are duped or pressurized into paying inordinate sums for sub-standard services, goods or

---

[44] *Seillon* (unreported) 14 May 1982.
[45] As expressed in *Re Cyona Distributors Ltd* [1967] Ch 889.
[46] Could one impute the same motives to those who drafted the Fraud Act 2006? The only problem may be having to choose which particular book a fraudster is brought to.
[47] *Grantham* [1984] Cr App R 79 at 86.
[48] *Re Patrick & Lyon Ltd* [1933] Ch 786 per Maugham J at 790.
[49] Per O'Connor LJ at 301.

materials.[50] The highest proportion of these cases relate to unnecessary tarmac or roofing work carried out by unregistered and unscrupulous workmen. These cases are currently prosecuted under the existing substantive offences under the Theft Acts, or indeed as conspiracy to defraud. There is no reason why they cannot now neatly be tried under s 9, even though the wrong-doing is quite different from that encountered by the Greene Committee in 1926.

---

[50] The suggestion was made in the OFT's Position Paper, *Legislative options for tackling bogus trading* (OFT 704), published 4 March 2004.

6

OBTAINING SERVICES DISHONESTLY

A. OVERVIEW

1. The New Offence

The new offence of obtaining services dishonestly, which replaces the old offence   6.01
of obtaining services by deception under Theft Act 1978, s 1 is expressed as
follows:

11 Obtaining services dishonestly

(1) A person is guilty of an offence under this section if he obtains services for himself or
another—
   (a) by a dishonest act, and
   (b) in breach of subsection (2).
(2) A person obtains services in breach of this subsection if—
   (a) they are made available on the basis that payment has been, is being or will be made
   for or in respect of them,
   (b) he obtains them without any payment having been made for or in respect of them
   or without payment having been made in full, and
   (c) when he obtains them, he knows—
      (i) that they are being made available on the basis described in paragraph (a), or
      (ii) that they might be,
   but intends that payment will not be made, or will not be made in full.

Subsection 3 provides that the maximum penalty on summary conviction for   6.02
the new offence is 12 months' imprisonment or a fine not exceeding the statutory
maximum or both, and the maximum penalty after conviction on indictment is five
years' imprisonment or a fine or both.

2. Significant Elements of the New Offence

6.03   The most important distinction between the new offence and the old offence is that the new offence does not include the element of operative deception. A person may be guilty of obtaining services dishonestly under the section where no-one has been deceived.

6.04   The emphasis of the consolidated law of fraud within the new Act has shifted towards the intention of the fraudster, and away from the concept of a victim being actively deceived, a concept upon which the 1968 and 1978 Acts heavily relied.

6.05   It has long been clear that s 1 of the 1978 Act is not capable of encompassing all types of dishonest behaviour in relation to the provision of services. Increasingly, services are obtained by means of the Internet and other machines in circumstances where there can be no deception. Alternatively, a person may dishonestly provide false credit card details to obtain services, the supplier of which neither knows nor cares whether they may have been deceived.

6.06   Section 11 therefore does away with the concept of an operative deception of a 'victim' in order to concentrate upon the dishonesty of the act, with the result that the offence is considerably widened. Two important elements of the offence, however, serve to restrict the application of the section. Firstly, the offence may only be committed by virtue of an act—an omission will not do. Secondly, the offence requires that a person committing it intends that payment will not be made for the services obtained.

6.07   Clearly, the offence of obtaining services dishonestly under s 11 overlaps to a certain extent with the offence of fraud by fraudulent representation in s 2 of the Act. Furthermore, some critics of the section have not been convinced by the Law Commission's rationale of the need for the new offence. However, there is an obvious benefit to abolishing the offence of obtaining services by deception as part of reforms which concentrate upon the intentions of fraudsters and not the effects of their actions upon their victims, if, indeed, there are any victims in the traditional sense.

B. BACKGROUND

1. Obtaining Services by Deception

6.08   The inadequacy of the previous provisions relating to obtaining services by deception has long been recognized, more clearly in some quarters than others. The 1968 Theft Act's definition of property did not include services. The Criminal Law Revision Committee made recommendations in their Thirteenth Report,[1] which were then implemented in the 1978 Theft Act.

6.09   However, the CLRC did not originally recommend the offence of 'obtaining services by deception', on account of the difficulty of defining 'services'.[2] The Committee instead proposed the narrower offence of 'deception as to prospect

---

[1] Cmnd 6733.   [2] Ibid, p 23.

of payment', which Parliament rejected. Subsequent case law has justified those concerns as to the proper interpretation of 'services'.

Section 1 of the 1978 Act, as amended by the Theft (Amendment) Act 1996, is   6.10
expressed in the following terms:

1. Obtaining services by deception

(1) A person who by any deception dishonestly obtains any services from another shall be guilty of an offence.

(2) It is an obtaining of services where the other is induced to confer a benefit by doing some act, or causing or permitting some act to be done, on the understanding that the benefit has been or will be paid for.

(3) Without prejudice to the generality of subsection (2) above, it is an obtaining of services where the other is induced to make a loan, or to cause or permit a loan to be made, on the understanding that any payment (whether by interest of otherwise) will be or has been made in respect of the loan.

Subsection 3 is the result of an amendment by virtue of the Theft (Amendment)   6.11
Act 1996. The amendment arose out of the decision of the Court of Appeal in *R v Halai*,[3] where it was held that the simple making of a loan, or a mortgage advance, or the opening of a bank account did not constitute 'services' within the meaning of the Act. The proper interpretation of 'services' in respect of the new Act is discussed below.

The maximum penalty under s 1 of the 1978 Act was five years' imprisonment.   6.12
The offence was triable either way.

2. The Need for Reform

The 1968 Act came into force as a result of the Law Commission's Eighth Report,   6.13
in which the minority expressed the view that it was undesirable for an offence of fraud to rely too heavily on the concept of an operative deception. There were then concerns, only too justified by subsequent case law, that such an offence would be vulnerable to technical and semantic arguments quite separate from the genuine merits of the case. The effect of the most recent reforms, evident in various sections of the Act, is to mark a significant departure from the concept of a deceived victim.

The Law Commission's 2002 report on fraud[4] identified various circumstances   6.14
in which someone could obtain services dishonestly without deceiving anyone. The first example it gave was where a defendant had obtained services by failing to disclose a material fact. An omission such as this would now be charged under s 3 of the Act (fraud by failing to disclose information).

An example is provided by the facts of the case in *R v Rai*.[5] The mother of the   6.15
defendant in that case had been awarded a grant by the council for the installation of

---

[3] [1983] Crim LR 624.
[4] Law Commission, *Fraud* (Law Com No 276, 2002), available at <http://www.lawcom. gov.uk/docs/lc276.pdf>.
[5] [2000] 1 Cr App R 242.

a bathroom in her house. The defendant failed to inform the council of his mother's death before the works had begun, and the bathroom was installed. The defendant was then charged under s 1 of the 1978 Act, but would now be charged under s 3.

6.16   The Law Commission gave further examples of obtaining services dishonestly but without deceiving anybody. A defendant climbs over a wall to watch a football match not intending to pay the admission charge. The 'service' is offered generally, and not to him in particular. His act of climbing over the wall has not deceived anyone, and his behaviour falls outside s 1 of the 1978 Act.

6.17   The Law Commission also recognized that, increasingly, services are not provided by people but by machines, or via the Internet. A person might use another person's credit card details to pay for a train ticket from a machine. The machine has not been deceived, and the person later checking the ticket is only interested in whether the ticket is valid, and not how the traveller has obtained it. The same concept applies to any service dishonestly obtained from the Internet or any other automated means. As the Attorney General put it during the second reading of the Bill in the House of Lords, 'the more we use machines to obtain goods and services, the more this difficulty arises'.[6]

6.18   The conclusion was that cases in line with these examples were not caught by the 1978 Act and notwithstanding that they may not involve 'misrepresentation, wrongful non-disclosure or secret abuse of a position of trust ... we think that they nevertheless ought to be criminal'.[7]

6.19   The Commission at first considered the concept of 'deeming' a machine to have been deceived, but dismissed it as too artificial for their purposes. The conclusion was that:

we should tackle the problem head on. Rather than requiring deception but diluting its meaning, we need to accept that deception should not be essential at all. This is because, where a person dishonestly obtains a service by giving false information to a machine, the gravamen of that person's conduct is not the provision of the false information but the taking of a valuable benefit without paying for it.[8]

6.20   The proposal, therefore, was not to extend the concept of deception but rather to create a new offence which was more akin to theft than the 1978 'deception' offences. All but one of the 28 bodies who responded to the Law Commission's Consultation Paper No 155 agreed. Liberty, dissenting, contended that the current law should be kept as it is because there is nearly always a human being who is deceived. The Law Commission disagreed, and proposed the new offence under s 11.

C. INGREDIENTS OF THE NEW OFFENCE

6.21   Whether the obtaining of services are criminal will depend upon whether the fact-finders consider whether the manner in which they were obtained was dishonest.

---

[6] *Hansard*, HL 22 June 2005 col 1653.   [7] Law Commission, *Fraud* (see n 4 above), para 8.2.
[8] Ibid, para 8.4.

1. A Dishonest Act

The offence specifically requires a dishonest act, so the offence cannot be made by 6.22
omission alone. However, dishonest omissions may still fall within the scope of s 3
(fraud by failing to disclose information).

Because analogous to theft, the new offence 'should not be inchoate in character. 6.23
It should require the actual obtaining of the service, not merely conduct intended
to result in the obtaining of the service'.[9]

The test for dishonesty under s 11, as with all such offences under the 1968, 6.24
1978, and 2006 Acts is that prescribed by Lord Lane in *R v Ghosh*.[10]

2. Services

The section itself does not define 'services', but it is clear that the intention was 6.25
for the term to be interpreted widely in accordance with the authorities that have
emerged since *Halai* (see paras 7.35–7.43, below):

The offence is not intended to apply to the obtaining of anything which cannot reasonably
be described as a service; but a service need not be provided by one person directly to another.
It may be provided through the medium of a machine.[11]

The implication is that anything that might reasonably be described as a service
would fall within the new offence.

The defining feature of services in the section is that the provider of those services 6.26
requires payment; in the terms of s 11(2), that 'they are made available on the basis
that payment has been, is being or will be made in respect of them'.

The offence under s 1(2) relied upon the concept of the service being provided 6.27
'on the understanding that the benefit has been or will be paid for'. The new Act
therefore modifies that element of the offence. Is a 'basis' for the provision of services
the same as an understanding in relation to them? Given that the Crown must still
prove dishonesty, the distinction between the two very similar terms does not seem
significant, and it is submitted that the authorities in respect of this ingredient of
the offence should apply the new offence.[12]

It is clear that Parliament intended the term 'services' to have very broad 6.28
application. In the Government response to consultations over the proposed
reforms, the Criminal Law Policy Unit noted that

examples of services which respondents [to the consultation] thought should be covered
include the opening of a bank account, the setting up of a company, downloading software
or music from the internet. We believe these are all covered within the normal meaning of
the term 'services'.[13]

---

[9] Ibid, para 8.8.   [10] [1982] QB 1053, 75 Cr App R 154.
[11] Law Commission, *Fraud* (see n 4 above), para 8.8.   [12] Ibid, para 7.39.
[13] *Fraud Law Reform; Government Response to Consultations* (Criminal Law Policy Unit, The
Home Office), para 36; available at <http://www.homeoffice.gov.uk/documents/cons-fraud-law-
reform/Government_response.pdf>.

3. Intention Not to Pay

6.29   The other way in which an otherwise very broad offence has been restricted by the terms of the section is that the offence is not committed unless the person obtaining the services formed an intention not to pay, either in part or in full. Section 11(2) requires that a person 'intends that payment will not be made, or will not be made in full' if he is to be guilty of the offence. This is more restrictive than the intention required for the commission of an offence under s 1 of the 1978 Act, by which services could be obtained by deception merely 'on the understanding that the benefit has been or will be paid for'. The old offence required no explicit intention not to pay.

6.30   The Law Commission gives the example of parents who lie about their child's religious upbringing in order to secure a place at a particular fee-paying school, but with every intention to pay the fees. Such behaviour would have been caught under s 1 of the 1978 Act but not s 11 of the new Act, on the basis that 'to impose liability for such a potentially wide offence where the defendant is willing to pay the full amount required would in our view allow dishonesty to do too much work'.[14]

6.31   Section 11(2)(c) extends the *mens rea* of the offence to those who dishonestly obtain services knowing that the services might be made available on the basis that payment has been, is being, or will be made in respect of them. This creates no difficulties where it is an obvious matter of fact that payment is required. However, there may arise a situation where someone provides services assuming that they will be paid for, whereas the recipient thinks payment might be required but is not sure. Whose understanding constitutes the 'basis' of the provision of the services? A similar difficulty arose out of the 'understanding that the benefit has been or will be paid for' under the old Act.[15]

6.32   The requirement of payment under s 11(2) is therefore two-fold. The services must be made available on the basis that they have been or will be paid for. That may be a matter of fact, or a mutual understanding. Secondly, the defendant must know that the services are, or might be, being provided on this basis.[16]

4. Summary of the Ingredients of the Offence

6.33   The key ingredients of the offence, therefore, are the obtaining of services:

(a) for which the provider requires payment,
(b) by a dishonest act,

---

[14] Law Commission, *Fraud* (see n 4 above), para 8.12.
[15] See discussion of *Sofroniou* [2004] QB 1218 at para 7.41 below.
[16] When the 'basis' upon which the services are supplied is not a matter of fact or explicit agreement, the section may not be sufficiently clear. A man may be offered, and avail himself of, sexual intimacy with the hostess of a champagne bar. There is no explicit discussion of payment and the 'rules of the house' are nowhere posted. The man hopefully ascribes the hostess's advances to his personal charm, but does not exclude the possibility that the hostess will require payment, in which case he will not pay. Subsection (2)(c)(ii) is satisfied, but can the Crown prove that the services are made available on the basis that payment will be made?

(c) knowing that the services are made on the basis that payment is required, or
    that they might be, and
(d) with the intention that payment will not be made in full, or at all.

D. PRINCIPLES ESTABLISHED BY CASE LAW

Although the new section dispenses with the concept of deception, authorities 6.34
relating to the old offence are instructive in the way in which they deal with other
ingredients of the offence.

1. Scope of the Term 'services'

Much of the case law dealing with the scope of 'services' stems from the much 6.35
criticized (and now discredited) case of *R v Halai*,[17] where the court held that the
simple making of a loan did not constitute a service. Furthermore, it was held that
the provision of a bank account could not amount to a service, because there was no
benefit to the customer. O'Connor LJ said that 'where a customer pays £500 into a
bank, by no stretch of the use of ordinary English can anyone suggest that the bank
is conferring a benefit on the customer'.

These remarks, effectively obiter, were responsible for a good deal of uncertainty 6.36
and confusion surrounding the scope of the term 'services'. They were criticized by
Lord Goff in *R v Preddy*,[18] who nevertheless expressed concern that the concept
of services might 'stretch far beyond what is ordinarily included in the notion of
services as generally understood' if, for example, loans were to be included within
the definition.

R v Halai had the effect of precluding the prosecution of mortgage frauds under 6.37
s 1 of the 1978 Act, and the section was subsequently amended by the addition of s
1(3) by the Theft (Amendment) Act 1996. This explicit statutory widening of the
concept of services, a piecemeal but necessary amendment, is not included in the
new Act. As discussed above, the authorities now suggest that the term 'services' is
to be applied generally and broadly.

In *R v Graham*[19] the Court of Appeal dismissed the obiter comments in *Halai*, 6.38
describing the decision as 'a sunken wreck, impeding navigation but difficult,
laborious and expensive to move'.[20] The court made it clear that the meaning of
'services' was sufficiently broad to include professional, financial, and commercial
services. The same must apply to the scope of the term 'services' under the new Act,
given that Parliament clearly intended the term to have a broad general application.

The Court of Appeal in *Graham* also identified the essential conditions of a 6.39
service. It must confer a benefit, and be rendered on the understanding that it has
been or will be paid for. That latter condition is made explicit in s 1(2)(a) of the
new Act. The term 'benefit', however, is not used in the new offence under s 11.

---

[17] [1983] Crim LR 624.   [18] [1996] AC 815.
[19] *Graham (HK)*; *Kansal*; *Ali (Sajid)*; *Marsh* [1997] 1 Cr App R 302.
[20] At 315–17.

6.40   The Court of Appeal in *R v Sofroniou*[21] considered that the caution urged by Lord Goff in *Preddy* in respect of the widened ambit of 'services' should be modified in light of the addition of subsection (3):

> Parliament was persuaded that dishonestly inducing a bank or building society to make a loan, on the understanding that interest or other payment would be made in respect of it, should constitute obtaining services within the section. In our judgment, there should no longer be any doubt but that dishonestly inducing a bank or building society to provide banking or credit card services is also within the section, provided the requirement as to payment is also satisfied.[22]

6.41   *Sofroniou* also makes it clear that the requirement as to payment need not be explicitly articulated, and may be satisfied 'where there is a common understanding that the services will not be provided gratuitously'. Recognizing that the understanding may not be mutual, the Court of Appeal suggested that s 1:

> 'envisages a putative objective mutual understanding as to payment on the assumption that the inducement [to provide a service] was not dishonest ... in our judgment, an understanding as to payment [under section 1] will not be satisfied unless there is an agreement or sufficient understanding that an identifiable payment or payments have been or will be made by or on behalf of the person receiving the services to the person providing them.[23]

6.42   However, the new offence is broader in this respect, because it may be committed when the defendant thinks that the services might be provided on the basis that payment is required.[24] This may be the case in the absence of 'sufficient understanding' that payment is required, although the Crown would still need to prove dishonesty.[25]

6.43   In *R v Widdowson* (1986) 82 Cr App R 314, the Court of Appeal rejected a submission that the obtaining of a hire purchase agreement could not amount to the obtaining of services. Saville J suggested that 'the hire purchasing of a vehicle on some such terms can be regarded as the conferring of a benefit by doing some act, or causing or permitting an act to be done, on the understanding that the benefit has been or will be paid for'.[26]

2. Services Obtained by Another

6.44   *R v Nathan* [1997] Crim LR 835, CA established that a person may be convicted of the offence under s 1 of the 1978 Act if the services were obtained for another. The same would apply under the new Act.

---

[21] [2004] QB 1218.   [22] At 1227.   [23] At 1228.   [24] Section 11(2)(c)(ii).
[25] The basis (or understanding) that services are provided in expectation of payment need not result in complicated directions to juries in terms of 'putative objective mutual understandings'. That phrase was coined in relation to an offence requiring an element of deception, where there could be no genuine understanding as to payment. Under the new Act, it will be obvious, more often than not, that the services were not provided *gratis*. In cases where there is a dispute as to the exact basis upon which the services were offered, a jury will still need to be satisfied that the defendant acted dishonestly. The position as to payment may be less clear in respect of services obtained via the Internet. Where, objectively speaking, it is difficult to determine whether payment is, in fact required, it will be very difficult to establish dishonesty.
[26] At 317–8.

3. Services Need Not be Lawful

Because 'services' are identified by the fact that they are provided on the basis 6.45
that payment is to be made for them, there is nothing to suggest that the services
obtained dishonestly need to be lawful for the offence to be committed. The facts of
the case of *R v Linekar* [1995] 2 Cr App R, where the defendant made off without
paying a prostitute for her services, would fall within s 11.

Commentators have extended this concept in theory to assassins not paid for 6.46
contract killings. It may be that assassins are sufficiently mindful of their privacy
not to pursue allegations of this sort through the courts. However, it is likely that
unlawful services will increasingly be obtained dishonestly via the Internet. It will
be a matter of judgment and common sense when to prosecute.[27]

4. Offence May be Continuous

In *R v Sofroniou*,[28] discussed in more detail above at paras 6.40 and 6.41, the 6.47
defendant had dishonestly operated several bank accounts by making use of the
overdraft facilities. The Court of Appeal held that the dishonest operation of
the account over a period of time 'was capable of being a continuous offence
encompassing the whole operation of the accounts'.[29] On the facts of that case, the
court also held that the fact that the particulars of the offence referred to a date
within that period was immaterial.

5. Summary

Given Parliament's stated intention to consolidate the law of fraud, the case for 6.48
retaining a modified 'obtaining services' offence has not been made convincingly,
or in any great detail. It is difficult to imagine many factual examples of behaviour
that would be caught by s 11, but not by s 2, of the Act.

It seems clear that the term 'services' should be given a wide and general 6.49
interpretation. Whilst the offence may not be invulnerable to technical assaults in
terms of what may constitute a service, one cannot anticipate the sort of troubled
case law which arose from the old offence.

The 'basis' of payment under s 11(2)(a), however, may cause confusion in certain 6.50
circumstances where the requirement to pay is not entirely clear. Section 2 may
then be a clearer option for prosecutors, and easier to prove.

---

[27] Where the service provided is unlawful but not immoral, it may be in the public interest to
prosecute. For example, the directors of an Internet gaming site may have inadvertently failed to renew
their permit, and thus be trading unlawfully. The criminality of a fraudster using their subscription
sites dishonestly is not diminished by their oversight.
[28] [2004] QB 1218.   [29] At 1228.

7

PROCEDURAL MATTERS

A. JURISDICTION

The Criminal Justice Act 1993 is amended by the Fraud Act 2006 to make the 7.01
following offences Group A offences for the purposes of that Act:

(a) Section 1 (fraud).
(b) Section 6 (possession, etc, of articles for use in frauds).
(c) Section 7 (making or supplying articles for use in frauds).
(d) Section 9 (participating in fraudulent business carried on by sole trader, etc).
(e) Section 11 (obtaining services dishonestly).

A person may be indicted for a Group A offence in England or Wales, if any 7.02
relevant event in relation to the offence took place in England or Wales; that is
to say, any act or omission or other event (including any result of one or more
acts or omissions), proof of which is required for conviction of the offence, took
place there.[1] In relation to the s 1 offence, 'relevant event' is deemed to include
the occurrence of any gain or loss intended by the defendant. This amendment is
intended to ensure that conduct which would have been caught by that Act under
the old legislation will continue to be so. For example, a false representation made
abroad, with the intention of obtaining property in England or Wales is indictable,
provided the property is actually obtained.

Conspiring to do conduct which would be a Group A offence is indictable in 7.03
England or Wales, whether or not the defendant became a party to the conspiracy
in the jurisdiction, and irrespective of whether any act pursuant to the conspiracy
actually takes place in the jurisdiction. Likewise, attempts to commit a Group A

---

[1] Criminal Justice Act 1993, s 2.

offence are indictable in England or Wales whether or not the attempt took place in the jurisdiction or its effects were felt there.

B. LIABILITY OF COMPANY OFFICERS

7.04　Section 12 of the Fraud Act 2006 sets out certain circumstances in which company officers are liable for an offence committed by a body corporate. The section states:

12 Liability of Company Officers for Offences by Company

(1) Subsection (2) applies if an offence under this Act is committed by a body corporate.

(2) If the offence is proved to have been committed with the consent or connivance of—
(a) a director, manager, secretary or other similar officer of the body corporate, or
(b) a person who was purporting to act in any such capacity,

he as well as the body corporate is guilty of the offence and liable to be proceeded against and punished accordingly.

(3) If the affairs of a body corporate are managed by its members, subsection (2) applies in relation to the acts and defaults of a member in connection with his functions of management as if he were a director of the body corporate.

7.05　This section mirrors s 18 of the Theft Act 1968. Under that provision where a director, etc, of a company either consents to or connives with an offence of false accounting by the company he is guilty of that offence. Originally s 18 of the Theft Act applied to the deception offences but these have now all been repealed.[2]

7.06　Section 12 of the Fraud Act 2006 is much wider than s 18 of the Theft Act in its application. It provides that if persons who have a specified corporate role 'consent or connive' with the commission of an offence under the Fraud Act 2006 by their body corporate, they will be guilty of the offence as well as the corporation. Thus the offence is much more widely drawn than under the Theft Act. This is especially significant when one considers how wide are the offences created by the Fraud Act 2006. It should be noted that the Companies Act of 2006 received Royal Assent on 8 November 2006. It repeals and replaces most of the Companies Act 1985. Its provisions are expected to be brought into force by October 2008. Part 36 of the 2006 Act contains specific criminal offences (sections 1121 to 1131), along with Schedule 3. Part 29 section 993 creates an offence of fraudulent trading in the same terms as is set out in section 458 of the Companies Act 1985.

7.07　This offence applies to directors, managers, secretaries, and other similar officers of companies and other bodies corporate. Subsection (3) provides that if the body corporate charged with an offence is managed by its members the members involved in management can be prosecuted too. Although the Fraud Act 2006 has abolished all the deception offences in the Theft Acts 1968 and 1978 the offence of false accounting (Theft Act 1968, s 17) remains.

---

[2] Namely, Theft Act 1968, ss 15 and 16 and Theft Act 1978, ss 1 and 2.

Section 733 of the Companies Act 1985 (offences by bodies corporate) contains a similar provision in the following terms: 7.08

where a body corporate is guilty of such an offence[3] and it is proved that the offence occurred with the consent or connivance of, or *was attributable to any neglect* on the part of any director, manager, secretary or other similar officer of the body, or any person who was purporting to act in any such capacity, he as well as the corporate body is guilty of that offence and is liable to be proceeded against and punished accordingly.

The Criminal Law Revision Committee, when recommending this provision in the original Theft Act of 1968, stated that its purpose was to place upon company officers a positive duty to prevent irregularities where they were aware of them. Generally speaking the criminal law does not make liable a person who has 'consented' to an act. The section is intended to make relevant individuals criminally liable where they have passively acquiesced to criminal conduct by a company for which they are responsible. In such a situation the 'director's responsibilities for his company require him to intervene to prevent fraud and where consent or connivance amount to guilt'.[4] However, such occasions are likely to be rare as in most circumstances a director will incur liability on the basis of joint enterprise. Where a person has a clear duty to oversee the actions of another (a fellow director) and does nothing to prevent the other from carrying out a criminal act and when he has knowledge of it he is likely to be guilty as an aider and abettor.[5] 7.09

The phrase 'a director, manager, secretary or other similar officer of the body corporate' contained in s 12 of the Fraud Act, s 18 of the Theft Act 1968, and s 733 of the Companies Act 1985 has been examined by the Court of Appeal in the case of *R v Boal*,[6] a case under s 23 of the Fire Precautions Act 1971 which contains the expression 'any director, manager, secretary or other similar officer of the body corporate'. The Court of Appeal quashed the conviction of the assistant general manager who had responsibility for running a shop on a day to day basis. The section was intended to make criminally liable 'only those who are in a position of real authority, the decision makers within the company who have both the power and the responsibility to decide corporate policy and strategy'.[7] 7.10

Section 12 of the Fraud Act 2006 thus restates an established principle that in certain circumstances officers of companies can be liable where the company itself has been guilty of a criminal offence and where they have 'connived' with or 'consented' to the criminal offence. 7.11

The principles concerning the criminal liability of corporations are relevant in this context. There is a degree of circularity about the position. Individuals through their actions can make a company criminally liable while individuals can become criminally liable if the company has committed an offence with their 'consent or 7.12

---

[3] An offence under ss 210, 216(3), 245(E)(3), 245(G)(7), 394(A)(1), 448, 449 to 451, and 453A.
[4] Cmnd 2977, para 104. [5] See *Tamm* [1973] Crim LR 115.
[6] [1992] 1 QB 591; 95 Cr App R 272. [7] Per Simon Brown J at 597–8; 276.

connivance'. The section is principally aimed at occasions when a company officer has a duty to intervene.

7.13   Companies (who are 'persons' within the definition of the Interpretation Act 1978[8]) may become criminally liable where the legislation creating the offence makes express provision for criminal liability,[9] through the principle of vicarious liability or where the natural person who performed the criminal act with the requisite state of mind was part of the controlling mind of the company. The classic statement of the latter principle is that a company will have transferred to it the acts and state of mind of those of its directors and managers who represent its 'directing mind and will'.[10] This does not mean that every responsible agent or executive will make a company criminally liable by his actions.[11]

C. EVIDENTIAL MATTERS

7.14   Section 13 of the Fraud Act 2006 protects a person from incriminating himself or his spouse or civil partner for the purposes of offences under the Act and related offences, while nonetheless being obliged to cooperate with certain civil proceedings relating to property. It reads as follows:

13 Evidence

(1) A person is not to be excused from—
    (a) answering any question put to him in proceedings relating to property, or
    (b) complying with any order made in proceedings relating to property,
    on the ground that doing so may incriminate him or his spouse or civil partner of an offence under this Act or a related offence.
(2) But, in proceedings for an offence under this Act or a related offence, a statement or admission made by the person in—
    (a) answering such a question, or
    (b) complying with such an order,
    is not admissible in evidence against him or (unless they married or became civil partners after the making of the statement or admission) his spouse or civil partner.
(3) "Proceedings relating to property" means any proceedings for—
    (a) the recovery or administration of any property,
    (b) the execution of a trust, or
    (c) an account of any property or dealings with property,

---

[8] 'Person' in a statute or subordinate legislation is to be construed, subject to the appearance of a contrary intention as including 'a body or persons corporate or incorporate': Interpretation Act 1978, ss 5 and 11, and Schedules 1 and 2, Pt 1, para 4.5.
[9] For example, Companies Act 1985, s 734.
[10] See *Lennard's Carrying Company v Asiatic Petroleum Co* [1915] AC 705, *Bolton Engineering Co v Graham* [1957] 1 QB 159 (Denning at p 172) and *Tesco Supermarkets Ltd v Nattrass* [1972] AC 153.
[11] *Andrews Weather-Foil Ltd* 56 Cr App R 31 and see also *Meridian Global Funds Management Asia Ltd* [1995] 2 AC 500, PC.

and "property" means money or other property whether real or personal (including things in action and other intangible property).

(4) "Related offence" means—

(a) conspiracy to defraud;

(b) any other offence involving any form of fraudulent conduct or purpose.

This section is similar to s 31(1) of the Theft Act 1968 and s 29(1) of the Theft Act (Northern Ireland) 1969. However, the section goes beyond those sections by removing privilege in relation to 'related offences'. 'Related offence' is defined in subsection (4) as meaning conspiracy to defraud and any other offence involving any form of fraudulent conduct or purpose. 7.15

The Fraud Act does not include an equivalent to s 30 of the Theft Act 1968. The effect of s 30 is to make spouses and civil partners liable in respect of each other's property. It follows that one spouse may steal property wholly or jointly owned by the other. The latter is the case as one co-owner may steal from the other. 7.16

Section 30 of the Theft Act 1968 arose out of the repeal of ss 12 and 16 of the Married Women's Property Act 1882. It was aimed at ensuring that a pre-1882 common law rule that husbands and wives could not steal from each other would not be resurrected. It is no longer necessary to include a provision of this sort, as it seems highly unlikely that this rule will be resurrected. 7.17

D. PENALTIES

1. Maximum Penalties

The maximum penalties upon conviction on indictment for the offences under the Act are as follows: 7.18

(a) Fraud: ten years.
(b) Possession of articles for use in fraud: five years.
(c) Making or supplying articles for use in fraud: ten years.
(d) Participating in a fraudulent business: ten years.
(e) Obtaining services dishonestly: five years.

The compares to the penalties for other fraud offences as follows: 7.19

(a) Theft (Theft Act 1968, s 1): seven years.
(b) Conspiracy to defraud: ten years.
(c) Fraudulent trading (Companies Act 1985, s 458): ten years.
(d) Principal money laundering offences (Proceeds of Crime Act 2002, ss 327–9): fourteen years.

2. Confiscation

Where an offender has benefited financially from his criminal conduct, and the prosecutor asks the court to do so, or the court of its own motion considers that it 7.20

is appropriate, the court will make a confiscation order under s 6 of the Proceeds of Crime Act 2002.

3. Directors' Disqualification

7.21 Where the offence is related to the operation of a company, the court may make a Directors' Disqualification Order. A Directors' Disqualification Order is an order that the offender shall not be a director of a company, act as a receiver of a company's property, or in any way, whether directly or indirectly, be concerned or take part in the promotion, formation, or management of a company unless (in each case) he has the leave of the court, and he shall not act as an insolvency practitioner. The power to disqualify is contained in the Company Directors Disqualification Act 1986:

2. Disqualification on conviction of indictable offence

(1) The court may make a disqualification order against a person where he is convicted of an indictable offence (whether on indictment or summarily) in connection with the promotion, formation, management or liquidation of a company, with the receivership of a company's property or with his being an administrative receiver of a company.

(2) "The court" for this purpose means—
 (a) any court having jurisdiction to wind up the company in relation to which the offence was committed, or
 (b) the court by or before which the person is convicted of the offence, or
 (c) in the case of a summary conviction in England and Wales, any other magistrates' court acting in the same local justice area;

and for the purposes of this section the definition of "indictable offence" in Schedule 1 to the Interpretation Act 1978 applies for Scotland as it does for England and Wales.

(3) The maximum period of disqualification under this section is—
 (a) where the disqualification order is made by a court of summary jurisdiction, five years, and
 (b) in any other case, 15 years.

8

FRAUD NOT COVERED
BY THE FRAUD ACT

A. THEFT

Although the Fraud Act 2006 will have a major impact on the way that 8.01
offences involving dishonesty are prosecuted it will sit alongside many existing offences. These include theft, false accounting, false statements by company
directors, the money laundering provisions, cheating the revenue, statutory tax
offences, and forgery and counterfeiting. This chapter sets out in outline these
offences.

1. Introduction

The Fraud Act 2006 does not amend or abolish the offence of theft contained in s 1 8.02
of the Theft Act 1968. Theft is defined as the dishonest appropriation of property
belonging to another with the intention of permanently depriving that other of it.
No description of the new fraud law would be complete without a summary of
the current state of the law of theft. Indeed the Law Commission when considering
the issue of fraud in 2002 was not directly concerned with theft as such, but as the
deception offences in the Theft Acts of 1968 and 1978 had elements in common
it was impossible for them to ignore it. It is clear from their report that as the
offence of theft is now so widely defined the Law Commission could see the need
for reform.

2. Appropriation

8.03   One important part of the definition of theft is that of 'appropriation' which is defined by s 3(1) of the Theft Act 1968 as 'any assumption ... of the rights of an owner'. The concept of defining 'appropriation' has caused great difficulty in the courts. The House of Lords held in *Gomez*[1] that even an act authorized by the owner of the property can be an appropriation and, if dishonest, can amount to theft. In Gomez an employee tricked his employer into accepting stolen cheques to pay for goods. Thus the owner's consent was actually obtained by deception and the transaction was therefore voidable as a matter of civil law. In the case of *Hinks*[2] the House of Lords held that even the acceptance of a gift is an appropriation and it is no defence that the gift is valid as a matter of civil law. In *Hinks* the question for the jury was whether the donor of a gift was so mentally incapable that the defendant herself must have realized that ordinary and decent people would regard it as dishonest to accept a gift from him. In effect this meant that whether Hinks was guilty of theft turned on whether a jury were sure that her conduct was dishonest. As the Law Commission in its report concluded:

> Theft is now an offence of dishonestly receiving property belonging to another by any means, lawful or unlawful.

3. Property Belonging to Another

8.04   'Property' is widely defined in s 4(1) of the Theft Act 1968 as including 'money and all other property, real or personal, including things in action and other intangible property'. Section 4 goes on to define property further so that land, wild flora, and untamed creatures cannot be stolen except in certain circumstances. The Fraud Act 2006 has a similar definition of property except that the limitations contained in s 4 of the Theft Act 1968 are not included. No difference was intended, as the Attorney General said when the Fraud Bill was in the House of Lords that 'we think it is highly desirable that the definitions of "property" for the purposes of theft and fraud are the same'.[3]

8.05   'Belonging to another' means that at the time when D dishonestly appropriates the property V must have some kind of proprietary right over it or a beneficial interest in it. In the case of *Hall*[4] D was a travel agent who was paid by clients to provide flights which he failed to do. There was no evidence that Hall acted dishonestly at the time when he agreed to make the travel arrangements. After the money had been paid by the customers they ceased to have any proprietary rights or beneficial interests in relation to it. What they had was a contractual right to the tickets for which they had made payment. Hall did not provide the tickets and was unable to reimburse the customers because he had spent the money. His theft

---

[1] [1993] AC 442.   [2] [2001] 2 AC 241.   [3] *Hansard*, HL 19 July 2005 col 1435.
[4] [1973] QB 126.

convictions were quashed because at the time he had dishonestly appropriated the money by spending it other than on the tickets it had not belonged to another.

If these circumstances arose again after the commencement of the Fraud Act   8.06
2006 Hall would be guilty of the offence of fraud by abuse of position. He occupied a position in which he was expected to safeguard, or not to act against, the financial interests of another person and he dishonestly abused that position, intending thereby to make a gain for himself or to expose another to the risk of economic loss.

4. With the Intention of Permanently Depriving the Other

This principle was central to the law of larceny and pre-dated the Theft Act 1968.   8.07
This was because D could not be guilty of larceny if he borrowed property and then abandoned it. English law did not recognize *furtum usus*, the theft of use. It had been held in earlier cases that the taking of someone's horse and riding it into town and then leaving it there was not theft. The Theft Acts incorporated this principle by providing in s 1(1) of the 1968 Act that the taking of an article for a temporary period was not theft.

Section 6(1) of the Theft Act 1968 defines the phrase 'with the intention of   8.08
permanently depriving the other of it'. It provides:

A person appropriating property belonging to another without meaning the other permanently to lose the thing itself is nevertheless to be regarded as having the intention of permanently depriving the other of it if his intention is to treat the thing as his own to dispose of regardless of the other's rights; and a borrowing or lending of it may amount to so treating it if, but only if, the borrowing or lending is for a period and in circumstances making it equivalent to an outright taking or disposal.

In the case of *Downes*[5] the defendant's conviction for theft of Inland Revenue   8.09
vouchers was upheld where he had sold them on to others who would later cash them in. Even though the Inland Revenue would get the vouchers back so that the defendant did not intend that they would be permanently deprived of them nevertheless he was guilty of theft as he had intended to treat the vouchers as his own to dispose of regardless of the Revenue's rights.

5. Dishonesty

Dishonesty is an essential element in both the offence of theft and the new fraud   8.10
offences created by the Fraud Act 2006. When dishonesty is a live issue the fact finders must approach it by way of a two-stage test laid down by the Court of Appeal in the case of *Ghosh*.[6] The first question is whether D's conduct was dishonest by the ordinary standards of reasonable and honest people. If the answer is no, then that is the end of the matter and D cannot be convicted. However, if the answer is yes, then the second question is whether the defendant must have been aware that his conduct was dishonest by the standards of reasonable, honest people.

---

[5] (1983) 77 Cr App R 260.   [6] [1982] QB 1053.

8.11   When the Fraud Bill was passing through Parliament the Attorney General, Lord Goldsmith, was asked by Lord Berwick whether the Bill was being enacted 'on the basis that *Ghosh* is the law as we understand it'.[7] The Attorney General refused to give such an assurance, stating that:

> I can say that is the current definition of dishonesty; it is referred to in the Explanatory Notes; no other definition is offered in the Bill. I cannot preclude your lordships from in due course taking a different view and saying that *Ghosh* was wrong all along, but I have no reason to think that it is. That is the most assurance that I can give.[8]

8.12   In fact, s 2 of the Theft Act 1968 limits dishonesty where D has appropriated property belonging to another in three separate situations. None of these is included in the Fraud Act 2006. A person's appropriation of property is not to be regarded as dishonest under the Theft Act 1968:

(a) where D has a genuine belief that he is entitled in law to the property, whether such belief is reasonable or otherwise,

(b) where he believes that the owner would have consented to the taking, or

(c) when he believes that the owner cannot be found.

The test of dishonesty is further tailored by s 2(2) of the Theft Act 1968, which states that D may be dishonest where he has appropriated property notwithstanding that he intended to pay for the property.

8.13   One criticism of the new fraud offences is that they rely too heavily on dishonesty. Several distinguished academics have criticized the way that the courts have defined dishonesty. Professor Griew[9] argued that *Ghosh* was erroneous because it leaves a question of law to the jury, assumes that there is a community-wide standard of honesty, leads to the possibility of inconsistent verdicts on the same facts, leads to longer trials because the issue is often live, and confuses the state of mind of the defendant with the concept of dishonesty.

8.14   It has also been argued that the *Ghosh* approach to dishonesty may fall foul of Article 7 of the ECHR, which prescribes a certainty of law test. The same may be said of the common law offences of conspiracy to defraud and cheating the Revenue. However, where the prosecution are careful to define the cheat or the conspiracy to defraud or where conduct is obviously dishonest such arguments are very weak. Where, however, the conduct that forms the basis of the criminal charge is not itself obviously dishonest or illegal then Article 7 certainty issues are more likely to arise. The principle behind Article 7, which also proscribes retrospective criminalization, is that citizens should be able to know what conduct is contrary to the criminal law.

8.15   The new fraud offences, although heavily reliant on dishonesty, are unlikely to fail the certainty of law test in Article 7. The Fraud Act has been declared compatible with the ECHR by the Attorney General and the Home Secretary, as is required by s 19 of the Human Rights Act 1998. The Joint Parliamentary Committee on

---

[7] *Hansard*, HL 22 June 2005 col 1666.   [8] *Hansard*, HL 22 June 2005 col 1674.

[9] In *The Theft Acts 1968 and 1978* (7th edn, 1995).

Human Rights in its Fourteenth Report[10] concluded that the new fraud offences were compatible with Article 7.

It concluded that the new fraud offence was not: 8.16

a general dishonesty offence rather it embeds as an element in the definition of the offence some identifiable morally dubious conduct to which the test of dishonesty may be applied, as the Law Commission correctly observed is required by the principle of legal certainty. We are therefore satisfied that, as defined in the Bill, the new general offence of fraud satisfies the common law and ECHR requirement that criminal offences be defined with sufficient clarity and precision to enable the public to predict with sufficient certainty whether or not they will be liable.[11]

Interestingly, the Joint Parliamentary Committee on Human Rights did say 8.17 that a 'general dishonesty offence would be incompatible with the common law principle of legal certainty'.[12] However, it did doubt the compatibility of conspiracy to defraud.

B. FRAUD OFFENCES PRESERVED

1. False Accounting (Theft Act 1968)

The offence of false accounting contained in s 17 of the Theft Act 1968 is not 8.18 amended or abolished by the Fraud Act 2006. It has proved to be a useful weapon for the Crown in cases where a wide class of documents used in a business have been falsified or destroyed to perpetrate fraud.

Section 17 creates an offence: 8.19

Where a person dishonestly, with a view to a gain for himself or another or with intent to cause loss to another,—

(a) destroys, defaces, conceals or falsifies any account or any record or document made or required for any accounting purpose; or
(b) in furnishing any information for any purpose produces or makes use of any account, or any such record or document as aforesaid, which to his knowledge is or may be misleading, false or deceptive in a material particular ...

The offence is punishable with a maximum of seven years' imprisonment.

The offence is widely drawn. It covers the dishonest use of 'any account, record 8.20 or document' required for an accounting purpose. The word 'record' has been held to cover, for example, a mechanical account such as a meter attached to a turnstile for recording the number of people passing through.[13] A large class of documents is required for an accounting purpose including false insurance cover notes,[14] housing benefit claim forms,[15] mortgage and other loan application forms,

---

[10] Available at <http://www.publications.parliament.uk/pa/jt200506/jtselect/jtrights/134/13402. htm>.
[11] Paragraph 2.14.   [12] Paragraph 2.2.   [13] *Edwards v Toombs* [1983] Crim LR 43, DC.
[14] *Manning* [1998] 2 Cr App R 461.   [15] *Osinuga v DPP* 162 JP 120, DC.

and any document either made specifically for an accounting purpose or those documents made for some other purpose but required for accounting purposes (such as personal loan proposal forms).[16]

8.21   The *mens rea* for the offence is falsifying, etc, the document 'with a view to gain or with intent to cause loss'. Section 34(2)(a) of the Theft Act 1968 sets out the following definition in the same terms as appears in the Fraud Act 2006:

(2) For the purposes of this Act—

(a) 'gain' and 'loss' are to be construed as extending only to gain or loss in money or other property, but as extending to any such gain or loss whether temporary or permanent; and—
    (i) 'gain' includes a gain by keeping what one has, as well as a gain by getting what one has not; and
    (ii) 'loss' includes a loss by not getting what one might get, as well as a loss by parting with what one has …

The Law Commission in 2002 decided that this definition should be used for the new offence fraud offence. It wrote:

We believe that it would be unrealistic and artificial to say that the new fraud offence requires proof of loss to others. The dishonest making of the financial gain should suffice. On the other hand we also believe that, where the defendant has dishonestly caused financial loss to another, it should not be a defence that the defendant acted out of malice or mischief and not for financial gain. It should be sufficient that the defendant either causes financial loss to another or makes a financial gain (or enables a third party to do so).[17]

8.22   In *R v Goleccha and Chorararia*[18] it was held that where a debtor D dishonestly falsifies a document required for an accounting purpose intending to induce a creditor thereby not to sue on a debt owed D does not have a 'view to a gain' within the meaning of s 34(2). D as a debtor was not possessed of any proprietary rights. He did not have money and the chose in action represented by the debt was owned by the creditor.

8.23   Although 'gain' and 'loss' must relate to money or other property it is not necessary for the Crown to prove that the defendant had no legal entitlement to the property. The Court of Appeal has held[19] that where a company director created two false invoices to improve the apparent financial status of a recently obtained company for the purpose of placating his fellow directors he did not act with a view to a gain within the meaning of s 34(2). A desire to improve relations with business partners did not involve monetary gain and an intent to retain his own resources was not sufficient in these circumstances as it was an artificial concept.

8.24   The offence is also committed where a person who has a duty to make a record in the course of their employment dishonestly fails to do so with a view to making

---

[16] *Attorney General's Reference (No 1 of 1980)* 72 Cr App R 60.
[17] Law Commission, *Fraud* (Law Com No 276, 2002), available at <http://www.lawcom.gov.uk/docs/lc276.pdf>, paras 7.51 and 7.52.
[18] 90 Cr App R 241.   [19] *Masterson* (unreported) 30 April 1996, CA 94 02221 X5.

a gain or intending to cause loss. In one case[20] an international telephone operator was required to record details of telephone calls to overseas subscribers on a number of identical forms, which were later used for accounting purposes. The Court of Appeal rejected a submission that an account had to be in existence before the offence of false accounting could be committed. The prosecution had to prove that D had dishonestly, with the appropriate *mens rea*, omitted material particulars from a document required for an accounting purpose.

2. Liability of Company Directors (Theft Act 1968)

Section 18 of the Theft Act 1968 provides that company officers who are party to the commission of an offence under s 17 by their body corporate will be liable to be charged for the offence as well as the company. A similar provision is included in s 12 of the Fraud Act 2006 and applies where an offence 'under this Act is committed by a body corporate' (s 12(1)).[21]   8.25

3. False Statements by Company Directors (Theft Act 1968)

Where any officer of a company or of an unincorporated association (or person purporting to act as such) with intent to deceive members or creditors publishes any written statement or account which to his knowledge is or may be misleading, false, or deceptive in a material particular he shall on conviction be liable to a term of imprisonment of up to seven years.   8.26

The offence does not include the word 'dishonestly' but requires an intent to deceive with knowledge that published information 'is or may be misleading' in a material particular. Section 744 of the Companies Act 1985 defines officer as director, manager, or secretary. An auditor of a company has been held to be an officer within the meaning of s 84 of the Larceny Act 1861.[22] The Fraud Act 2006 defines a false representation in similar terms. Section 2 states that a representation is false if 'it is untrue or misleading and the person making it knows that it is or might be untrue or misleading'.   8.27

It is an essential element of the offence that D either published or concurred in publishing a written statement or account which to his knowledge was or might be misleading, false, or deceptive in a material particular. A statement or account may be false on account of what it omits even if literally true.[23]   8.28

The Crown must also prove that D published the written statement or account with intent to deceive 'members or creditors of the body corporate or unincorporated association' about its affairs.   8.29

---

[20] *Shama* 91 Cr App R 138.   [21] See para 7.04 ff, above.
[22] *Shacter* [1960] 2 QB 252.
[23] *Lord Kylsant* [1932] 1 KB 442, 23 Cr App R 83 and *Bishirgian* 25 Cr App R 176.

4. Dishonest Destruction of Documents (Theft Act 1968)

8.30 Although the Fraud Act 2006 abolishes the offence of obtaining a valuable security by deception contained in s 20(2) of the Theft Act 1968 the offence of dishonestly destroying documents in s 20(1) is preserved. Section 20 (1) of the Theft Act 1968 states:

> A person who dishonestly, with a view to gain for himself or another or with intent to cause loss to another, destroys, defaces or conceals any valuable security, any will or other testamentary document or any original document of or belonging to, or filed or deposited in, any court of justice or any government department shall on conviction on indictment be liable to imprisonment for a term not exceeding seven years.

C. MONEY LAUNDERING

8.31 Although a full description of the current money laundering laws is outside the scope of this work much fraud is connected to this relatively new and developing area of law. Thus it is necessary and expedient to set out the main provisions. In the UK money laundering criminal legislation (first contained in the Drug Trafficking Act 1986, followed by the Criminal Justice Act 1993 and more recently the Proceeds of Crime Act 2002) has been driven by international obligations, particularly European Directives.[24] There have been three EC Directives: in 1991, 2001, and 2005. These led to criminal anti-money laundering laws and the creation of the Money Laundering Regulations 1993, 2001, and 2003.

8.32 The main UK money laundering laws are set out in the Proceeds of Crime Act 2002. These offences consolidate existing drug and non-drug money laundering laws in one statute and introduce sweeping new offences. The relevant provisions are set out in POCA 2002, Pt 7, ss 327–340. These sections became law on 24 February 2003. However, the principal offences do not apply 'where the conduct constituting an offence under those provisions began before 24 February 2003 and ended after that date and the old principal money laundering offences shall continue to have effect in such circumstances'.[25] Thus for a considerable time the old law will apply.

8.33 POCA 2002, s 327 creates offences of 'concealing, disguising, converting, transferring or removing criminal property from the jurisdiction'. POCA 2002, s 328 creates an offence of entering into or becoming concerned in an arrangement which the defendant knows or suspects facilitates by whatever means the acquisition, retention, use, or control of criminal property by or on behalf of another person. POCA 2002, s 329 creates an offence of 'acquiring, using or possessing criminal property'. All three principal money laundering offences now apply to the laundering of an offender's own proceeds of crime as well as those of someone else.

---

[24] 1991 EC Directive 91/308/EC; EC Directive 2001/97/EC; and EC Directive 2005/60/EC.
[25] The Proceeds of Crime Act 2002 (Commencement No 4 Transitional Provisions and Savings) Order 2003, SI 2003/120.

A person does not commit any offence under POCA 2002, ss 327, 328, or 329   8.34
if he has made a disclosure under s 338 and has the appropriate consent, or he
intended to do so but had a reasonable excuse for not doing so. In addition, no
offence under s 329 is committed if the person 'acquired or used or had possession
of the property for adequate consideration'.

POCA 2002, s 330 imposes upon those working in the 'regulated sector'[26] a   8.35
duty to make a disclosure if they know or suspect or have reasonable grounds
for knowing or suspecting that another person is engaged in money laundering,
where such knowledge came to them in the course of their business. Subject
to the statutory defences, it is an offence to fail to make such a disclosure as
soon as is practicable after information is received. Those nominated to receive
disclosures commit offences if they fail to comply with the requirements for onward
disclosure as set out in POCA 2002, s 331 (regulated sector) or s 332 (non-regulated
sector).

POCA 2002 makes provision for consent to be given to an individual to perform   8.36
acts prohibited by POCA 2002, ss 327, 328, or 329, and an offence is committed
if consent is given otherwise than in compliance with POCA 2002, s 336.

POCA 2002, s 333 creates an offence of 'tipping off' or making a disclosure   8.37
which is likely to prejudice an investigation. There is also an offence of prejudicing
an investigation, which is set out at POCA 2002, s 342.

Sections 102 to 107 of the Serious Organised Crime Act 2005 have amended   8.38
the POCA money laundering offences in important respects. The amendments fall
into the following categories. Section 102 creates a defence where overseas conduct
is legal under local law. Section 103 establishes threshold amounts below which
banks and other deposit taking bodies need not make disclosures. Section 104 takes
away the obligation to make reports where the identity of a culprit or whereabouts
of criminal property are unknown. Section 105 details the form and manner of
disclosures and creates an offence of not using them.

1. Conspiracy to Money Launder

Money laundering is defined in POCA 2002, s 340(11) as an act which constitutes   8.39
an offence under this section (and POCA 2002, ss 328, 329) and includes 'an
attempt, conspiracy or incitement to commit' such offences. Thus a person can
only be guilty of a substantive offence under this section if he has knowledge or
suspicion. The Criminal Law Act 1977, s 1(2) requires that:

where any liability for any offence may be incurred without knowledge on the part of the
person committing it of any particular fact or circumstance necessary for the commission of
the offence, a person shall nevertheless not be guilty of conspiracy to commit the offence
by virtue of subsection (1) above unless he and at least one other party to the agreement
intend or know that that fact or circumstance shall or will exist at the time when the conduct
constituting the offence is to take place.

---

[26] As defined in Sch 9 of POCA 2002.

8.40   This raises the issue as to what is the *mens rea* for an offence of conspiracy to commit an offence contrary to this section. What are the 'facts or circumstances' which the offender must 'know' for the commission of the offence? Can an offender be guilty of conspiracy if he knows of primary facts but his mental state is one of suspicion? Is all that is required knowledge of the primary facts which lead to his suspicion?

8.41   One of the points which *Hussain* appeared to decide was that on a conspiracy to money launder charge the prosecution did not have to prove that the defendant knew that the relevant money was the proceeds of crime or drug trafficking.[27] It was sufficient for the Crown to show that a defendant knew or suspected that it was. This has now been overruled by the effect of the House of Lords decision in *R v Montilla* [2004] UKHL 50, [2004] 1 All ER 113 and the case of *R v Liaquat Ali, Akhtar Hussain, Mohsin Khan* and *Shaid Bhatti* [2005] EWCA 87. The former case established that the Crown must prove that the relevant property was in fact the proceeds of drug trafficking or other criminal conduct. It is not enough that the defendant has reasonable grounds to suspect that the property is the proceeds of drug trafficking or of other criminal conduct when in fact it is not (or cannot be proved to be so).

8.42   In *R v Ali and Others* the Court of Appeal held that on a conspiracy to money launder charge under both the CJA 1988 and the DTA 1994 it was necessary for the prosecution to prove that the property in question was the proceeds of crime or was intended to be and that the defendant knew this to be the case. Suspicion was not enough.

8.43   In *R v Abdul Rahman Saik* [2006] UKHL it was held that a defendant would not be guilty of conspiracy to commit the substantive money laundering offence where he did not know, and therefore did not intend, that the money which he agreed to convert would be the proceeds of crime when at a date in the future he performed his part of the agreement with his co-conspirators. Reasonable grounds for suspicion were sufficient for the substantive offence but not for conspiracy.

D. CHEATING THE REVENUE

8.44   Cheating as a common law offence was abolished by s 32(1) of the Theft Act 1968 except in relation to Revenue offences. Cheating the Revenue is very widely defined and includes any type of fraudulent conduct which results in money being diverted away from the Revenue. The offence can be committed either by a positive act or even an omission. The offence does require an intent to defraud. As the offence is contrary to common law sentence is at large.

8.45   In *R v Hudson*[28] D had falsely stated the profits of his business to the Revenue and as a result paid less tax. The defence submitted that an offence of cheating the

---

[27] *Hussain* [2002] EWCA Crim 06 at para [33].   [28] [1956] 2 QB 252.

Revenue against a private individual (as opposed to a public officer) was unknown to law. The Court of Appeal rejected this and upheld the conviction.

In the later case of *Mavji*[29] it was held that D could be guilty of cheating the 8.46 Revenue where he had omitted to fill in VAT returns when he had a statutory duty to do so. Deception is not a necessary ingredient of the offence. The court also held that even though there was an equivalent statutory offence contrary to the VAT Act 1994, s 72(1) it was not improper to charge a cheat. It was said that the offence of cheating the Revenue may properly be charged in serious and unusual tax offences.

A further attempt was made to strike down the offence of cheating the Revenue in 8.47 the case of *R v Redford*.[30] In this case the Court of Appeal held that the common law offence of cheating the Revenue was still indictable even though D could have been tried on statutory charges which were available on the facts. The Court of Appeal confirmed that the offence could be committed by an omission to act rather than through any positive action. The court placed reliance on the eighteenth century case of *Bembridge* in which Mansfield CJ said 'so long ago as the reign of Edward III it was taken to be clear that an indictment would lie for an omission or concealment of a pecuniary nature, to the prejudice of the king'. Hudson had both failed to register for VAT and not made any returns or payments to the Commissioners of Customs and Excise. It is, however, to be noted that Lord Bingham of Cornhill in the recent case of *Rimmington v Goldstein*[31] said that 'good practice and respect for the primacy of statute do in my judgment require that conduct falling within the terms of a specific statutory provision should be prosecuted under that provision unless there is good reason for doing otherwise'.[32] That case involved a prosecution for the common law offence of public nuisance in which the House of Lords held that the statutory offence should have been charged.

The English courts on other occasions have confirmed the offence. In *R v Hunt*[33] 8.48 the Court of Appeal held that cheating the Revenue is a 'conduct' offence and so there is no requirement to prove resultant loss. *Hudson* was followed in *R v Mulligan*[34] which quoted with approval the words of Hawkins, *Pleas of the Crown* (8th edn) p 1322 that 'all frauds affecting the Crown and public at large are indictable as cheats at common law'. In *R v Litzanzios*[35] the Court of Appeal emphasized that a count of cheating the Revenue must be drafted with sufficient particularity to inform the court and the defence of the exact nature of the factual allegation and so as to eliminate the possibility of conviction on either of two alternative bases.

The Court of Appeal has not yet given approval to the offence of cheating the 8.49 public revenue since the coming into force of the Human Rights Act 1998. A Crown Court judge held[36] in a VAT evasion case relating to gold that the charge of cheating the Revenue, as drafted, was sufficiently precise to pass the 'certainty of

---

29 84 Cr App R 34.   30 89 Cr App R 1.   31 [2006] 1 AC 459.
32 At para 30.   33 [1994] Crim LR 747.   34 [1990] Crim LR 747.
35 [1999] Crim LR 667 CA.
36 *Pattni and Others* Southwark Crown Court [2001] Crim LR 570.

law' test contained within Article 7 of the ECHR. On the facts of the case, if the conduct as alleged by the Crown had occurred then a tax fraud was proved. The defendant's case was that he did not carry out the specified conduct. Human rights principles attach to an individual's position in each case. It may well be that the Court of Appeal will have to consider this issue at some stage. For example, where the conduct is agreed but the defence is that there was no fraudulent intent to cheat the situation may be different. The principle behind Article 7 is that a citizen is entitled to know with sufficient certainty at the time that he carries out an offence that the conduct is subject to the criminal law.

E. FORGERY AND COUNTERFEITING

8.50   Forgery and counterfeiting were the subject of Law Commission recommendations in 1973.[37] These recommendations formed the basis of the Forgery and Counterfeiting Act 1981. The common law offence of forgery was abolished and the Coinages Offences Act 1936 and the Forgery Act 1913 were repealed.

8.51   A person is guilty of forgery if 'he makes a false instrument, with the intention that he or another shall use it to induce somebody to accept it as genuine, and by reason of so accepting it to do some act to his own or another person's prejudice'.[38] The offence carries a maximum sentence of ten years' imprisonment. The Law Commission had recommended this definition in its draft Bill. The 1981 Act was aimed at simplifying the law while at the same time preserving the basic concept of forgery. A forgery does not arise because a document contains lies but when it tells lies about itself. This common law principle is preserved in the 1981 Act. It was perhaps best expressed by Blackburn J in *R v Windsor*[39] when he said:

Forgery is the false making of an instrument purporting to be that which it is not, it is not the making of an instrument which purports to be what it really is, but which contains false statements. Telling a lie does not become a forgery because it is reduced into writing.

8.52   'Instrument' means:

(a) any document, whether of a formal or informal character;
(b) any stamp issued or sold by a postal operator;
(c) any Inland Revenue stamp;
(d) any disc, tape, sound track, or other device on or in which information is recorded or stored by mechanical, electronic, or other means.

8.53   The necessity at common law for a forgery to be of a 'document or writing' had caused difficulty. An earlier common law authority[40] had established that the painting of a false signature of an artist in the corner of a picture which was a

---

[37] Law Commission, *Forgery and Counterfeit Currency* (Law Com No 55, 1973).
[38] Forgery and Counterfeiting Act 1981, s 1.   [39] (1865) 10 Cox 118, 123.
[40] *Closs* (1858) Dears & B 460.

fake purporting to be by a well known artist did not make the defendant guilty of forgery. This was because the forgery must be of some 'document or writing'. Cockburn CJ said that the painting of the name was 'merely in the nature of the mark put upon the painting with a view to identifying it, and was no more than if the painter put any other arbitrary mark as a recognition of the picture being his'. Another case had appeared to decide the opposite. In *R v Douce* on very similar facts the Court of Appeal decided that the signature was an 'instrument in writing' as it purported to convey information about the picture.[41] The Law Commission in its draft Bill intended that the law should be as decided in *Closs*, not *Douce*.

Section 9 of the 1981 Act defines the meaning of 'false' and 'making' in respect of the 'instrument' in various ways: 8.54

(1) An instrument is false for the purposes of this Part of this Act—
   (a) if it purports to have been made in the form in which it is made by a person who did not in fact make it in that form; or
   (b) if it purports to have been made in the form in which it is made on the authority of a person who did not in fact authorise its making in that form; or
   (c) if it purports to have been made in the terms in which it is made by a person who did not in fact make it in those terms; or
   (d) if it purports to have been made in the terms in which it is made on the authority of a person who did not in fact authorise its making in those terms; or
   (e) if it purports to have been altered in any respect by a person who did not in fact alter it in that respect; or
   (f) if it purports to have been altered in any respect on the authority of a person who did not in fact authorise the alteration in that respect; or
   (g) if it purports to have been made or altered on a date on which, or at a place at which, or otherwise in circumstances in which, it was not in fact made or altered; or
   (h) if it purports to have been made or altered by an existing person but he did not in fact exist.

In the case of *R v Moore*[42] the House of Lords confirmed that the repeated use of the word 'purports' in s 9 meant that for an instrument to be false it must tell a lie about itself. In *Moore* D had stolen a cheque payable to someone else, Mark Jessel. He then opened an account at a building society in that false name. He later withdrew money from the account by filling in a withdrawal slip in the name of Mark Jessel. The House of Lords held that the withdrawal slip did not come within s 9(1)(g) above as the form was purported to be signed by the person who originally opened the account albeit in a false name. Thus the document was not a forgery because it did not tell a lie about itself.   8.55

Sections 2 to 5 of the 1981 Act create various other offences involving forgery. These include copying a false instrument (s 2), using a false instrument (s 3), using a copy of a false instrument (s 4), and various offences of having custody or control of certain false instruments (such as passports, money orders, and share certificates) or control of equipment or materials with which such instruments may be made (s 5).   8.56

---

41 *Douce* [1972] Crim LR 105.   42 86 Cr App R 234.

8.57   Most of these offences require D to 'induce' somebody to accept the false instrument as genuine. D must intend that V should be *induced*, by reason of accepting the false instrument as genuine, to do some act to his own or another's *prejudice*. Section 10 of the 1981 Act defines 'prejudice' and 'induce'.

F. MISCELLANEOUS PROVISIONS

8.58   There are a variety of other criminal laws which deal with specific types of fraud. These include insider dealing contrary to s 52 of the Criminal Justice Act 1993; misleading market practices under s 397 of the Financial Services and Markets Act 2000; the intellectual property offences under s 107 of the Copyright, Designs and Patents Act 1988, s 92 of the Trade Marks Act 1994, and ss 1 to 3 of the Computer Misuse Act 1990; and tax offences contrary to s 72(8) of the Value Added Tax Act 1994.

9

FRAUD MANAGEMENT AND THE FUTURE OF FRAUD TRIALS

A. INTRODUCTION

There is a consensus that an overhaul in the way in which fraud trials are investigated   9.01
and prosecuted is necessary. A combination of factors has contributed towards a
system of trying frauds that is widely regarded as mismanaged, ineffective, and
unduly expensive.

The purpose of this chapter is two-fold; first, to set out the statutory provisions   9.02
and guidelines which should ensure the effectiveness and expediency of the trial
process, and, secondly, to consider reforms and innovations that are likely to change
the landscape of large and complex fraud trials and associated legal proceedings
over the next few years. A raft of reforms is currently in the process of review and
consultation, and the practical consequences to the practitioner are likely to be
more widespread and fundamental than those flowing from the Fraud Act itself.
Of course, at the time of publication there can be no certainty as to which of the
reforms currently under review will be enacted.

The perceived failings of the current system and the scale of the proposed reviews   9.03
are, of course, related. The Government expects a change of culture in respect
of the way large fraud trials are conducted. The Labour Party's manifesto for the
2005 election featured prominently a pledge to overhaul the laws on fraud, 'to
update them for the 21st century'. In July 2006 the report of the Fraud Review
was published after extensive research by a range of specialist parties.[1] The public
consultation finished in October 2006. The practitioner will need to be alert to the
final decisions taken in respect of the review. The most significant proposals within
the review are discussed below.

---

[1] The final report can be downloaded at <http://www.lslo.gov.uk//fraud_review.htm>.

9.04   The reforms are aimed at achieving the refinement and resolution of agreed issues, and the isolation of contested issues, a great deal earlier in the trial process than is presently the case. Various efforts made in the last twenty years to achieve this goal have enjoyed mixed success. The relevant provisions of the Criminal Procedure Rules, the Criminal Justice Act 2003, the Disclosure Protocol, and the Lord Chief Justice's Protocol on the control and management of heavy fraud cases have not yet combined to create a sea-change in the prosecution of serious frauds. Over the last few years the necessary concentration of minds and resources to manage trials more effectively at an early stage has been compromised by a concurrent debate about legal aid. It seems beyond doubt, for example, that the 'front-loading' of preparation required by the Criminal Procedure Rules has not taken full effect because of concerns about funding. The recent substantial cuts in legal aid funding announced as part of the Carter Review in serious fraud cases can only have the effect of frustrating the aims of achieving shorter trials.

B. MANAGEMENT OF FRAUD TRIALS

9.05   There are already in existence statutes, guidelines, and codes of practice which, if properly considered and applied, would avert many of the problems associated with long fraud trials.[2] This part of the chapter aims to set out in summary the existing measures in place to try to ensure the effective management of long and complex fraud trials.

1. Disclosure

Disclosure is one of the most important—as well as the most abused—of the procedures relating to criminal trials … For too long, a wide range of serious misunderstandings has existed, both as to the exact ambit of the unused material to which the defence is entitled, and the role to be played by the judge ensuring that the law is properly applied.[3]

9.06   Disclosure problems may be the fault of either side of a fraud prosecution. There had in recent years developed a tendency to hand over the keys to the warehouse. The duty of each prosecutor is to recognize his duties under the relevant statutes,[4] and disclose material only when those duties dictate. Whatever the details of the reforms which actually come to pass, judges are certain to be handed new powers to penalize and prevent improper uses of the disclosure test.

9.07   Practitioners must also be fully acquainted with the Disclosure Protocol issued on 20 February 2006.[5] The protocol requires a complete culture change in the

---

[2] For example, the CPR (see Appendix 7) and the Fraud Protocol (see Appendix 3).

[3] *Disclosure: A protocol for the control and management of unused material in the Crown Court* (20 February 2006), para 1. The protocol is available at <http://www.hmcourts-service.gov.uk/publications/guidance/disclosure.htm>.

[4] The Criminal Procedure and Investigations Act 1996 (CPIA); the Code of Practice issued under s 23 of the CPIA; Parts 25–28 of the Criminal Procedure Rules 2005; and the CPIA 1996 (Defence Disclosure Time Limits) Regulations 1997.

[5] See n 3, above.

form, detail, and scope of defence statements, and generally a proper regard to the requirements of the primary legislation and the Criminal Procedure Rules. Judges are encouraged to make wasted costs orders where applications are unmeritorious and ill-conceived. If judges seize the initiative to manage disclosure in the way that the protocol encourages, disclosure of unused material may cease to be the albatross that it so often proves to be in more complex cases.

Prosecutors must also be familiar with the Attorney General's Guidelines on Disclosure,[6] revised in April 2005 following the House of Lords case *R v H and C.*[7] 9.08

2. The Disclosure Provisions

The following paragraphs seek to identify the most common abuses of the disclosure provisions, and draw to the practitioner's attention the more salient provisions. The Government has indicated that the present disclosure regime, as amended, is being very closely monitored, and practitioners should acquaint themselves fully with the relevant provisions, protocols, and guidelines. 9.09

The provisions of the Criminal Procedure and Investigations Act 1996 as amended by the Criminal Justice Act 2003 create a single test for disclosure. The single test is applicable to cases where the criminal investigation commenced on or after 4 April 2005. The test conflates the tests for primary and secondary disclosure under the un-amended CPIA. The test for disclosure is set out at s 3 of the CPIA 1996 as amended by s 32 of the CJA: 9.10

(1) The prosecutor must
  (a) disclose to the accused any prosecution material which has not previously been disclosed to the accused and which *might reasonably be considered capable of undermining* the case for the prosecution against the accused *or of assisting the case for the accused.*[8]

Under s 7A of the CPIA the prosecutor is under a continuing obligation to keep under review whether there is any material that falls to be disclosed according to the same test. The expectation is that prosecutors will apply this test carefully and responsibly, ensuring to serve material that does satisfy the test whilst refusing to serve material which does not. 9.11

Defence practitioners frequently fail to observe the obligations in relation to defence statements and defence disclosure under s 6A, B, and C of the CPIA as amended. Those provisions must be carefully followed with regard to the detail and particularity of defence statements submitted to the court. The requirement to notify the court of defence witnesses under s 6C is often overlooked. The courts will also seek to enforce time limits. 9.12

---

[6] Available at <http://www.lslo.gov.uk/pdf/disclosure.doc>.
[7] [2004] UKHL 3. Paragraphs 13–17 of the judgment provide a concise summary of the development of disclosure in the last 25 years.
[8] CPIA 1996 as amended. The italics show the amendments made by s 32 of the CJA 2003. The old test referred to material which 'in the prosecutor's opinion' undermined the case. The new test is objective.

9.13   As discussed below, a more rigid enforcement of these provisions is under way with a view to a culture change in respect of disclosure and defence statements. Ad hoc requests for disclosure should not be entertained or granted. That is likely to prompt many more applications for disclosure under s 8 of the CPIA. Such applications should be made in a detailed and particular fashion with close reference to the details of the defence case if the court is to order disclosure of the requested material.

3. Attorney General's Guidelines

9.14   The Attorney General's guidelines on disclosure were updated in April 2005, and emphasize the need to observe closely the disclosure provisions, and also the relevant Criminal Procedure Rules.[9] In respect of cases involving large amounts of data, a realistic view is taken:

> ... exceptionally the extent and manner of inspecting, viewing or listening will depend on the nature of material and its form. For example, it might be reasonable to examine digital material by using software search tools, or to establish the contents of large volumes of material by dip sampling. If such material is not examined in detail, it must nonetheless be described on the disclosure schedules accurately and as clearly as possible.[10]

9.15   The guidelines in relation to defence statements make it clear that bald assertions of innocence and pro forma requests for material will no longer do:

> A comprehensive defence statement assists the participants in the trial to ensure that it is fair. The trial process is not well served if the defence make general and unspecified allegations and then seek far-reaching disclosure in the hope that material may turn up to make them good. The more detail a defence statement contains the more likely it is that the prosecutor will make an informed decision ... It also helps in the management of the trial by narrowing down and focussing on the issues in dispute.[11]

4. The Disclosure Protocol

9.16   'Disclosure: A protocol for the control and management of unused material in the Crown Court' was published in February 2006,[12] a further attempt to effect the necessary 'sea-change' in respect of the widespread abuse of the disclosure system:

> ... it is essential that the trial process is not overburdened or diverted by erroneous and inappropriate disclosure of unused prosecution material, or by misconceived applications in relation to such material.[13]

9.17   The protocol is aimed as much at judges as practitioners, recognizing that a firm judicial hand is the best means of ensuring stringent application of the provisions.

---

[9] The guidelines are available at: <http://www.lslo.gov.uk/pdf/disclosure.doc>.
[10] Attorney General's Guidelines on Disclosure, para 27.   [11] Ibid, para 15.
[12] Available at <http://www.judiciary.gov.uk/judgment_guidance/protocols/crown_unused_material.htm>.
[13] Paragraph 3 of the protocol.

Judges are under a duty to apply the statutory scheme. The protocol emphasizes the need to follow the relevant provisions of the Criminal Procedure Rules under Part 25 in respect of disclosure, and Part 3 in respect of trial management (see below).

Applying the statutory regime should not mean that judges start to apply 9.18 unrealistic timetables for the disclosure of material. Sometimes, judicial muscles are flexed in a way that is clearly counter-productive, and the protocol advises against making orders that parties are unlikely to be able to satisfy:

In order to ensure that the listing of the PCMH is appropriate, judges should not impose time limits for service of case papers or initial/primary disclosure unless and until they are confident that the prosecution advocate has taken the requisite instructions from those who are actually going to do the work specified. It is better to impose a realistic timetable from the outset than to set unachievable limits.[14]

To this end, practitioners need to be informed when addressing the court on 9.19 appropriate timetables, and avoid suggesting arbitrary timetables. The protocol, and the other guidelines, are moving towards a much more formal structure with regard to disclosure. The prosecution advocate must be in an informed position about the disclosure exercise at all stages of the case. By the same token, the protocol reminds defence representatives of their duties. If the defence have failed to satisfy their disclosure obligations, judges will ask why nothing has been done, and what arrangements have been made to put the matter right:

Delays and failures by the defence are as damaging to the timely, fair and efficient hearing of the case as delays and failures by the prosecution, and judges should identify and deal with such failures firmly and fairly.[15]

The consequence of defence practitioners failing to observe the requirements in 9.20 relation to defence statements may be the drawing of an adverse inference under s 11 of the amended CPIA. In the past some practitioners have considered the drawing of inferences from legal documents (which the defendant has agreed to but not drafted) as hitting below the belt. Paragraph 42 of the protocol envisages an increase in such inferences:

In suitable cases, the prosecution should consider commenting upon failures in defence disclosure, with a view to such an inference, more readily than has been the case under the old CPIA regime, subject to any views expressed by the judge.

In order to curb the enthusiasm of prosecutors seeking to draw inferences, the 9.21 protocol recommends that the matter is canvassed before the judge before any comment may be made.

Paragraph 46 of the protocol signals the death knell for the practice of blanket 9.22 disclosure:

... the practice of making blanket orders for disclosure in all cases should cease, since such orders are inconsistent with the statutory framework of disclosure laid down by the CPIA, and which was endorsed by the House of Lords in *R v H and C*.

---

[14] Paragraph 26.   [15] Paragraph 29.

9.23   *R v H and C* also provides authoritative guidance on the proper approach to PII applications.[16] Once again, the relevant Criminal Procedure Rules (r 25.1 to r 25.5) are emphasized.

5. Serious Fraud Protocol

9.24   The protocol for the control and management of heavy fraud and other complex criminal cases was issued by the Lord Chief Justice on 22 March 2005.[17] As discussed elsewhere in this chapter, it remains to be seen whether the ever-growing raft of guidelines and protocols will achieve the desired effect. For the present purposes, the desired effect is to keep trials to a reasonable length, to enable the jury to assess and understand the evidence that they have heard, and to make proper use of limited public resources.[18]

9.25   The protocol stresses the crucial role of the judge, expecting that 'judges should exert a substantial and beneficial influence'[19] in managing trials and keeping them within reasonable limits. Most cases should aim to be complete within three months, although the protocol recognizes that an exceptional few cases will take longer.

9.26   In respect of disclosure, the protocol advises that it is 'most undesirable to give the warehouse key to the defence for two reasons':

(a) this amounts to an abrogation of the responsibility of the prosecution;
(b) the defence solicitors may spend a disproportionate amount of time and incur disproportionate costs trawling through a morass of documents.[20]

9.27   The protocol in fact does little more than repeat and gently expand upon the existing statutory provisions, on the basis that they have been largely abused, ignored, or mis-applied. The case management provisions in the CPR (discussed below) are applied to the letter by some enthusiastic judges, but largely ignored by others, so that cases rumble on with little respect for the obligations they impose upon all parties.

9.28   The protocol recognizes that the measures within the CPR relating to case management 'are salutary provisions which should bring to an end interminable criminal trials of the kind which the court of appeal criticised in *Jisl* [2004] EWCA 696'.[21]

9.29   These salutary provisions involve the judge making positive steps to reduce the length of the trial. The Crown may be asked why they have elected to prosecute the case in a particular way, which will be interesting in cases where the Crown elect to use the retained conspiracy to defraud as opposed to the new offence of fraud. The judge can aim to persuade the Crown to do away with particular counts on the indictment, or refrain from relying on particular areas of evidence. The case

---

[16] *H and C* [2004] 2 AC 134.
[17] Available at <http://www.dca.gov.uk/criminal/procrules_fin/contents/pd_protocol/pd_protocol.htm>.
[18] See *Jisl* [2004] EWCA Crim 696.   [19] Paragraph 1(i)(b) of the protocol.
[20] Paragraph 4(iii).   [21] Paragraph 3(vii).

management process is ongoing before and after the trial, so that matters are not left to drift.

However, the protocol does recognize that the Criminal Procedure Rules do not have to be used on every occasion, particularly if all parties are getting on perfectly well without them: 9.30

Where the advocates have done their job properly, by narrowing the issues, pruning the evidence and so forth, it may be quite inappropriate for the judge to 'weigh in' and start cutting out more evidence or more charges of his own volition. It behoves the judge to make a careful assessment of the degree of judicial intervention which is warranted in each case.[22]

The conduct of interviews comes in for particular criticism, and there is no doubt that shapeless and interminable interviews protract and confuse a trial. Interviews should be 'an opportunity for suspects to respond to the allegations. They should not be an occasion to discuss every document in the case'.[23] 9.31

Given the contents of the Fraud Review, which are discussed in detail below, it will increasingly be the case that the investigation and the prosecution of serious frauds are conducted in much greater harmony. It may increasingly fall to the prosecution advocate to determine the proper limits of questions to be asked in interview. 9.32

The protocol also encourages judges to regulate the prolixity of counsel on both sides, 'indicating when cross examination is irrelevant, unnecessary or time wasting'.[24] 9.33

6. Case Management and Criminal Procedure Rules

Parts 1 and 3 of the Criminal Procedure Rules should be familiar to practitioners, and are appended to this text. The rules are extensive and wide ranging, and it is not appropriate to descend into their detail in this context. The overriding objective set out in Part 1 of the rules provides a very broad ambit for the rules. Of particular relevance is CPR 1.1(e), 'dealing with cases efficiently and expeditiously'. 9.34

To that end, Part 3 of the CPR sets out a series of measures in respect of case management. The rules require the early identification of relevant issues and witnesses, of what needs to be done by whom and when. Progress of the case is constantly monitored, with the potential for unspecified consequences in the event of non-compliance. The court has a wide range of powers to ensure and enforce the efficient conduct of the trial. Under rule 3.5(2)(e), the court may make a direction without a hearing. This power, if judiciously used in non-contentious matters, should reduce the need for listing cases for mention. 9.35

7. Preparatory Hearings under the Criminal Justice Act 1987

Section 7 of the Criminal Justice Act 1987 provides for preparatory hearings in long and complex cases. Under s 7(1) the judge may order such a hearing in cases 9.36

---

[22] Paragraph 3(vii)(b).   [23] Paragraph 1(ii)(a).   [24] Paragraph 6(v).

where 'an indictment reveals a case of fraud of such seriousness and complexity that substantial benefits are likely to accrue from a hearing'.

9.37   The purpose of such a hearing is set out in s 7(1):

(a) identifying issues which are likely to be material to the determinations and findings which are likely to be required during the trial;
(b) if there is to be a jury, assisting their comprehension of those issues and expediting the proceedings before them;
(c) determining an application to which s 45 of the Criminal Justice Act 2003 applies;
(d) assisting the judge's management of the trial;
(e) considering questions as to the severance or joinder of charges.

9.38   The case law makes it clear that 'the purpose' to be achieved by a preparatory hearing is the purpose of the trial judge in managing the trial.[25]

9.39   Section 7 has been amended by the Criminal Justice Act 2003, so that under s 7(c) the preparatory hearing would have been the appropriate time to argue whether the case should be tried without a jury, if s 45 of the CJA 2003 had been enacted.

9.40   Section 7(e), allowing a judge to consider severance and joinder at a preparatory hearing, was added by s 310 of the Criminal Justice Act 2003. Before that amendment was made, it was not clear whether decisions as to joinder and severance were within the scope of the purpose of a preparatory hearing, a good illustration of the great potential for overlap between matters relating to trial management and other matters which fall outside the scope of s 7.

9.41   In *R v G*,[26] before s 7(e) was added, the Court of Appeal was asked to consider whether consideration of joinder and severance could properly be dealt with at a preparatory hearing. Henry LJ held that 'severance is an important case management weapon. Where the judge uses it for that purpose, then an interlocutory appeal will, in appropriate cases, lie'.[27]

9.42   The proper ambit of what may be subject to a preparatory hearing is sometimes challenged by parties in the case seeking to press other matters for the judge's determination. However, the Court of Appeal has emphasized that a preparatory hearing should not develop beyond the case management purposes of the section:

We cannot bring ourselves to believe that Parliament can possibly ... have intended to allow a preparatory hearing to commence for a certain specified purpose and then permit, once a preparatory hearing for that purpose is in being, argument to range around all manner of issues which cannot be said to relate to any of the specified purposes.[28]

9.43   Section 9 of the Criminal Justice Act 1987 gives a judge the power to adjourn a preparatory hearing from time to time (s 9(2)), and sets out the range of powers which a judge may exercise in the course of a preparatory hearing:

---

[25] 'The governing purposes set out in s 7(1) relate to the trial judge's management of the trial, that is to say, on matters facilitating the trial. The purpose is the judge's purpose.' Henry LJ in *R v G* (Interlocutory Appeal: Jurisdiction) [2002] 1 WLR 200.

[26] *G* (Interlocutory Appeal: Jurisdiction) [2002] 1 WLR 200.

[27] At para 36 of the judgment.

[28] *In re Gunawardena, Harbutt and Banks* [1990] 1 WLR 703 at 707.

(3) He may determine–
    (a) a question arising under s 6 of the Criminal Justice Act 1993 (relevance of external law to certain charges of conspiracy, attempt and incitement);
    (b) any question relating to the admissibility of evidence; and
    (c) any question of law relating to the case; and
    (d) any question as to the severance or joinder of charges.

In the case of *Gunawardena*, the Court of Appeal was asked to decide whether s 9(3) was subordinate to the provisions in s 7(1). The court strongly confirmed that to be the case, so that a judge's powers under s 9(3) were to be used pursuant to the limited case management scope of s 7:   **9.44**

… we think that the material legislation means that the set purposes and no other may be served throughout the existence of the preparatory hearing and in respect of every application which is made to the judge during the hearing. Care must be taken to avoid confusion between a preparatory hearing under the Act and the informal pre-trial review.[29]

Section 9(11) of the Criminal Justice Act 1987 makes provision for interlocutory appeals as follows: **9.45**

An appeal shall lie to the Court of Appeal from any order or ruling of a judge under subsection 3(b)(c) or (d) above from the refusal by a judge of an application to which section 45 of the Criminal Justice Act 2003 applies or from an order under section 43 or 44 of that Act which is made on the determination of such an application, but only with the leave of the judge or the Court of Appeal.

Because the powers under s 9 are subordinate to those of s 7(1), a ruling must fall within s 7(1) and s 9(3) to be the proper subject of an appeal.[30] The Court of Appeal has been traditionally reluctant to entertain interlocutory appeals, and this is likely to continue with the increasing emphasis placed on judges' obligations proactively to manage their trials.   **9.46**

Before severance was included in a judge's powers by the addition of s 7(1)(e), *R v Jennings*[31] considered whether a judge's decision to sever an indictment fell to be appealed. The general rule stated in that case, and supported subsequently, was that there was no prima facie right to appeal a decision to sever because that power was not included in s 7(1). However, the Court of Appeal accepted that it would be possible to argue that severance was a decision relating to 'the judge's management of the trial' under s 7(d), and that argument in fact succeeded in the application of the Crown in the subsequent case of *R v G*.   **9.47**

Section 9(3) restricts the appeals to rulings on questions of law, admissibility, and severance. It is not therefore clear whether the exercise of judicial discretion in using case management powers can be appealed, but the Court of Appeal has discouraged appeals against decisions arising from a judge exercising his discretion.   **9.48**

---

[29] [1990] 1 WLR 707.
[30] The cases reviewed in *G* (Interlocutory Appeal: Jurisdiction) [2002] 1 WLR 200 'make it clear beyond argument that an interlocutory appeal under s 9(11) only lies when the section 9(3)(b)(c) powers are exercised for section 7(1) purposes'. Henry LJ at 208.
[31] (1993) 98 Cr App R 308.

9.49   The effect of ss 7(1) and 9(3) is not certain in limiting what may or may not be appealed under s 9(11), particularly since matters of case management often overlap with rulings in law. Given the Court of Appeal's traditional reluctance to entertain appeals of this kind, practitioners should consider very carefully whether the decision they wish to appeal falls within ss 7(1) and 9(3). If the decision arises from improper use of a judge's discretion, or does not relate to case management issues, it is most unlikely that an appeal can arise.

C. REFORMING THE APPROACH TO FRAUD

... the sheer size and complexity of cases produced by the modern economic and commercial environment continues to test, even to breaking point, the criminal justice system.[32]

1. Long and Complex Fraud Trials Conducted Without Juries?

9.50   Part 7 of the Criminal Justice Act 2003 provided for trials on indictment without juries in cases involving long and complex frauds or the risk of jury tampering. Section 43 of the Act allowed the Crown to apply for a long and complex fraud to be tried without a jury. The judge would have to consider whether 'the complexity of the trial or the length of the trial (or both) is likely to make the trial so burdensome to the members of a jury hearing the trial that the interests of justice require that serious consideration should be given to the question of whether the trial should be conducted without a jury'.[33] Under s 43(4) a judge could not make an order to try the case without a jury without the approval of the Lord Chief Justice or a judge nominated by him. The decision could then be the subject of an appeal.

9.51   The measure, unsurprisingly, provoked a great deal of controversy. As a concession to get the Bill through Parliament, Part 7 of the Act required an affirmative resolution by both Houses of Parliament before it could take effect.[34] In June 2005 the Attorney General announced in the House of Lords that the Government intended to propose the necessary affirmative resolutions by autumn 2005, seeking to downplay the significance of the measure:

To put it into perspective, there are around 40,000 jury trials in England and Wales annually, and this provision will affect a handful—perhaps 15 to 20.[35]

9.52   The affirmative resolutions were never proposed, and the Government was pressured into undertaking that jury trials would not be removed except through a separate stand-alone measure. As a consequence the Fraud (Trials without a Jury) Bill was introduced into Parliament on 16 November 2006 and received its

---

[32] HM Chief Inspector Stephen Wooler CB, *Review of the Investigation and Criminal Proceedings in relation to the Jubilee Line case*, para 3.2, available at <http://www.hmcpsi.gov.uk/reports/JubileeLineReponly.pdf>.

[33] Criminal Justice Act 2003, s 43(5).   [34] Criminal Justice Act 2003, s 330(5)(b).

[35] *Hansard*, HL 21 June 2005.

second reading on 29 November. The Bill would provide for fraud trials conducted without juries by 'a judge of the High Court exercising the jurisdiction of the Crown Court'.

As could have been expected, the measure continues to face implacable opposition on both sides of the house. The provision of non-jury trials seems to be an important element of the Government's 'coordinated approach' to tackling the problems of fraud, and part of a move towards a single financial jurisdiction for fraud cases (see below). Critics of the proposal, and there are many, seek to persuade the Government that other measures can ensure more efficient trials without compromising the right to trial by jury. The principal issue to be determined in most serious fraud cases is dishonesty. That is likely to continue under the provisions of the Fraud Act, given that dishonesty has a determinative function in respect of the principal offences created by the Act. It is argued that the variety and scope of moral codes encompassed by a jury are a fairer way of determining the issue of dishonesty than a professional, and perhaps cynical, judge. In contrast, others suggest that defence practitioners have for too long traded on the naivety of jurors, most of whom come cold to the industry of fraud.   9.53

On a practical level, critics of the proposal argue that the effect of various protocols and reforms designed to manage fraud cases more effectively (as discussed above) has yet to be seen, and that this measure is premature. Many speakers in the debate in the House of Commons after the second reading of the Bill said they were in no doubt that the Government would invoke the Parliament Act if the measures failed to pass through the House of Lords. There are real concerns expressed privately by the judiciary that judge-alone trials would in practice be unworkable.   9.54

2. The Final Report of the Fraud Review

The Final Report of the Fraud Review seeks to analyse the failings of the current methods of measuring, preventing, investigating, and trying fraud cases and proposes recommendations for the reform of these methods. The most significant proposals are discussed below. Many of the recommendations of the review relate to the more rigid enforcement of rules, procedures for which are already on the statute books, and these are also discussed below.   9.55

3. Measuring, Preventing, and Investigating Fraud

The ambit of the Fraud Review is extensive, dealing as much with preventative measures to avoid and combat fraud as investigating and prosecuting it. It is not proposed to deal in any detail with aspects of the Fraud Review that do not relate directly to the trial process, but an overview provides a useful context in terms of the scale of the challenge facing the Government.   9.56

The Fraud Review was unable to quantify the scale of the problem of fraud in the UK because of the lack of any consistent national strategy for recording the cost of fraud to the economy. There is no consistent national strategy to combat fraud,   9.57

and so the Review unleashes the usual management-speak vocabulary—holistic approaches, upstream thinking—to emphasize the coordinated approach it will take in combating fraud. A key recommendation of the Review is that the Government should establish a National Fraud Strategic Authority ('the NFSA'), which would coordinate the work of existing organizations and serve as a centre of expertise to assist organizations in the private and public sectors. The Review also urges the sharing of data between organizations with a view to preventing fraud, and the widening of legislative gateways to allow this. This proposal is likely to be welcomed by most 'stakeholders' as an essential means of ensuring consistency throughout the system for monitoring, investigating, prosecuting, and punishing fraud, and making the fullest use of the available resources, data, and experience.

9.58   The fragmentation of the resources available to prevent and to investigate fraud is a serious impediment to the coordinated approach for which the Government strives. For example, there are in the region of 50 bodies who have the responsibility to investigate and prosecute fraud in the UK, few (if any) of which would claim to enjoy sufficient resources for their task. It is a massive challenge to strive for a consistent approach across these agencies, both in terms of investigation and of prosecution.

9.59   The quality and integrity of fraud prosecutions will depend upon the agency which investigates and prosecutes any particular fraud. The Serious Fraud Office, which effectively chooses the cases it wishes to prosecute, ensures early cooperation and communication between investigators, accountants, and lawyers. A well-managed investigation, with a close view to the eventual shape of the prosecution, is the sort of approach large fraud trials will have to take in the future. That cannot happen without a significant increase in integration between investigators and prosecutors, and a clear strategy in handling the largest types of case. The official review into the failure of the *Jubilee Line* case is a graphic and detailed account of what can happen when the prosecuting authority lacks a clear strategy, in terms of both specific investigations and the broader systems in place to prevent cases spiralling out of control.[36]

9.60   The Fraud Review highlights a depressing decrease in the amount of police resources outside London dedicated to the combat and investigation of fraud, which is described as 'a Cinderella function'. The National Policing Plan does not even list the combat of fraud as a priority. Although the combat of fraud is the third strategic priority for the Serious Organized Crime Agency (after Class A drugs and organized immigration crime), police resources clearly need to increase to provide support. To that end, the Review recommends that the Home Secretary should consider making fraud a policing priority, and ensure that each police fraud squad is able to obtain pre-charge advice from specialist area fraud prosecutors. There are also recommendations to the effect that fraud squads nationwide should have sufficient computer capacity to handle the large amounts of digital data generated by large fraud investigations, and that a uniform system exists throughout the regions.

---

[36] See n 2, above.

A more controversial suggestion is the proposed scope for increased public/private 9.61
partnership in the investigation of fraud. Many fraud investigations at the moment
depend on the investigative work of organizations which fall victim to fraud—banks,
building societies, local authorities. Some critics fear that the Government is shaping
up to design a PPP whereby private bodies directly allocate funds to augment police
resources in investigating particular frauds, notwithstanding the Court of Appeal's
recent depiction of the dangers implicit in such schemes:[37]

In our judgment, soliciting by the police of funds from potential victims of fraud, or any
other crime, quite apart from being *ultra vires* police powers, is a practice which is fraught
with danger. It may compromise the essential independence and objectivity of the police
when carrying out an investigation. It might lead to police officers being selective as to which
crimes to investigate and which not to investigate. It might lead to victims persuading a
police investigating team to act partially. It might also lead to investigating officers carrying
out a more thorough preparation of the evidence in a case of a 'paying' victim; or a less
careful preparation of the evidence in the case of a non-contributing victim.

That passage is quoted at some length because the 'rent-an-investigation' concept 9.62
may be sufficiently economically alluring to the Government to override concerns
about impartiality, fairness, and proportionality. Although the Review recognizes
the dangers of direct business support for individual investigations, it seeks to
increase initiatives 'in which police investigative units were directly financed by
the organizations which benefited from them'.[38] The example given is that of the
Vehicle Leasing Squad, which is financed by the Financing and Leasing Association.
If such initiatives are to increase, there must be a danger that corporate bodies which
fund the means to investigate and prosecute frauds against their interest will have a
greater protection against fraud than those who do not. The resources available to
try and punish frauds, and to recover illicit assets, will always be finite. Will 'private'
frauds be ushered through the courts with greater ease than the frauds perpetrated
against those who cannot contribute towards the costs of an investigation?

4. A Single Financial Jurisdiction

The principal recommendations of the Fraud Review relate to the largest and most 9.63
complex fraud cases, recognizing that for every *Jubilee Line* there are hundreds of
efficiently tried cases of fraud which prompt no cause for concern:

Fraud trials can range from very straightforward 1 or 2 day cases involving a couple of
forged cheques to cases involving highly complex business or financial issues, or sophisticated
criminal gangs, often with an international dimension. The majority of fraud cases are straightforward and tried routinely in our courts by magistrates or judges with no particular expertise
in fraud. We have not identified any real concern in the way that these cases are handled.[39]

---

[37] *Hounsham, Mayes, Blake* [2005] EWCA Crim 1366. The case involved three insurance companies
providing financial assistance to the police in an investigation into an insurance scam involving the
theft of cars, their use in staged crashes, and fraudulent insurance claims.
[38] Fraud Review, Final Report, p 147 (see n 1, above, for reference).   [39] Ibid, p 203.

9.64   Heavy and complex frauds, by contrast, are increasingly difficult to manage. The concern does not relate solely to the volume and complexity of evidence, but also to the increasing overlap between criminal frauds, confiscation proceedings, and associated civil proceedings. One of the most eye-catching proposals of the Review is to establish 'what could be described as a financial court jurisdiction in the Queen's Bench Division, linking the Crown Court and the High Court to handle and co-ordinate civil and criminal fraud work':

> This would enable more frequent allocation of High Court or long trial specialist judges to complex Crown Court fraud trials and the allocation of ancillary High Court matters arising from a fraud offence to the Crown Court, where it would be just and appropriate to do so. The joinder of jurisdiction would eliminate much of the current wasteful duplication of court and judicial resources by enabling related ancillary civil matters to be based on a single basic facts hearing, and to be heard by the same (trial) judge.[40]

9.65   This recommendation appears to have been made on the assumption that there will be a provision for fraud trials to be heard without juries. A single jurisdiction court may indeed save resources, but it may be too radical and complicated a goal to achieve.

5. Wide Sentencing Powers

9.66   The Fraud Review, in the wake of various recommendations of the Auld Review,[41] envisages a more extensive combination of sentencing powers with the court's regulatory function. The most radical realization of that would be the creation of a single financial jurisdiction (see above), but even in the absence of that the Review seeks to achieve more of a 'one-stop shop' in respect of penalizing fraudsters and compensating victims:

> The 'new' powers … are based entirely on those already exercised; albeit in different proceedings in different courts. The Fraud Review does not propose any changes to the essential nature of the proceedings or their remedies, merely to rationalize their uses and the fora in which they are deployed. In short, we are proposing to augment the criminal court's sentencing powers with remedies borrowed from the civil courts. Fraud is unique as an offence that invariably spawns regulatory action and satellite proceedings in the civil courts. In these circumstances, a certain amount of one stop shopping is bound to bring benefits to offenders, victims, witnesses and the justice system.[42]

9.67   The Review recommends extending the range of non-custodial options available to the court, including powers to wind up companies, disqualify persons from engaging in particular professional or commercial activities, appoint a receiver, dissolve partnerships, and award compensation to the victims of fraud. The consolidation of powers currently wielded by a large range of regulatory bodies in

---

[40] Fraud Review, Final Report, p 197.
[41] Auld LJ, *Review of the Criminal Courts of England and Wales*, 2001. Available at <http://www.criminal-courts-review.org.uk>.
[42] Fraud Review, p 178.

one place would certainly make for brisk justice, but the Government can expect a good deal of opposition from those existing regulatory bodies, who may feel that their functions are being usurped. Many of those consulted have stressed the fact that satellite issues arising from criminal frauds may often be too extensive or complex to be dealt with in the criminal jurisdiction. The Government must also monitor the impact these increased powers may have on the legal aid budget. Perhaps the most significant benefit in terms of the resources would be the reduction in serial proceedings which all depend on the same facts.

6. Fraud Trials

The risks associated with complex fraud trials have been discussed above, and it is clear that there exists something of a cultural failure amongst practitioners to abide by the laws, rules, guidelines, and protocols that have appeared in the last ten or fifteen years to try to achieve efficient trial management. An efficient and fair trial will depend to a great extent on the efficiency and focus of the investigation, and if reforms to the investigative process succeed, the management of certain trials may become less problematic. Those lawyers who advise pre-charge, or even at an early stage in the investigation, will do so with a mind to the practicality of proving the offences and the volume and scope of used and unused material. Whilst prosecutors will wish to reflect the full criminality of the case, a little discrimination at an early stage may ward off serious disclosure issues further down the line. 9.68

In respect of recent fraud prosecutions, the Fraud Review indicated serious concerns in respect of disclosure, trial management, and the electronic presentation of evidence. 9.69

7. Disclosure and Trial Management

The current provisions in relation to disclosure, and the common abuses thereof, have been discussed in part B of this chapter. The Review identifies disclosure as being 'a major cost driver in complex fraud cases', and cites an example of a trial at Wood Green requiring 6,000 prosecution man hours dealing with disclosure.[43] Furthermore, the potential labour and time spent (or wasted) on disclosure issues act as a disincentive to police forces to accept or further investigate cases. 9.70

The increase in digital data gives even the most experienced and well-organized prosecution agencies potential disclosure difficulties which may spiral beyond practical control. By way of example, the Computer Forensic Unit at the SFO calculated that the average case it dealt with involved the analysis of over five terabytes of digital material, roughly equivalent to a pile of paper twelve times the height of Mount Everest.[44] The scale of that problem can only increase with the further proliferation of electronic data in frauds, and the Government sensibly proposes to continue to monitor the problem. 9.71

---

[43] Ibid, paras 9.44 and 9.55.   [44] Ibid, para 9.49.

9.72   Beyond recommending the more rigid enforcement of the existing provisions in respect of disclosure, the Fraud Review does not recommend amending or replacing them, electing instead to keep them under review. Indeed, the Review resists a recommendation by the Fraud Advisory Panel to remove the obligation upon the investigating authority to pursue all reasonable lines of enquiry, which the FAP regarded as 'wholly unrealistic in the circumstances of a serious fraud case'.[45]

9.73   There is a clear emphasis in the Review upon the defence justifying any request for material with reference to the particulars of their case. The Review does not propose any amendments to the existing disclosure regime on the basis that 'a great deal of work has been done in this area and the impact of this work, and the more general work on trial management, cannot yet be assessed'.[46] The Review does recommend that a study be carried out into the effectiveness of the sanctions available to the judges. If they are shown to be ineffective or insufficient, they may be increased. The Review summarizes what the system seeks to achieve, emphasizing the role that the defence will be required to play:

> The general principle that runs through the initiatives and protocols in place is that when a case actually comes to trial the issue in dispute should be clear, the expert evidence should have been narrowed down to focus on those issues, disclosure of unused material should have been dealt with and only those prosecution witnesses whose evidence is likely to be challenged should have to attend court. This can only be achieved if the Defence is obliged to play its full part in both the trial management and disclosure processes. There should be no place for ambush defences in fraud trials.[47]

9.74   The Fraud Review's analysis of the role of the defence in the disclosure and trial management processes is the starting point for what appears to be a proposal to shift the burden of proof in complex criminal cases:

> The time may now be right to move towards a full 'civil' degree of mutual disclosure between prosecution and defence and other complex trials. The prosecution are now bound to provide pleadings in the form of a case outline, lists of admissions and issues and they must select relevant unused material to disclose. For the court, the picture can only be complete when the defence is also obliged to provide more than an 'outline' of its case.[48]

9.75   There is clearly scope for a good deal of controversy to arise from this line of thinking, particularly when one considers the proposed single financial jurisdiction combining criminal and civil powers, and the potential removal of juries for certain trials. Whether or not there is a hidden agenda to find a way to secure high-profile convictions in big fraud trials whilst saving money and shaving away ancient rights and protections afforded to a defendant, the Government is considering tackling serious problems with radical solutions. The debates, and the outcome of those debates, will be interesting to observe. The new disclosure regime is on probation.

---

[45] Fraud Review, para 9.57. See also the Fraud Advisory Panel's *Improving the Investigation and Prosecution of Serious Fraud*, published 25 May 2006, available at <http://www.fraudadvisorypanel.org>. In response to the Fraud Review on this point, the FAP emphasizes the importance of prosecutors being allowed to close down an unpromising line of investigation.
[46] Fraud Review, para 9.79.   [47] Ibid, para 9.31.   [48] Ibid, para 9.32.

In the meantime, the Fraud Review emphasizes the need for a robust judicial 9.76
approach to the issues of disclosure and trial management, and the greater use of
the available sanctions.

8. Training and Strategy

To enforce the proper implementation of the existing provisions, the Review seeks 9.77
to create a mechanism for coordinating the oversight of long and complex fraud
trials, in order 'to promote a consistent and co-ordinated approach to the training
of judges authorised to hear serious fraud cases, oversee any appraisal in relation
to the "fraud" judges and provide a valuable link with the Very High Cost Case
Review Board'.[49]

Even if the ambitious proposal to create a single financial jurisdiction does not 9.78
come to pass, there will be clear and coordinated requirements for judges to be
specialized and trained. Consideration will be given to a specialist panel of judges,
comprising a mix of High Court and Crown Court judges with fraud tickets. If it is
the case that some judges are cowed by the experience or persuasion of senior silks to
the detriment of case management, this procedure would ensure that the nominated
trial judges are up to the job and have stiff resolve. The Review does not support
the proposal that these judges should only try fraud cases, on the basis that 'the best
judges tend to be good trial managers across the board'.[50] The early appointment
of a specialist judge for long and complex fraud cases will be an important priority,
in the same way that the Review recommends consistency and continuity in the
investigation and prosecution teams.

In addition to annual training courses, it is proposed that specialist fraud judges 9.79
attend compulsory training courses which deal with disclosure in high volume cases
and case management skills.

9. Electronic Presentation of Evidence

The Review regards as inevitable the introduction of a common system for managing 9.80
case documents during the investigation, and at all stages in the run-up to and
including the trial. The electronic preparation and presentation of evidence (or
'EPPE', as the acronym goes) is already a feature of some complex trials. In 2001
the Court Service completed a pilot scheme which was regarded as positive, but it
was clear that a large amount of analysis and research was still required. The Review
claims that 'there is a growing body of credible anecdotal evidence to suggest that
EPPE can save between 10% and 25% of the time',[51] although that sounds less
than convincing, and the Review is devoid of any detailed or practical suggestions
as to how to implement such a system, recognizing that the lack of a rigorous cost
analysis has prevented any significant progress in the last few years. Consequently,
the Review recommends that a cost benefit analysis into the viability of EPPE

---

[49] Ibid, para 9.61.   [50] Ibid, para 9.62.   [51] Ibid, para 9.38.

be commissioned. This slow-pedal approach does not inspire confidence in the 'inevitable' implementation of a common system any time soon.

10. The Approach to Sentencing

9.81 As the Fraud Act 2006 has only recently passed into law, there are no guidelines as to the appropriate levels of sentence in fraud cases. Furthermore, the authors of the Fraud Review were frustrated at the 'poorly organized sentencing data' available to them.[52] The Review refers to a general perception that fraudsters get off lightly, particularly considering the fact that many frauds will be perpetrated in breach of trust. The SFO's statistics, which clearly refer to serious and complex cases of fraud where the loss exceeds £1m, indicate that the average length of imprisonment of the most severely sentenced defendant between 2000 and 2005 was 31.7 months.[53] The principal deterrence to people considering the commission of fraud appears not to be the level of eventual sentence, but the likelihood of detection.

9.82 The unpredictability of the sentences handed down does not sit easily with the Government's enthusiasm for consistency and predictability. Even where Court of Appeal guidelines recommend appropriate 'brackets' for certain types of sentencing, judicial discretion, and the particular aggravating or mitigating circumstances of individual cases, can create a wide disparity in the sentences passed. The Review indicates a move towards 'a robust, transparent sentencing framework',[54] and its authors are clearly seduced to a degree by the certainty and automatism of the US model of sentencing, in comparison to the unpredictability and variety of our system. This may transpire to mean an effort to render the sentencing process more of an exact science than it is, which would certainly be in tune with the proposals in respect of plea-bargaining and alternative disposals:

> … an advisory matrix for fraud cases, which the courts are advised to follow unless there are specific mitigating or aggravating circumstances, together with specific sentencing and prosecutorial guidelines may constitute a more transparent system which would assist with plea bargaining.[55]

9.83 Accordingly, the Review recommends that specific guidelines should be published in respect of offences committed under the Fraud Act, and that further research into an 'advisory matrix system' to assist with plea bargaining should be commissioned. The Review also recommends that consideration be given to increasing the maximum penalty for the most serious cases of fraud to fourteen years.

11. Plea Bargaining

9.84 Sections 71–73 of the Serious Crime and Police Act 2005 ('SOCPA') lay out statutory provision for offenders to be subject to reduced sentences and immunity from

---

[52] Fraud Review, para 10.55.   [53] Ibid, para 10.37.   [54] Ibid, para 10.55.
[55] Ibid, para 10.78.

prosecution in return for providing assistance to specified prosecuting authorities.[56] A judge, in reducing the sentence of a defendant who has provided assistance to the prosecuting authority, must state in open court that the sentence has been reduced, and specify what the sentence would have been had the assistance not been provided. (Section 73)

Under section 74 of SOCPA, the court has the power to review a sentence. In circumstances where a defendant has failed to provide the assistance he undertook to provide, the court may increase the sentence. Contrarily, if a defendant who has already assisted the prosecuting authority undertakes to provide further assistance, the court may reduce the sentence. The court also has the power to reduce the sentence of a defendant who, not having previously assisted the prosecuting authority, provides assistance after the original sentence has been passed. By virtue of section 75 of SOCPA, the sentencing judge has the power to exclude the public from the proceedings. 9.85

It is undoubtedly the case that these provisions will play an increasingly prominent role in the conduct of fraud trials. Assuming that criminal fraud trials will increasingly resemble those conducted in the United States, these provisions may represent the foundation of a formal system of plea-bargaining which would surely reduce the number of contested trials. 9.86

Furthermore, in the case of *R v Goodyear*[57] the Deputy Lord Chief Justice issued guidelines formalizing the practice of a judge indicating the maximum sentence that would be passed in the event of a guilty plea at the time the indication was requested. Both the guidelines issued in the case and the Attorney General's guidelines emphasize that no indication should be given unless a plea has been agreed, and the issues between parties have been resolved. The Attorney General also states that in difficult or complicated cases (which would obviously include serious fraud cases) at least seven days' notice in writing must be given to the court that an indication will be sought.[58] The prosecutor is obliged to draw to the sentencing judge's attention any maximum, minimum, or mandatory sentences in respect of the relevant offence. 9.87

Formal provisions akin to plea-bargaining are therefore evolving, only without a structured system. The Review aims to speed up that process of evolution by recommending that a formal plea-bargaining system be agreed in principle, for the time being only in relation to fraud cases, with a working party to set out the legal framework. The plea-bargaining system would apply pre-charge, as the Review explains: 9.88

… from our discussion we have concluded that it is time for a change of approach so that a formal system of plea-bargaining be introduced at an early stage and, enabling discussions to take place between the prosecuting authorities and the defence to see whether acceptable

---

[56] The DPP, the SFO and HM Revenue and Customs are all specified prosecutors (SOCPA 2006, s 71).
[57] [2005] EWCA 888.
[58] *Attorney General's Guidelines on the Acceptance of Pleas and the Prosecutor's Role in the Sentencing Exercise*, available at <http://www.lslo.gov.uk/pdf/acceptance_of_pleas_guidance.doc>, section D.

pleas can be agreed at that stage, and, if so, allow access to the courts before charge so that judicial approval can be sought.[59]

9.89　　This system aims to achieve financial savings to the public purse, by allowing the disposal of cases at a much earlier stage in the proceedings—pre-trial, or even pre-charge. Suspects who wish to assist investigations could obtain immunity at an earlier stage in the proceedings, so that the investigators and prosecutors could carry out a far more focused and efficient investigation. Their hand would also be strengthened with regard to other suspects who do not agree to assist the investigation in a positive manner. The system envisaged in the Fraud Review would result in genuine incentives for cooperation. Once again, the thinking behind the system derives principally from the US. The US model of plea-bargaining is nothing if not effective, in that 95% of cases plead. There is no doubt that in the US the severe consequences awaiting uncooperative defendants serve to speed the plough. The Sarbanes Oxley Act of 2002 further increased the range of sanctions in criminal fraud cases, and increased the level of fines and terms of imprisonment.

9.90　　In this jurisdiction, defendants who may wish to assist and cooperate are often prevented from doing so because of the lack of certainty in relation to their eventual sentences, *Goodyear* directions notwithstanding. A more predictable, matrix-style system would allow defendants to plead guilty and assist an investigation knowing the eventual outcome. The prosecution would inevitably play a significant role in the process of plea-bargaining, both as to acceptability of pleas and the appropriate sentence in the case.

9.91　　The Fraud Review recommends 'that there be a formal plea bargaining system agreed in principle specifically for cases dealt with by the Serious Fraud Office, the Fraud Prosecution Service and the CPS and serious and complex fraud cases brought by other prosecuting authorities'.[60] The details of such a system are to be devised by a specialist working party, but the framework involves greater concentration of disputed areas at an earlier stage of the process. Legal aid will be provided to suspects in pre-charge negotiations. Prosecutors will consider supplying pre-charge statements of case to defendants identifying their alleged role. The suspect would then be given an option of replying to this statement with a 'without prejudice' statement:

... and then for both sides to engage in 'without prejudice' negotiation to see whether an early agreement as to criminality can be reached; this negotiation to include a recommended realistic sentencing package, to include consideration of the extended sentencing options [as considered above].[61]

9.92　　Parties could have recourse to a specialist judge during (or as a result of) these pre-charge negotiations, to approve the result of a plea-bargain or indicate a likely sentence. Given that the plea-bargaining framework will derive at least in part from the US model, it seems that an inevitable consequence for practitioners will be fewer trials, earlier disposals, and an even more labyrinthine sentencing regime.

---

[59] Fraud Review, para 11 summary, p 250.　　[60] Ibid, para 11.76.　　[61] Ibid.

APPENDIX 1

Fraud Act 2006

CONTENTS

FRAUD ACT 2006

An Act to make provision for, and in connection with, criminal liability for fraud and obtaining services dishonestly. [8th November 2006]

BE IT ENACTED by the Queen's most Excellent Majesty, by and with the advice and consent of the Lords Spiritual and Temporal, and Commons, in this present Parliament assembled, and by the authority of the same, as follows:—

Fraud

1 Fraud

(1) A person is guilty of fraud if he is in breach of any of the sections listed in subsection (2) (which provide for different ways of committing the offence).

(2) The sections are—

    (a) section 2 (fraud by false representation),

    (b) section 3 (fraud by failing to disclose information), and

    (c) section 4 (fraud by abuse of position).

(3) A person who is guilty of fraud is liable—

    (a) on summary conviction, to imprisonment for a term not exceeding 12 months or to a fine not exceeding the statutory maximum (or to both);

    (b) on conviction on indictment, to imprisonment for a term not exceeding 10 years or to a fine (or to both).

(4) Subsection (3)(a) applies in relation to Northern Ireland as if the reference to 12 months were a reference to 6 months.

2 Fraud by false representation

(1) A person is in breach of this section if he—

    (a) dishonestly makes a false representation, and

    (b) intends, by making the representation—

        (i) to make a gain for himself or another, or

        (ii) to cause loss to another or to expose another to a risk of loss.

(2) A representation is false if—

    (a) it is untrue or misleading, and

    (b) the person making it knows that it is, or might be, untrue or misleading.

(3) "Representation" means any representation as to fact or law, including a representation as to the state of mind of—

    (a) the person making the representation, or

    (b) any other person.

(4) A representation may be express or implied.

(5) For the purposes of this section a representation may be regarded as made if it (or anything implying it) is submitted in any form to any system or device designed to receive, convey or respond to communications (with or without human intervention).

3 Fraud by failing to disclose information

A person is in breach of this section if he—

(a) dishonestly fails to disclose to another person information which he is under a legal duty to disclose, and

(b) intends, by failing to disclose the information—

    (i) to make a gain for himself or another, or

    (ii) to cause loss to another or to expose another to a risk of loss.

4 Fraud by abuse of position

(1) A person is in breach of this section if he—

    (a) occupies a position in which he is expected to safeguard, or not to act against, the financial interests of another person,

    (b) dishonestly abuses that position, and

    (c) intends, by means of the abuse of that position—

        (i) to make a gain for himself or another, or

        (ii) to cause loss to another or to expose another to a risk of loss.

(2) A person may be regarded as having abused his position even though his conduct consisted of an omission rather than an act.

5 "Gain" and "loss"

(1) The references to gain and loss in sections 2 to 4 are to be read in accordance with this section.

(2) "Gain" and "loss"—

    (a) extend only to gain or loss in money or other property;

    (b) include any such gain or loss whether temporary or permanent; and "property" means any property whether real or personal (including things in action and other intangible property).

(3) "Gain" includes a gain by keeping what one has, as well as a gain by getting what one does not have.

(4) "Loss" includes a loss by not getting what one might get, as well as a loss by parting with what one has.

6 Possession etc. of articles for use in frauds

(1) A person is guilty of an offence if he has in his possession or under his control any article for use in the course of or in connection with any fraud.

(2) A person guilty of an offence under this section is liable—

    (a) on summary conviction, to imprisonment for a term not exceeding 12 months or to a fine not exceeding the statutory maximum (or to both);

    (b) on conviction on indictment, to imprisonment for a term not exceeding 5 years or to a fine (or to both).

(3) Subsection (2)(a) applies in relation to Northern Ireland as if the reference to 12 months were a reference to 6 months.

7 Making or supplying articles for use in frauds

(1) A person is guilty of an offence if he makes, adapts, supplies or offers to supply any article—

    (a) knowing that it is designed or adapted for use in the course of or in connection with fraud, or

    (b) intending it to be used to commit, or assist in the commission of, fraud.

(2) A person guilty of an offence under this section is liable—

   (a) on summary conviction, to imprisonment for a term not exceeding 12 months or to a fine not exceeding the statutory maximum (or to both);

   (b) on conviction on indictment, to imprisonment for a term not exceeding 10 years or to a fine (or to both).

(3) Subsection (2)(a) applies in relation to Northern Ireland as if the reference to 12 months were a reference to 6 months.

8 "Article"

(1) For the purposes of—

   (a) sections 6 and 7, and

   (b) the provisions listed in subsection (2), so far as they relate to articles for use in the course of or in connection with fraud,

"article" includes any program or data held in electronic form.

(2) The provisions are—

   (a) section 1(7)(b) of the Police and Criminal Evidence Act 1984 (c. 60),

   (b) section 2(8)(b) of the Armed Forces Act 2001 (c. 19), and

   (c) Article 3(7)(b) of the Police and Criminal Evidence (Northern Ireland) Order 1989 (S.I. 1989/1341 (N.I. 12));

(meaning of "prohibited articles" for the purposes of stop and search powers).

9 Participating in fraudulent business carried on by sole trader etc.

(1) A person is guilty of an offence if he is knowingly a party to the carrying on of a business to which this section applies.

(2) This section applies to a business which is carried on—

   (a) by a person who is outside the reach of section 458 of the Companies Act 1985 (c. 6) or Article 451 of the Companies (Northern Ireland) Order 1986 (S.I. 1986/1032) (N.I. 6)) (offence of fraudulent trading), and

   (b) with intent to defraud creditors of any person or for any other fraudulent purpose.

(3) The following are within the reach of section 458 of the 1985 Act—

   (a) a company (within the meaning of that Act);

   (b) a person to whom that section applies (with or without adaptations or modifications) as if the person were a company;

   (c) a person exempted from the application of that section.

(4) The following are within the reach of Article 451 of the 1986 Order—

   (a) a company (within the meaning of that Order);

   (b) a person to whom that Article applies (with or without adaptations or modifications) as if the person were a company;

   (c) a person exempted from the application of that Article.

(5) "Fraudulent purpose" has the same meaning as in section 458 of the 1985 Act or Article 451 of the 1986 Order.

(6) A person guilty of an offence under this section is liable—

   (a) on summary conviction, to imprisonment for a term not exceeding 12 months or to a fine not exceeding the statutory maximum (or to both);

(b) on conviction on indictment, to imprisonment for a term not exceeding 10 years or to a fine (or to both).

(7) Subsection (6)(a) applies in relation to Northern Ireland as if the reference to 12 months were a reference to 6 months.

10 Participating in fraudulent business carried on by company etc.: penalty

(1) In Schedule 24 to the Companies Act 1985 (punishment of offences), in column 4 of the entry relating to section 458 of that Act, for "7 years" substitute "10 years".

(2) In Schedule 23 to the Companies (Northern Ireland) Order 1986 (punishment of offences), in column 4 of the entry relating to Article 451 of that Order, for "7 years" substitute "10 years".

Obtaining services dishonestly

11 Obtaining services dishonestly

(1) A person is guilty of an offence under this section if he obtains services for himself or another—
   (a) by a dishonest act, and
   (b) in breach of subsection (2).

(2) A person obtains services in breach of this subsection if—
   (a) they are made available on the basis that payment has been, is being or will be made for or in respect of them,
   (b) he obtains them without any payment having been made for or in respect of them or without payment having been made in full, and
   (c) when he obtains them, he knows—
       (i) that they are being made available on the basis described in paragraph (a), or
       (ii) that they might be,
   but intends that payment will not be made, or will not be made in full.

(3) A person guilty of an offence under this section is liable—
   (a) on summary conviction, to imprisonment for a term not exceeding 12 months or to a fine not exceeding the statutory maximum (or to both);
   (b) on conviction on indictment, to imprisonment for a term not exceeding 5 years or to a fine (or to both).

(4) Subsection (3)(a) applies in relation to Northern Ireland as if the reference to 12 months were a reference to 6 months.

Supplementary

12 Liability of company officers for offences by company

(1) Subsection (2) applies if an offence under this Act is committed by a body corporate.

(2) If the offence is proved to have been committed with the consent or connivance of—
   (a) a director, manager, secretary or other similar officer of the body corporate, or
   (b) a person who was purporting to act in any such capacity, he (as well as the body corporate) is guilty of the offence and liable to be proceeded against and punished accordingly.

(3) If the affairs of a body corporate are managed by its members, subsection (2) applies in relation to the acts and defaults of a member in connection with his functions of management as if he were a director of the body corporate.

13 Evidence

(1) A person is not to be excused from—
   (a) answering any question put to him in proceedings relating to property, or
   (b) complying with any order made in proceedings relating to property,
   on the ground that doing so may incriminate him or his spouse or civil partner of an offence under this Act or a related offence.

(2) But, in proceedings for an offence under this Act or a related offence, a statement or admission made by the person in—
   (a) answering such a question, or
   (b) complying with such an order,
   is not admissible in evidence against him or (unless they married or became civil partners after the making of the statement or admission) his spouse or civil partner.

(3) "Proceedings relating to property" means any proceedings for—
   (a) the recovery or administration of any property,
   (b) the execution of a trust, or
   (c) an account of any property or dealings with property,
   and "property" means money or other property whether real or personal (including things in action and other intangible property).

(4) "Related offence" means—
   (a) conspiracy to defraud;
   (b) any other offence involving any form of fraudulent conduct or purpose.

14 Minor and consequential amendments etc.

(1) Schedule 1 contains minor and consequential amendments.
(2) Schedule 2 contains transitional provisions and savings.
(3) Schedule 3 contains repeals and revocations.

15 Commencement and extent

(1) This Act (except this section and section 16) comes into force on such day as the Secretary of State may appoint by an order made by statutory instrument; and different days may be appointed for different purposes.

(2) Subject to subsection (3), sections 1 to 9 and 11 to 13 extend to England and Wales and Northern Ireland only.

(3) Section 8, so far as it relates to the Armed Forces Act 2001 (c. 19), extends to any place to which that Act extends.

(4) Any amendment in section 10 or Schedule 1, and any related provision in section 14 or Schedule 2 or 3, extends to any place to which the provision which is the subject of the amendment extends.

16 Short title

This Act may be cited as the Fraud Act 2006.

SCHEDULES

SCHEDULE 1

Section 14(1)

MINOR AND CONSEQUENTIAL AMENDMENTS

Abolition of various deception offences

1. Omit the following provisions—
   (a) in the Theft Act 1968 (c. 60)—
       (i)   section 15 (obtaining property by deception);
       (ii) section 15A (obtaining a money transfer by deception);
       (iii) section 16 (obtaining pecuniary advantage by deception);
       (iv) section 20(2) (procuring the execution of a valuable security by deception);
   (b) in the Theft Act 1978 (c. 31)—
       (i) section 1 (obtaining services by deception);
       (ii) section 2 (evasion of liability by deception);
   (c) in the Theft Act (Northern Ireland) 1969 (c. 16 (N.I.))—
       (i)   section 15 (obtaining property by deception);
       (ii) section 15A (obtaining a money transfer by deception);
       (iii) section 16 (obtaining pecuniary advantage by deception);
       (iv) section 19(2) (procuring the execution of a valuable security by deception);
   (d) in the Theft (Northern Ireland) Order 1978 (S.I. 1978/1407 (N.I. 23))—
       (i) Article 3 (obtaining services by deception);
       (ii) Article 4 (evasion of liability by deception).

Visiting Forces Act 1952 (c. 67)

2 In the Schedule (offences referred to in section 3 of the 1952 Act), in paragraph 3 (meaning of "offence against property"), after sub-paragraph (l) insert—"(m) the Fraud Act 2006."

Theft Act 1968 (c. 60)

3 Omit section 15B (section 15A: supplementary).
4 In section 18(1) (liability of company officers for offences by company under section 15, 16 or 17), omit "15, 16 or".
5 In section 20(3) (suppression etc. of documents—interpretation), omit ""deception" has the same meaning as in section 15 of this Act, and".
6 (1) In section 24(4) (meaning of "stolen goods") for "in the circumstances described in section 15(1) of this Act" substitute ", subject to subsection (5) below, by fraud (within the meaning of the Fraud Act 2006)".
   (2) After section 24(4) insert—
   "(5) Subsection (1) above applies in relation to goods obtained by fraud as if—
       (a) the reference to the commencement of this Act were a reference to the commencement of the Fraud Act 2006, and

(b) the reference to an offence under this Act were a reference to an offence under section 1 of that Act."

7 (1) In section 24A (dishonestly retaining a wrongful credit), omit subsections (3) and (4) and after subsection (2) insert—

"(2A) A credit to an account is wrongful to the extent that it derives from—

    (a) theft;

    (b) blackmail;

    (c) fraud (contrary to section 1 of the Fraud Act 2006); or

    (d) stolen goods."

(2) In subsection (7), for "subsection (4)" substitute "subsection (2A)".

(3) For subsection (9) substitute—

"(9) "Account" means an account kept with—

    (a) a bank;

    (b) a person carrying on a business which falls within subsection (10) below; or

    (c) an issuer of electronic money (as defined for the purposes of Part 2 of the Financial Services and Markets Act 2000).

(10) A business falls within this subsection if—

    (a) in the course of the business money received by way of deposit is lent to others; or

    (b) any other activity of the business is financed, wholly or to any material extent, out of the capital of or the interest on money received by way of deposit.

(11) References in subsection (10) above to a deposit must be read with—

    (a) section 22 of the Financial Services and Markets Act 2000;

    (b) any relevant order under that section; and

    (c) Schedule 2 to that Act;

but any restriction on the meaning of deposit which arises from the identity of the person making it is to be disregarded.

(12) For the purposes of subsection (10) above—

    (a) all the activities which a person carries on by way of business shall be regarded as a single business carried on by him; and

    (b) "money" includes money expressed in a currency other than sterling."

8 In section 25 (going equipped for burglary, theft or cheat)—

    (a) in subsections (1) and (3) for "burglary, theft or cheat" substitute "burglary or theft", and

    (b) in subsection (5) omit ", and "cheat" means an offence under section 15 of this Act".

Theft Act (Northern Ireland) 1969 (c. 16 (N.I.))

9 Omit section 15B (section 15A: supplementary).

10 In section 19(3) (suppression etc. of documents—interpretation), omit "deception" has the same meaning as in section 15, and".

11 (1) In section 23(5) (meaning of "stolen goods") for "in the circumstances described in section 15(1)" substitute ", subject to subsection (6), by fraud (within the meaning of the Fraud Act 2006)".

(2) After section 23(5) insert—"(6) Subsection (1) applies in relation to goods obtained by fraud as if—

    (a) the reference to the commencement of this Act were a reference to the commencement of the Fraud Act 2006, and

(b) the reference to an offence under this Act were a reference to an offence under section 1 of that Act."

12 (1) In section 23A (dishonestly retaining a wrongful credit), omit subsections (3) and (4) and after subsection (2) insert—

"(2A) A credit to an account is wrongful to the extent that it derives from—
  (a) theft;
  (b) blackmail;
  (c) fraud (contrary to section 1 of the Fraud Act 2006); or
  (d) stolen goods."

(2) In subsection (7), for "subsection (4)" substitute "subsection (2A)".

(3) For subsection (9) substitute—

"(9) "Account" means an account kept with—
  (a) a bank;
  (b) a person carrying on a business which falls within subsection (10); or
  (c) an issuer of electronic money (as defined for the purposes of Part 2 of the Financial Services and Markets Act 2000).

(10) A business falls within this subsection if—
  (a) in the course of the business money received by way of deposit is lent to others; or
  (b) any other activity of the business is financed, wholly or to any material extent, out of the capital of or the interest on money received by way of deposit.

(11) References in subsection (10) to a deposit must be read with—
  (a) section 22 of the Financial Services and Markets Act 2000;
  (b) any relevant order under that section; and
  (c) Schedule 2 to that Act; but any restriction on the meaning of deposit which arises from the identity of the person making it is to be disregarded.

(12) For the purposes of subsection (10)—
  (a) all the activities which a person carries on by way of business shall be regarded as a single business carried on by him; and
  (b) "money" includes money expressed in a currency other than sterling."

13 In section 24 (going equipped for burglary, theft or cheat)—
  (a) in subsections (1) and (3), for "burglary, theft or cheat" substitute "burglary or theft", and
  (b) in subsection (5), omit ", and "cheat" means an offence under section 15".

Theft Act 1978 (c. 31)

14 In section 4 (punishments), omit subsection (2)(a).
15 In section 5 (supplementary), omit subsection (1).

Theft (Northern Ireland) Order 1978 (S.I. 1978/1407 (N.I. 23))

16 In Article 6 (punishments), omit paragraph (2)(a).
17 In Article 7 (supplementary), omit paragraph (1).

Limitation Act 1980 (c. 58)

18 In section 4 (special time limit in case of theft), for subsection (5)(b) substitute—
  "(b) obtaining any chattel (in England and Wales or elsewhere) by—

     (i) blackmail (within the meaning of section 21 of the Theft Act 1968), or
     (ii) fraud (within the meaning of the Fraud Act 2006);".

Finance Act 1982 (c. 39)

19 In section 11(1) (powers of Commissioners with respect to agricultural levies), for "or the Theft (Northern Ireland) Order 1978," substitute ", the Theft (Northern Ireland) Order 1978 or the Fraud Act 2006".

Nuclear Material (Offences) Act 1983 (c. 18)

20 In section 1 (extended scope of certain offences), in subsection (1)(d), omit "15 or" (in both places).

Police and Criminal Evidence Act 1984 (c. 60)

21 In section 1 (power of constable to stop and search persons, vehicles etc.), in subsection (8), for paragraph (d) substitute—
"(d) fraud (contrary to section 1 of the Fraud Act 2006)."

Limitation (Northern Ireland) Order 1989 (S.I. 1989/1339 (N.I. 11))

22 In Article 18 (special time limit in case of theft), for paragraph (5)(b) substitute—
"(b) obtaining any chattel (in Northern Ireland or elsewhere) by—blackmail (within the meaning of section 20 of the Theft Act (Northern Ireland) 1969), or
     (ii) fraud (within the meaning of the Fraud Act 2006);".

Police and Criminal Evidence (Northern Ireland) Order 1989 (S.I. 1989/1341 (N.I. 12))

23 In Article 3 (power of constable to stop and search persons, vehicles etc.), in paragraph (8), for sub-paragraph (d) substitute—
"(d) fraud (contrary to section 1 of the Fraud Act 2006)."

Criminal Justice Act 1993 (c. 36)

24 (1) In section 1(2) (Group A offences), omit the entries in paragraph (a) relating to sections 15, 15A, 16 and 20(2) of the Theft Act 1968.
(2) Omit section 1(2)(b).
(3) Before section 1(2)(c) insert—
"(bb) an offence under any of the following provisions of the Fraud Act 2006—
     (i)   section 1 (fraud);
     (ii) section 6 (possession etc. of articles for use in frauds);
     (iii) section 7 (making or supplying articles for use in frauds);
     (iv) section 9 (participating in fraudulent business carried on by sole trader etc.);
     (v) section 11 (obtaining services dishonestly)."
25 (1) Amend section 2 (jurisdiction in respect of Group A offences) as follows.
(2) In subsection (1), after "means" insert "(subject to subsection (1A))".
(3) After subsection (1) insert—
"(1A) In relation to an offence under section 1 of the Fraud Act 2006 (fraud), "relevant event" includes—
     (a) if the fraud involved an intention to make a gain and the gain occurred, that occurrence;

(b) if the fraud involved an intention to cause a loss or to expose another to a risk of loss and the loss occurred, that occurrence."

Criminal Justice (Northern Ireland) Order 1994 (S.I. 1994/2795 (N.I. 15))

26 In Article 14 (compensation orders), in paragraphs (3) and (4)(a) for "or Article 172 of the Road Traffic (Northern Ireland) Order 1981" substitute ", Article 172 of the Road Traffic (Northern Ireland) Order 1981 or the Fraud Act 2006".

Criminal Justice (Northern Ireland) Order 1996 (S.I. 1996/3160 (N.I. 24))

27 (1) In Article 38(2) (Group A offences), omit the entries in sub-paragraph (a) relating to sections 15, 15A, 16 and 19(2) of the Theft Act (Northern Ireland) 1969.
(2) Omit Article 38(2)(b).
(3) Before Article 38(2)(c) insert—
"(bb) an offence under any of the following provisions of the Fraud Act 2006—
    (i) section 1 (fraud);
    (ii) section 6 (possession etc. of articles for use in frauds);
    (iii) section 7 (making or supplying articles for use in frauds);
    (iv) section 9 (participating in fraudulent business carried on by sole trader etc.);
    (v) section 11 (obtaining services dishonestly)."
28 (1) Amend Article 39 (jurisdiction in respect of Group A offences) as follows.
(2) In paragraph (1), after "means" insert "(subject to paragraph (1A))".
(3) After paragraph (1) insert—
"(1A) In relation to an offence under section 1 of the Fraud Act 2006 (fraud), "relevant event" includes—
    (a) if the fraud involved an intention to make a gain and the gain occurred, that occurrence;
    (b) if the fraud involved an intention to cause a loss or to expose another to a risk of loss and the loss occurred, that occurrence."

Powers of Criminal Courts (Sentencing) Act 2000 (c. 6)

29 In section 130 (compensation orders), in subsections (5) and (6)(a), after "Theft Act 1968" insert "or Fraud Act 2006".

Terrorism Act 2000 (c. 11)

30 (1) In Schedule 9 (scheduled offences), in paragraph 10, at the end of subparagraph (d) insert "and" and omit paragraph (e).
(2) After paragraph 22A of that Schedule insert—
    '*Fraud Act 2006*
    23 Offences under section 1 of the Fraud Act 2006 (fraud) subject to note 2 below."
(3) In note 2 to Part 1 of Schedule 9, for "paragraph 10(a), (c) or (e)" substitute "paragraph 10(a) or (c) or 23".
31 (1) In Schedule 12 (compensation), in paragraph 12(1), omit "(within the meaning of section 15(4) of the Theft Act (Northern Ireland) 1969)".
(2) After paragraph 12(1) of that Schedule insert—

"(1A) "Deception" means any deception (whether deliberate or reckless) by words or conduct as to fact or as to law, including a deception as to the present intentions of the person using the deception or any other person."

Criminal Justice and Court Services Act 2000 (c. 43)

32 (1) In Schedule 6 (trigger offences), in paragraph 1, omit the entry relating to section 15 of the Theft Act 1968.

(2) After paragraph 2 of Schedule 6 insert—

"3 Offences under the following provisions of the Fraud Act 2006 are trigger offences—

section 1 (fraud)

section 6 (possession etc. of articles for use in frauds)

section 7 (making or supplying articles for use in frauds)."

Armed Forces Act 2001 (c. 19)

33 In section 2(9) (definition of prohibited articles for purposes of powers to stop and search), for paragraph (d) substitute—

"(d) fraud (contrary to section 1 of the Fraud Act 2006)."

Licensing Act 2003 (c. 17)

34 In Schedule 4 (personal licence: relevant offences), after paragraph 20 insert—

"21 An offence under the Fraud Act 2006."

Asylum and Immigration (Treatment of Claimants, etc.) Act 2004 (c. 19)

35 (1) In section 14(2) (offences giving rise to immigration officer's power of arrest), omit paragraph (g)(ii) and (iii), in paragraph (h), "15, 16" and paragraphs (i) and (j).

(2) After section 14(2)(h) insert—

"(ha) an offence under either of the following provisions of the Fraud Act 2006—

(i) section 1 (fraud);

(ii) section 11 (obtaining services dishonestly),"."

Serious Organised Crime and Police Act 2005 (c. 15)

36 In section 76 (financial reporting orders: making), in subsection (3), for paragraphs (a) and (b) substitute—

"(aa) an offence under either of the following provisions of the Fraud Act 2006—

(i) section 1 (fraud),

(ii) section 11 (obtaining services dishonestly),"."

37 In section 78 (financial reporting orders: making in Northern Ireland), in subsection (3), for paragraphs (a) and (b) substitute—

"(aa) an offence under either of the following provisions of the Fraud Act 2006—

(i) section 1 (fraud),

(ii) section 11 (obtaining services dishonestly),"."

Gambling Act 2005 (c. 19)

38 After paragraph 3 of Schedule 7 (relevant offences) insert—

"3A An offence under the Fraud Act 2006."

SCHEDULE 2

Section 14 (2)

TRANSITIONAL PROVISIONS AND SAVINGS

Maximum term of imprisonment for offences under this Act

1 In relation to an offence committed before the commencement of section 154(1) of the Criminal Justice Act 2003 (c. 44), the references to 12 months in sections 1(3)(a), 6(2)(a), 7(2)(a), 9(6)(a) and 11(3)(a) are to be read as references to 6 months.

Increase in penalty for fraudulent trading

2 Section 10 does not affect the penalty for any offence committed before that section comes into force.

Abolition of deception offences

3 (1) Paragraph 1 of Schedule 1 does not affect any liability, investigation, legal proceeding or penalty for or in respect of any offence partly committed before the commencement of that paragraph.

(2) An offence is partly committed before the commencement of paragraph 1 of Schedule 1 if—

(a) a relevant event occurs before its commencement, and

(b) another relevant event occurs on or after its commencement.

(3) "Relevant event", in relation to an offence, means any act, omission or other event (including any result of one or more acts or omissions) proof of which is required for conviction of the offence.

Scope of offences relating to stolen goods under the Theft Act 1968 (c. 60)

4 Nothing in paragraph 6 of Schedule 1 affects the operation of section 24 of the Theft Act 1968 in relation to goods obtained in the circumstances described in section 15(1) of that Act where the obtaining is the result of a deception made before the commencement of that paragraph.

Dishonestly retaining a wrongful credit under the Theft Act 1968

5 Nothing in paragraph 7 of Schedule 1 affects the operation of section 24A(7) and (8) of the Theft Act 1968 in relation to credits falling within section 24A(3) or (4) of that Act and made before the commencement of that paragraph.

Scope of offences relating to stolen goods under the Theft Act (Northern Ireland) 1969 (c. 16 (N.I.))

6 Nothing in paragraph 11 of Schedule 1 affects the operation of section 23 of the Theft Act (Northern Ireland) 1969 in relation to goods obtained in the circumstances described in section 15(1) of that Act where the obtaining is the result of a deception made before the commencement of that paragraph.

Dishonestly retaining a wrongful credit under the Theft Act (Northern Ireland) 1969

7 Nothing in paragraph 12 of Schedule 1 affects the operation of section 23A(7) and (8) of the Theft Act (Northern Ireland) 1969 in relation to credits falling within section 23A(3) or (4) of that Act and made before the commencement of that paragraph.

Limitation periods under the Limitation Act 1980 (c. 58)

8 Nothing in paragraph 18 of Schedule 1 affects the operation of section 4 of the Limitation Act 1980 in relation to chattels obtained in the circumstances described in section 15(1) of the Theft Act 1968 where the obtaining is a result of a deception made before the commencement of that paragraph.

Limitation periods under the Limitation (Northern Ireland) Order 1989 (S.I. 1989/1339 (N.I. 11))

9 Nothing in paragraph 22 of Schedule 1 affects the operation of Article 18 of the Limitation (Northern Ireland) Order 1989 in relation to chattels obtained in the circumstances described in section 15(1) of the Theft Act (Northern Ireland) 1969 where the obtaining is a result of a deception made before the commencement of that paragraph.

Scheduled offences under the Terrorism Act 2000 (c. 11)

10 Nothing in paragraph 30 of Schedule 1 affects the operation of Part 7 of the Terrorism Act 2000 in relation to an offence under section 15(1) of the Theft Act (Northern Ireland) 1969 where the obtaining is a result of a deception made before the commencement of that paragraph.

Powers of arrest under Asylum and Immigration (Treatment of Claimants, etc.) Act 2004 (c. 19)

11 (1) Nothing in paragraph 35 of Schedule 1 affects the power of arrest conferred by section 14 of the Asylum and Immigration (Treatment of Claimants, etc.) Act 2004 in relation to an offence partly committed before the commencement of that paragraph.

(2) An offence is partly committed before the commencement of paragraph 35 of Schedule 1 if—
   (a) a relevant event occurs before its commencement, and
   (b) another relevant event occurs on or after its commencement.

(3) "Relevant event", in relation to an offence, means any act, omission or other event (including any result of one or more acts or omissions) proof of which is required for conviction of the offence.

SCHEDULE 3

Section 14(3)

REPEALS AND REVOCATIONS

Title and number	Extent of repeal or revocation
Theft Act 1968 (c. 60)	Sections 15, 15A, 15B and 16. In section 18(1), "15, 16 or". Section 20(2). In section 20(3), ""deception" has the same meaning as in section 15 of this Act, and". In section 25(5), ", and "cheat" means an offence under section 15 of this Act". Section 24A(3) and (4). In section 25(5), ", and "cheat" means an offence under section 15 of this Act".
Theft Act (Northern Ireland) 1969 1969 (c. 16 (N.I.))	Sections 15, 15A, 15B and 16. Section 19(2). In section 19(3), ""deception" has the same meaning as in section 15, and". Section 23A(3) and (4). In section 24(5), ", and "cheat" means an offence under section 15".
Theft Act 1978 (c. 31)	Sections 1 and 2. Section 4(2)(a). Section 5(1).
Theft (Northern Ireland) Order 1978 (S.I. 1978/1407 (N.I. 23))	Articles 3 and 4 Article 6(2)(a). Article 7(1).
Nuclear Material (Offences) Act 1983 (c. 18)	In section 1(1)(d), "15 or" (in both places).
Criminal Justice Act 1993 (c. 36)	In section 1(2), the entries in paragraph (a) relating to sections 15, 15A, 16 and 20(2) of the Theft Act 1968. Section 1(2)(b).
Theft (Amendment) Act 1996 (c. 62)	Sections 1, 3(2) and 4.
Criminal Justice (Northern Ireland) Order 1996 (S.I. 1996/3160 (N.I. 24))	In Article 38(2), the entries in sub-paragraph (a) relating to sections 15, 15A, 16 and 19(2) of the Theft Act (Northern Ireland) 1969. Article 38(2)(b).
Theft (Amendment) (Northern Ireland) Order 1997 (S.I. 1997/277 (N.I. 3))	Articles 3, 5(2) and 6.

Title and number	Extent of repeal or revocation
Terrorism Act 2000 (c. 11)	In Schedule 9, paragraph 10(e).
	In Schedule 12, in paragraph 12(1), "(within the meaning of section 15(4) of the Theft Act (Northern Ireland) 1969)".
Criminal Justice and Court Services Act 2000 (c. 43)	In Schedule 6, in paragraph 1, the entry relating to section 15 of the Theft Act 1968
Asylum and Immigration (Treatment of Claimants, etc.) Act 2004 (c. 19)	In section 14(2), paragraph (g)(ii) and (iii), in paragraph (h), "15, 16" and paragraphs (i) and (j).

APPENDIX 2

Pre-Legislative Materials

A. THE LAW COMMISSION REPORTS

In *Pepper (Inspector of Taxes) v Hart and related appeals* [1993] AC 593, [1993] 1 All ER 42, Lord Browne-Wilkinson said:

[The rule which prohibits the court from looking at reports made by commissioners on which legislation was based] has now been relaxed so as to permit reports of commissioners, including Law Commissioners, and white papers to be looked at for the purpose solely of ascertaining the mischief which the statute is intended to cure but not for the purpose of discovering the meaning of the words used by Parliament to effect such cure (see *Eastman Photographic Materials Co Ltd v Comptroller-General of Patents Designs and Trade-marks* [1898] AC 571 and *Assam Railways and Trading Co Ltd v IRC* [1935] AC 445 at 457–458, [1934] All ER Rep 646 at 655). Indeed, in *Factortame Ltd v Secretary of State for Transport* [1989] 2 All ER 692, [1990] 2 AC 85 your Lordships' House went further than this and had regard to a Law Commission report not only for the purpose of ascertaining the mischief but also for the purpose of drawing an inference as to parliamentary intention from the fact that Parliament had not expressly implemented one of the Law Commission's recommendations.

The Law Commission (<http://www.lawcom.gov.uk>) published the following reports, the most important being (e):

(a) Law Com No 76: *Conspiracy and Criminal Law Reform* (published 1976).
(b) Law Com No 228: *Criminal Law: Conspiracy to Defraud* (published December 1994).
(c) Law Com No 277: *The Effective Prosecution of Multiple Offending* (published October 2002; available at:<http://www.lawcom.gov.uk/docs/lc277.pdf>); introduces the measures behind the fraudulent business provisions.
(d) Law Commission Consultation Paper No 155: *Legislating the Criminal Code: Fraud and Deception* (published March 1999; available at:<http://www.lawcom. gov.uk/docs/cp155.pdf>.
(e) Law Com No 276: Fraud (published July 2002; available at:<http://www.lawcom. gov.uk/docs/lc276.pdf>.
(f) Draft Fraud Bill (published July 2002; available at:<http://www.lawcom.gov.uk/ docs/lc276bill.pdf>.

B. THE GOVERNMENT PROPOSALS

The Home Office produced a consultation paper in response to the Bill, *Fraud Law Reform - Consultation on proposals for legislation*, in May 2004, and a response, *Fraud Law Reform - Government Response to Consultations*, in September 2004, both available at:<http://www.homeoffice.gov.uk/documents/cons-fraud-law-reform/?version=1>.

C. PASSAGE THROUGH PARLIAMENT

In *Pepper v Hart* Lord Browne-Wilkinson went on:

I therefore reach the conclusion, subject to any question of parliamentary privilege, that the exclusionary rule should be relaxed so as to permit reference to parliamentary materials where:

(a) legislation is ambiguous or obscure, or leads to an absurdity;
(b) the material relied on consists of one or more statements by a minister or other promoter of the Bill together if necessary with such other parliamentary material as is necessary to understand such statements and their effect;
(c) the statements relied on are clear ...

1. Dramatis Personae

(Titles and positions as at the time of the debates).

(a) House of Lords

Lord Goldsmith	Government (Attorney General) — promoting the Bill
Lord Clinton-Davis	Labour
Lord Goodhart	Liberal Democrat shadow Lord Chancellor
Lord Kingsland	Conservative shadow Lord Chancellor
Lord Lloyd of Berwick	Cross-bencher (former Law Lord)
Lord Lyell of Markyate	Conservative (former Attorney General)
Lord Thomas of Gresford	Liberal Democrat shadow Attorney General

(b) House of Commons

O'Brien, Mr Mike	Government (Solicitor General) — promoting the Bill
Amess, Mr David	Chair of Committee B; Conservative MP (Southend West)
Brown, Ms Lyn	Labour MP (West Ham)
Campbell, Mr Alan	Government (Lord Commissioner of Her Majesty's Treasury)
Cox, Mr Geoffrey	Conservative MP (Torridge and West Devon)
Cunningham, Mr Jim	Labour MP (Coventry, South)
Fabricant, Mr Michael	Conservative MP (Lichfield)
Garnier, Mr Edward	Conservative MP (Harborough)
Grieve, Mr Dominic	Shadow Solicitor General; Conservative MP (Beaconsfield)
Gwynne, Mr Andrew	Labour MP (Denton and Reddish)
Hands, Mr Greg	Conservative MP (Hammersmith and Fulham)
Heath, Mr David	Shadow Spokesman for Department of Constitutional Affairs; Liberal Democrat MP (Somerton and Frome)
Johnson, Ms Diana R	Labour MP (Kingston upon Hull North) (Lab)
Jones, Mr Martyn	Chair of Committee B; Labour MP (Clwyd South)
Llwyd, Mr Elfyn	Plaid Cymru MP (Meirionnydd Nant Conwy)
Lucas, Mr Ian	Labour MP (Wrexham)
Snelgrove, Ms Anne	Labour MP (South Swindon)

Sutcliffe, Mr Gerry	Government (Parliamentary Under-Secretary of State for the Home Department)
Wright, Mr Jeremy	Conservative MP (Rugby and Kenilworth)

(c) Ministers promoting the Bill

The Bill was promoted by Lord Goldsmith, the Attorney General, in the House of Lords and Mike O'Brien, the Solicitor General, in the House of Commons.

2. Passage through Parliament

(a) First reading, House of Lords: 25 May 2005.
(b) Second reading, House of Lords: 22 June 2005.
(c) Committee stage, House of Lords: 19 July 2005.
(d) Report stage, House of Lords: 14 March 2006.
(e) Third reading, House of Lords: 29 March 2006.
(f) Second reading, House of Commons: 12 June 2006.
(g) Committee stage, House of Commons: 20 and 22 June 2006.
(h) Report stage and third reading, House of Commons: 26 October 2006.
(i) Royal assent: 8 November 2006.

D. THE DEBATES

1. First reading, House of Lords: 25 May 2005

<http://www.publications.parliament.uk/pa/ld200506/ldhansrd/vo050525/text/50525–04.htm#50525–04_head1>

The Attorney General, Lord Goldsmith, introduced the Bill 'to make provision for, and in connection with, criminal liability for fraud and obtaining services dishonestly'.[1]

2. Second reading, House of Lords: 22 June 2005

<http://www.publications.parliament.uk/pa/ld200506/ldhansrd/vo050622/text/50622–04.htm#50622–04_head2>

Section/clause		Col
Act	Attorney General sets out the purpose of the Bill	1651
1–4	The fraud offence	1653
6	Possession of articles for use in frauds	1654
7	Making or supplying articles	1654
9	Fraudulent business	1654
	Repeal of common law conspiracy to defraud	1654–57
	Baroness Anelay of St Johns for the Opposition	1657–61
	Lord Thomas of Gresford for the Liberal Democrats	1661–64

---

[1] 25 May 2005 col 463.

153

3. Committee stage, House of Lords: 19 July 2005

<http://www.publications.parliament.uk/pa/ld200506/ldhansrd/vo050719/text/
50719–16.htm#50719–16_head1>

Section/clause		Col
3	Lord Kingsland questions why there is a need for a non-disclosure offence. Reference to the facts of *R v Firth*. Lord Goldsmith said there was a need to clearly define non-disclosure as an offence rather than the law being that silence could in certain circumstances amount to a representation.	1411
2	Intending to make a gain or cause a loss or to expose. Discussion of 'intention'.	1413
2(2)	Complaint made that the phrase 'knows that it might be misleading' is too wide. Proposed by Lord Kingsland that the word 'reckless' be added.	1416–19
2(2)	Amendment to leave out 'might' from 'might be misleading' withdrawn.	1422
3	Failure to disclose.	1423–24
3	Failure to disclose reasons for not including moral duty to disclose.	1426
3	Legal duty to disclose.	1428–30
4	Amendment proposed to add 'secretly'.	1432–33
	Definition of property within the Fraud Bill does not include confidential information.	1435
	Abolition of the common law offence of conspiracy to defraud	1437–50
6	Possession of articles for use in fraud *mens rea*.	1451–52
	Husband and wife as conspirators.	1452–56
	Amendment to abolish common law offence of cheating the Revenue by leave withdrawn. Complaint made by Lord Kingsland that cheating the Revenue may be in breach of Article 7 of the ECHR (as it may fail the certainty of law test).	1457–59

4. Report stage, House of Lords: 14 March 2006

<http://www.publications.parliament.uk/pa/ld199900/ldhansrd/pdvn/lds06/text/
60314–05.htm#60314–05_head0>

Section/clause		Col
2(2)	Government amendment carried to delete 'by words or conduct' from 2(3). The reason was to make it clear that a false representation could be made to a machine.	1107–09
2(5)	Subsection 5 added to make clear that a representation may be made to a machine and may be submitted in any form to any system or device designed to receive, convey, or respond to communications.	1109
	Opposition amendment to abolish conspiracy to defraud by leave withdrawn.	1111–17

Opposition amendment to preserve jury trials in fraud cases   1118–33
and to bring in new rules to expedite such cases and make
them more manageable.

5. *Third reading, House of Lords: 29 March 2006*

<http://www.publications.parliament.uk/pa/ld199900/ldhansrd/pdvn/lds06/text/
60329–04.htm>

Section/clause		Col
—	Proposed amendment that the AG should issue guidance as to when conspiracy to defraud should be charged.	779
	Lord Goldsmith in response says that he will issue formal guidance at or around the time of Royal Assent. The AG said there was no need for the Bill to be amended as 'I have quite a powerful weapon to enforce it myself: the ability to intervene in any case and to stop that case using my powers of *noli prosequi* if I were not satisfied with the way in which the prosecuting authority was acting.'	783
	The amendment is by leave withdrawn.	783

6. *Second reading, House of Commons: 12 June 2006*

<http://www.publications.parliament.uk/pa/cm200506/cmhansrd/cm060612/
debtext/60612–0450.htm>

Section/clause		Col
Act	Solicitor General sets out the purpose of the Bill.	534
1	Aim of new law is to replace provisions in daily use in our courts.	535
2	Representation is meant to be very widely defined.	535
3	Reasons why Government did not pursue 'moral duty' to disclose, quoting Association of Chief Police Officers.	536
4	It applies in situations where the defendant has been put in a privileged position and by virtue of that position is expected to safeguard another's financial interests, or at least not to act against those interests.	536
	Complaints that the phrase 'expected to safeguard' is too wide.	538
11	Reason for new offence. At present, it is questionable what crime is committed by a person who dishonestly obtains services from a machine. Under current law, the problem is not only that fraud must involve deception, but that services cannot be stolen.	539
6	This offence proposed during the consultation process. Complaints that the offence does not contain on its face any necessity for *mens rea*. Solicitor General makes clear general intention is required as with the offence of going equipped; reference to *R v Ellames*.	541
7		542

Section/clause		*Col*
9	Fraudulent trading is an activity offence and should not just apply to those using the vehicles of corporations.	543
Conspiracy to defraud		
	Government have decided not to abolish conspiracy to defraud because of the opposition to this in the consultation process. It is desirable that there be a 'seamless transition' to the new fraud law	543
	Dominic Grieve (shadow Solicitor General): general support for the new law. Expresses reservations about retention of conspiracy to defraud and support for juries.	546
	Brian Jenkins	552
	David Heath	556

7. Committee stage, House of Commons: 20 and 22 June 2006

The House of Commons Standing Committee B considered the Bill on 20 June 2006 and 22 June 2006.

(a) 20 June 2006 am

<http://www.publications.parliament.uk/pa/cm200506/cmstand/b/st060620/am/60620s01.htm>

Section/clause		*Col*
1	The Solicitor General introduced the new law as being widely supported and being aimed at doing away with the need to prove deception. He went on: 'The simplified and rationalised fraud offence will provide those working on the frontline with the necessary tools to be able to tackle fraud more effectively'.	4
2	Dominic Grieve welcomes the new law but warns that there is a danger that it my be too wide.	5 and 7
3	Discussion about meaning of 'legal duty' as being prescribed by law and not by morality. 'Let the buyer beware' is still the case.	8–10
4	Opposition amendment to omit 'expected' and to add the words 'under a fiduciary duty' (ie, no offence of failure to disclose unless D was *under a fiduciary duty* to safeguard V's financial interests). Opposition proposal put but defeated by 8 votes to 6.	11–28
5	Definition of 'gain and loss'.	29
6	Possessing articles for use in fraud. Opposition proposed amendment that 'intends' be added. Amendment by leave withdrawn.	37–40

(b) 20 June 2006 pm

<http://www.publications.parliament.uk/pa/cm200506/cmstand/b/st060620/pm/60620s01.htm>

(c) 22 June 2006 am

<http://www.publications.parliament.uk/pa/cm200506/cmstand/b/st060622/am/
60622s01.htm>

8. Report stage and third reading, House of Commons: 26 October 2006

<http://www.publications.parliament.uk/pa/cm200506/cmhansrd/cm061026/
debtext/61026–0005.htm#06102646001671>

(a) Report stage

(b) Third Reading

The Fraud Protocol: Control and Management of Heavy Fraud and Other Complex Criminal Cases

A Protocol issued by the Lord Chief Justice of England and Wales—22 March 2005

INTRODUCTION

There is a broad consensus that the length of fraud and trials of other complex crimes must be controlled within proper bounds in order:

(i) To enable the jury to retain and assess the evidence which they have heard. If the trial is so long that the jury cannot do this, then the trial is not fair either to the prosecution or the defence.

(ii) To make proper use of limited public resources: see *Jisl* [2004] EWCA Crim 696 at [113]— [121].

There is also a consensus that no trial should be permitted to exceed a given period, save in exceptional circumstances; some favour 3 months, others an outer limit of 6 months. Whatever view is taken, it is essential that the current length of trials is brought back to an acceptable and proper duration.

This Protocol supplements the Criminal Procedure Rules and summarises good practice which experience has shown may assist in bringing about some reduction in the length of trials of fraud and other crimes that result in complex trials. Flexibility of application of this Protocol according to the needs of each case is essential; it is designed to inform but not to prescribe.

This Protocol is primarily directed towards cases which are likely to last eight weeks or longer. It should also be followed, however, in all cases estimated to last more than four weeks. This Protocol applies to trials by jury, but many of the principles will be applicable if trials without a jury are permitted under s. 43 of the Criminal Justice Act 2003.

The best handling technique for a long case is continuous management by an experienced Judge nominated for the purpose.

It is intended that this Protocol be kept up to date; any further practices or techniques found to be successful in the management of complex cases should be notified to the office of the Lord Chief Justice.

A. THE INVESTIGATION

(i) The role of the prosecuting authority and the judge

(a) Unlike other European countries, a judge in England and Wales does not directly control the investigative process; that is the responsibility of the Investigating Authority, and in turn the Prosecuting Authority and the prosecution advocate. Experience has shown that a prosecution lawyer (who must be of sufficient experience and who will be a member of the team at trial) and the prosecution advocate, if different, should be involved in the investigation as soon as it appears that a heavy fraud trial or other complex criminal trial is likely to ensue. The costs that this early preparation will incur will be saved many times over in the long run.

(b) The judge can and should exert a substantial and beneficial influence by making it clear that, generally speaking, trials should be kept within manageable limits. In most cases 3 months should be the target outer limit, but there will be cases where a duration of 6 months, or in exceptional circumstances, even longer may be inevitable.

(ii) Interviews

(a) At present many interviews are too long and too unstructured. This has a knock-on effect on the length of trials. Interviews should provide an opportunity for suspects to respond to the allegations against them. They should not be an occasion to discuss every document in the case. It should become clear from judicial rulings that interviews of this kind are a waste of resources.

(b) The suspect must be given sufficient information before or at the interview to enable them to meet the questions fairly and answer them honestly; the information is not provided to give the suspect the opportunity to manufacture a false story which fits undisputable facts.

(c) It is often helpful if the principal documents are provided either in advance of the interview or shown as the interview progresses; asking detailed questions about events a considerable period in the past without reference to the documents is often not very helpful.

(iii) The prosecution and defence teams

(a) *The Prosecution Team*

While instructed, it is for the lead advocate for the prosecution to take all necessary decisions in the presentation and general conduct of the prosecution case in court. The prosecution lead advocate will be treated by the court as having that responsibility.

However, in relation to policy decisions, the lead advocate for the prosecution must not give an indication or undertaking which binds the prosecution without first discussing the issue with the Director of the Prosecuting authority or other senior officer.

"Policy" decisions should be understood as referring to non-evidential decisions on: the acceptance of pleas of guilty to lesser counts or groups of counts or available alternatives: offering no evidence on particular counts; consideration of a re-trial; whether to lodge an appeal; certification of a point of law; and the withdrawal of the prosecution as a whole (for further information see the 'Farquharson Guidelines' on the role and responsibilities of the prosecution advocate).

(b) *The Defence Team*

In each case, the lead advocate for the defence will be treated by the court as having responsibility to the court for the presentation and general conduct of the defence case.

(c) In each case, a case progression officer must be assigned by the court, prosecution and defence from the time of the first hearing when directions are given (as referred to in paragraph 3 (iii)) until the conclusion of the trial.

(d) In each case where there are multiple defendants, the LSC will need to consider carefully the extent and level of representation necessary.

(iv) Initial consideration of the length of a case

If the prosecutor in charge of the case from the Prosecuting Authority or the lead advocate for the prosecution consider that the case as formulated is likely to last more than 8 weeks, the case should be referred in accordance with arrangements made by the Prosecuting Authority to a more senior prosecutor. The senior prosecutor will consider whether it is desirable for the case to be prosecuted in that way or whether some steps might be taken to reduce its likely length, whilst at the same time ensuring that the public interest is served.

Any case likely to last 6 months or more must be referred to the Director of the Prosecuting Authority so that similar considerations can take place.

(v) Notification of cases likely to last more than 8 weeks

Special arrangements will be put in place for the early notification by the CPS and other Prosecuting Authorities, to the LSC and to a single designated officer of the Court in each Region (Circuit) of any case which the CPS or other Prosecuting Authority consider likely to last over 8 weeks.

(vi) Venue

The court will allocate such cases and other complex cases likely to last 4 weeks or more to a specific venue suitable for the trial in question, taking into account the convenience to witnesses, the parties, the availability of time at that location, and all other relevant considerations.

B. DESIGNATION OF THE TRIAL JUDGE

(i) The assignment of a judge

(a) In any complex case which is expected to last more than four weeks, the trial judge will be assigned under the direction of the Presiding Judges at the earliest possible moment.

(b) Thereafter the assigned judge should manage that case "from cradle to grave"; it is essential that the same judge manages the case from the time of his assignment and that arrangements are made for him to be able to do so. It is recognised that in certain court centres with a large turnover of heavy cases (e.g. Southwark) this objective is more difficult to achieve. But in those court centres there are teams of specialist judges, who are more readily able to handle cases which the assigned judge cannot continue with because of unexpected events; even at such courts, there must be no exception to the principle that one judge must handle all the pre-trial hearings until the case is assigned to another judge.

C. CASE MANAGEMENT

(i) Objectives

(a) The number, length and organisation of case management hearings will, of course, depend critically on the circumstances and complexity of the individual case. However, thorough, well-prepared and extended case management hearings will save court time and costs overall.

(b) Effective case management of heavy fraud and other complex criminal cases requires the judge to have a much more detailed grasp of the case than may be necessary for many other Plea and Case Management Hearings (PCMHs). Though it is for the judge in each case to decide how much pre-reading time he needs so that the judge is on top of the case, it is not always a sensible use of judicial time to allocate a series of reading days, during which the judge sits alone in his room, working through numerous boxes of ring binders.

See paragraph 3 (iv) (e) below.

(ii) Fixing the trial date

Although it is important that the trial date should be fixed as early as possible, this may not always be the right course. There are two principal alternatives:

(a) The trial date should be fixed at the first opportunity—i.e. at the first (and usually short) directions hearing referred to in subparagraph (iii). From then on everyone must work to that date. All orders and pre-trial steps should be timetabled to fit in with that date. All advocates and the judge should take note of this date, in the expectation that the trial will proceed on the date determined.

(b) The trial date should not be fixed until the issues have been explored at a full case management hearing (referred to in subparagraph (iv), after the advocates on both sides have done some serious work on the case. Only then can the length of the trial be estimated.

Which is apposite must depend on the circumstances of each case, but the earlier it is possible to fix a trial date, by reference to a proper estimate and a timetable set by reference to the trial date, the better.

It is generally to be expected that once a trial is fixed on the basis of the estimate provided, that it will be **increased** if, and only if, the party seeking to extend the time justifies why the original estimate is no longer appropriate.

(iii) The first hearing for the giving of initial directions

At the first opportunity the assigned judge should hold a short hearing to give initial directions. The directions on this occasion might well include:

(a) That there should be a full case management hearing on, or commencing on, a specified future date by which time the parties will be properly prepared for a meaningful hearing and the defence will have full instructions.

(b) That the prosecution should provide an outline written statement of the prosecution case at least one week in advance of that case management hearing, outlining in simple terms:

(i) The key facts on which it relies.

(ii) The key evidence by which the prosecution seeks to prove the facts.

The statement must be sufficient to permit the judge to understand the case and for the defence to appreciate the basic elements of its case against each defendant. The prosecution may be invited to highlight the key points of the case orally at the case management hearing by way of a short mini-opening. The outline statement should not be considered binding, but it will serve the essential purpose in telling the judge, and everyone else, what the case is really about and identifying the key issues.

(c) That a core reading list and core bundle for the case management hearing should be delivered at least one week in advance.

(d) Preliminary directions about disclosure: see paragraph 4.

(iv) The first Case Management Hearing

(a) At the first case management hearing:

(i) The prosecution advocate should be given the opportunity to highlight any points from the prosecution outline statement of case (which will have been delivered at least a week in advance).

(ii) Each defence advocate should be asked to outline the defence.

If the defence advocate is not in a position to say what is in issue and what is not in issue, then the case management hearing can be adjourned for a short and limited time and to a fixed date to enable the advocate to take instructions; such an adjournment should only be necessary in exceptional circumstances, as the defence advocate should be properly instructed by the time of the first case management hearing and in any event is under an obligation to take sufficient instructions to fulfil the obligations contained in S 33–39 of Criminal Justice Act 2003.

(b) There should then be a real dialogue between the judge and all advocates for the purpose of identifying:

(i) The focus of the prosecution case.

(ii) The common ground.

(iii) The real issues in the case. (Rule 3.2 of the Criminal Procedure Rules.)

(c) The judge will try to generate a spirit of co-operation between the court and the advocates on all sides. The expeditious conduct of the trial and a focussing on the real issues must be in the interests of **all** parties. It cannot be in the interests of any defendant for his good points to become lost in a welter of uncontroversial or irrelevant evidence.

(d) In many fraud cases the primary facts are not seriously disputed. The real issue is what each defendant knew and whether that defendant was dishonest. Once the judge has identified what is in dispute and what is not in dispute, the judge can then discuss with the advocate how the trial should be structured, what can be dealt with by admissions or agreed facts, what uncontroversial matters should be proved by concise oral evidence, what timetabling can be required under Rule 3.10 Criminal Procedure Rules, and other directions.

(e) In particularly heavy fraud or complex cases the judge may possibly consider it necessary to allocate a whole week for a case management hearing. If that week is used wisely, many further weeks of trial time can be saved. In the gaps which will inevitably arise during that week (for example while the advocates are exploring matters raised by the judge) the judge can do a substantial amount of informed reading. The case has come "alive" at this stage. Indeed, in a really heavy fraud case, if the judge fixes one or more case management hearings on this scale, there will be need for fewer formal reading days. Moreover a huge amount can be achieved in the pre-trial stage, if all trial advocates are gathered in the same place, focussing on the case **at the same time**, for several days consecutively.

(f) Requiring the defence to serve proper case statements may enable the court to identify:
(i) what is common ground and
(ii) the real issues.

It is therefore important that proper defence case statements be provided as required by the Criminal Procedure Rules; Judges will use the powers contained in ss 28–34 of the Criminal Proceedings and Evidence Act 1996 (and the corresponding provisions of the CJA 1987, ss. 33 and following of the Criminal Justice Act 2003) and the Criminal Procedure Rules to ensure that realistic defence case statements are provided.

(g) Likewise this objective may be achieved by requiring the prosecution to serve draft admissions by a specified date and by requiring the defence to respond within a specified number of weeks.

(v) Further Case Management Hearings

(a) The date of the next case management hearing should be fixed at the conclusion of the hearing so that there is no delay in having to fix the date through listing offices, clerks and others.

(b) If one is looking at a trial which threatens to run for months, pre-trial case management on an intensive scale is essential.

(vi) Consideration of the length of the trial

(a) Case management on the above lines, the procedure set out in paragraph 1 (iv), may still be insufficient to reduce the trial to a manageable length; generally a trial of 3 months should be the target, but there will be cases where a duration of 6 months or, in exceptional circumstances, even longer may be inevitable.

(b) If the trial is not estimated to be within a manageable length, it will be necessary for the judge to consider what steps should be taken to reduce the length of the trial, whilst still ensuring that the prosecution has the opportunity of placing the full criminality before the court.

(c) To assist the judge in this task,

    (i) The lead advocate for the prosecution should be asked to explain why the prosecution have rejected a shorter way of proceeding; they may also be asked to divide the case into sections of evidence and explain the scope of each section and the need for each section.

    (ii) The lead advocates for the prosecution and for the defence should be prepared to put forward in writing, if requested, ways in which a case estimated to last more than three months can be shortened, including possible severance of counts or defendants, exclusions of sections of the case or of evidence or areas of the case where admissions can be made.

(d) One course the judge may consider is pruning the indictment by omitting certain charges and/or by omitting certain defendants. The judge must not usurp the function of the prosecution in this regard, and he must bear in mind that he will, at the outset, know less about the case than the advocates. The aim is achieve fairness to all parties.

(e) Nevertheless, the judge does have two methods of pruning available for use in appropriate circumstances:

    (i) Persuading the prosecution that it is not worthwhile pursuing certain charges and/or certain defendants.

    (ii) Severing the indictment. Severance for reasons of case management alone is perfectly proper, although judges should have regard to any representations made by the prosecution that severance would weaken their case. Indeed the judge's hand will be strengthened in this regard by rule 1.1 (2) (g) of the Criminal Procedure Rules. However, before using what may be seen as a blunt instrument, the judge should insist on seeing full defence statements of all affected defendants. Severance may be unfair to the prosecution if, for example, there is a cut-throat defence in prospect. For example, the defence of the principal defendant may be that the defendant relied on the advice of his accountant or solicitor that what was happening was acceptable. The defence of the professional may be that he gave no such advice. Against that background, it might be unfair to the prosecution to order separate trials of the two defendants.

(vii) The exercise of the powers

(a) The Criminal Procedure Rules require the court to take a more active part in case management. These are salutary provisions which should bring to an end interminable criminal trials of the kind which the Court of Appeal criticised in *Jisl* [2004] EWCA 696 at [113]— [121].

(b) Nevertheless these salutary provisions do not have to be used on every occasion. Where the advocates have done their job properly, by narrowing the issues, pruning the evidence and so forth, it may be quite inappropriate for the judge to "weigh in" and start cutting out more evidence or more charges of his own volition. It behoves the judge to make a careful assessment of the degree of judicial intervention which is warranted in each case.

(c) The note of caution in the previous paragraph is supported by certain experience which has been gained of the Civil Procedure Rules (on which the Criminal Procedure Rules are based). The CPR contain valuable and efficacious provisions for case management by the judge on his own initiative which have led to huge savings of court time and costs. Surveys by the Law Society have shown that the CPR have been generally welcomed by court users and the profession, but there have been reported to have been isolated instances in which the parties to civil litigation have faithfully complied with both the letter and the spirit of the CPR, and have then been aggrieved by what was perceived to be unnecessary intermeddling by the court.

(viii) Expert Evidence

(a) Early identification of the subject matter of expert evidence to be adduced by the prosecution and the defence should be made as early as possible, preferably at the directions hearing.

(b) Following the exchange of expert evidence, any areas of disagreement should be identified and a direction should generally be made requiring the experts to meet and prepare, after discussion, a joint statement identifying points of agreement and contention and areas where the prosecution is put to proof on matters of which a positive case to the contrary is not advanced by the defence. After the statement has been prepared it should be served on the court, the prosecution and the defence. In some cases, it might be appropriate to provide that to the jury.

(ix) Surveillance Evidence

(a) Where a prosecution is based upon many months' observation or surveillance evidence and it appears that it is capable of effective presentation based on a shorter period, the advocate should be required to justify the evidence of such observations before it is permitted to be adduced, either substantially or in its entirety.

(b) Schedules should be provided to cover as much of the evidence as possible and admissions sought.

D. DISCLOSURE

In fraud cases the volume of documentation obtained by the prosecution is liable to be immense. The problems of disclosure are intractable and have the potential to disrupt the entire trial process.

(i) The prosecution lawyer (and the prosecution advocate if different) brought in at the outset, as set out in paragraph 1 (i)(a), each have a continuing responsibility to discharge the prosecution's duty of disclosure, either personally or by delegation, in accordance with the Attorney General's Guidelines on Disclosure.

(ii) The prosecution should only disclose those documents which are relevant (i.e. likely to assist the defence or undermine the prosecution—see s. 3 (1) of CPIA 1996 and the provisions of the CJA 2003).

(iii) It is almost always undesirable to give the "warehouse key" to the defence for two reasons:

  (a) This amounts to an abrogation of the responsibility of the prosecution;

  (b) The defence solicitors may spend a disproportionate amount of time and incur disproportionate costs trawling through a morass of documents.

The Judge should therefore try and ensure that disclosure is limited to what is likely to assist the defence or undermine the prosecution.

(iv) At the outset the judge should set a timetable for dealing with disclosure issues. In particular, the judge should fix a date by which all defence applications for specific disclosure must be made. In this regard, it is relevant that the defendants are likely to be intelligent people, who know their own business affairs and who (for the most part) will know what documents or categories of documents they are looking for.

(v) At the outset (and before the cut-off date for specific disclosure applications) the judge should ask the defence to indicate what documents they are interested in and from what source. A general list is not an acceptable response to this request. The judge should insist upon a list which is specific, manageable and realistic. The judge may also require justification of any request.

(vi) In non-fraud cases, the same considerations apply, but some may be different:

   (a) It is not possible to approach many non-fraud cases on the basis that the defendant knows what is there or what they are looking for. But on the other hand this should not be turned into an excuse for a "fishing expedition"; the judge should insist on knowing the issue to which a request for disclosure applies.

   (b) If the bona fides of the investigation is called into question, a judge will be concerned to see that there has been independent and effective appraisal of the documents contained in the disclosure schedule and that its contents are adequate. In appropriate cases where this issue has arisen and there are grounds which show there is a real issue, consideration should be given to receiving evidence on oath from the senior investigating officer at an early case management hearing.

E. ABUSE OF PROCESS

(i) Applications to stay or dismiss for abuse of process have become a normal feature of heavy and complex cases. Such applications may be based upon delay and the health of defendants.

(ii) Applications in relation to absent special circumstances tend to be unsuccessful and not to be pursued on appeal. For this reason there is comparatively little Court of Appeal guidance: but see: *Harris and Howells* [2003] EWCA Crim 486. It should be noted that abuse of process is not there to discipline the prosecution or the police.

(iii) The arguments on both sides must be reduced to writing. Oral evidence is seldom relevant.

(iv) The judge should direct full written submissions (rather than "skeleton arguments") on any abuse application in accordance with a timetable set by him; these should identify any element of prejudice the defendant is alleged to have suffered.

(v) The Judge should normally aim to conclude the hearing within an absolute maximum limit of one day, if necessary in accordance with a timetable. The parties should therefore prepare their papers on this basis and not expect the judge to allow the oral hearing to be anything more than an occasion to highlight concisely their arguments and answer any questions the court may have of them; applications will not be allowed to drag on.

F. THE TRIAL

(i) The particular hazard of heavy fraud trials

A heavy fraud or other complex trial has the potential to lose direction and focus. This is a disaster for three reasons:

(a) The jury will lose track of the evidence, thereby prejudicing both prosecution and defence.

(b) The burden on the defendants, the judge and indeed all involved will become intolerable.

(c) Scarce public resources are wasted. Other prosecutions are delayed or—worse—may never happen. Fraud which is detected but not prosecuted (for resource reasons) undermines confidence.

(ii) Judicial mastery of the case

(a) It is necessary for the judge to exercise firm control over the conduct of the trial at all stages.

(b) In order to do this the judge must read the witness statements and the documents, so that the judge can discuss case management issues with the advocates on—almost—an equal footing.

(c) To this end, the judge should not set aside weeks or even days for pre-reading (see paragraph 3 (i)(b) above). Hopefully the judge will have gained a good grasp of the evidence during the case management hearings. Nevertheless, realistic reading time must be provided for the judge in advance of trial.

(d) The role of the judge in a heavy fraud or other complex criminal trial is different from his/her role in a "conventional" criminal trial. So far as possible, the judge should be freed from other duties and burdens, so that he/she can give the high degree of commitment which a heavy fraud trial requires. This will pay dividends in terms of saving weeks or months of court time.

(iii) The order of the evidence

(a) By the outset of the trial at the latest (and in most cases very much earlier) the judge must be provided with a schedule, showing the sequence of prosecution (and in an appropriate case defence) witnesses and the dates upon which they are expected to be called. This can only be prepared by discussion between prosecution and defence which the judge should expect, and say he/she expects, to take place: See: Criminal Procedure Rule 3.10. The schedule should, in so far as it relates to Prosecution witnesses, be developed in consultation with the witnesses, via the Witness Care Units, and with consideration given to their personal needs. Copies of the schedule should be provided for the Witness Service.

(b) The schedule should be kept under review by the trial judge and by the parties. If a case is running behind or ahead of schedule, each witness affected must be advised by the party who is calling that witness at the earliest opportunity.

(c) If an excessive amount of time is allowed for any witness, the judge can ask why. The judge may probe with the advocates whether the time envisaged for the evidence-in-chief or cross-examination (as the case may be) of a particular witness is really necessary.

(iv) Case management sessions

(a) The order of the evidence may have legitimately to be departed from. It will, however, be a useful for tool for monitoring the progress of the case. There should be periodic case management sessions, during which the judge engages the advocates upon a stock-taking exercise: asking, amongst other questions, "where are we going?" and "what is the relevance of the next three witnesses?". This will be a valuable means of keeping the case on track. Rule 3.10 of the Criminal Procedure Rules will again assist the judge.

(b) The judge may wish to consider issuing the occasional use of "case management notes" to the advocates, in order to set out the judge's tentative views on where the trial may be going off track, which areas of future evidence are relevant and which may have become irrelevant (e.g. because of concessions, admissions in cross-examination and so forth). Such notes from the judge plus written responses from the advocates can, cautiously used, provide a valuable focus for debate during the periodic case management reviews held during the course of the trial.

(v) Controlling prolix cross-examination

(a) Setting **rigid** time limits in advance for cross-examination is rarely appropriate—as experience has shown in civil cases; but a timetable is essential so that the judge can exercise control and so that there is a clear target to aim at for the completion of the evidence of each witness. Moreover the judge can and should indicate when cross-examination is irrelevant, unnecessary or time wasting. The judge may limit the time for further cross-examination of a particular witness.

(vi) Electronic presentation of evidence

(a) Electronic presentation of evidence (EPE) has the potential to save huge amounts of time in fraud and other complex criminal trials and should be used more widely.

(b) HMCS is providing facilities for the easier use of EPE with a standard audio visual facility. Effectively managed, the savings in court time achieved by EPE more than justify the cost.

(c) There should still be a core bundle of those documents to which frequent reference will be made during the trial. The jury may wish to mark that bundle or to refer back to particular pages as the evidence progresses. EPE can be used for presenting all documents not contained in the core bundle.

(d) Greater use of other modern forms of graphical presentations should be made wherever possible.

(vii) Use of interviews

The Judge should consider extensive editing of self serving interviews, even when the defence want the jury to hear them in their entirety; such interviews are not evidence of the truth of their contents but merely of the defendant's reaction to the allegation.

(viii) Jury Management

(a) The jury should be informed as early as possible in the case as to what the issues are in a manner directed by the Judge.

(b) The jury must be regularly updated as to the trial timetable and the progress of the trial, subject to warnings as to the predictability of the trial process.

(c) Legal argument should be heard at times that causes the least inconvenience to jurors.

(d) It is useful to consider with the advocates whether written directions should be given to the jury and, if so, in what form.

(ix) Maxwell hours

(a) Maxwell hours should only be permitted after careful consideration and consultation with the Presiding Judge.

(b) Considerations in favour include:
  (i) Legal argument can be accommodated without disturbing the jury;
  (ii) There is a better chance of a representative jury;
  (iii) Time is made available to the judge, advocates and experts to do useful work in the afternoons.

(c) Considerations against include:
  (i) The lengthening of trials and the consequent waste of court time;
  (ii) The desirability of making full use of the jury once they have arrived at court;
  (iii) Shorter trials tend to diminish the need for special provisions e.g. there are fewer difficulties in empanelling more representative juries;
  (iv) They are unavailable if any defendant is in custody.

(d) It may often be the case that a maximum of one day of Maxwell hours a week is sufficient; if so, it should be timetabled in advance to enable all submissions by advocates, supported by skeleton arguments served in advance, to be dealt with in the period after 1:30 pm on that day.

(x) Livenote

If Livenote is used, it is important that all users continue to take a note of the evidence, otherwise considerable time is wasted in detailed reading of the entire daily transcript.

G. OTHER ISSUES

(i) Defence representation and defence costs

(a) Applications for change in representation in complex trials need special consideration; the ruling of HH Judge Wakerley QC (as he then was) in *Asghar Ali* has been circulated by the JSB.

(b) Problems have arisen when the Legal Services Commission have declined to allow advocates or solicitors to do certain work; on occasions the matter has been raised with the judge managing or trying the case.

(c) The Legal Services Commission has provided guidance to judges on how they can obtain information from the LSC as to the reasons for their decisions; further information in relation to this can be obtained from *Nigel Field, Head of the Complex Crime Unit, Legal Services Commission, 29–37 Red Lion Street, London, WC1R 4PP.*

(ii) Assistance to the Judge

Experience has shown that in some very heavy cases, the judge's burden can be substantially offset with the provision of a Judicial Assistant or other support and assistance.

Guidance on the Use of the Common Law Offence of Conspiracy to Defraud

Summary

1. This guidance concerns the issues which the Attorney General asks prosecuting authorities in England and Wales to consider before using the common law offence of conspiracy to defraud, in the light of the implementation of the Fraud Act 2006. It may be supplemented by Departmental-specific guidance issued by individual Directors of the prosecuting authorities.

Background

2. When the Fraud Act 2006 comes into force on 15 January 2007, the prosecution will be able to use modern and flexible statutory offences of fraud. The 2006 Act replaces the deception offences contained in the Theft Acts 1968–1996 with a general offence of fraud that can be committed in three ways:
   - fraud by false representation;
   - fraud by failing to disclose information; and
   - fraud by abuse of position.

   It also introduces other offences which can be used in particular circumstances, notably;
   - new offences to tackle the possession and supply of articles for use in fraud; and
   - a new offence of fraudulent trading applicable to sole traders and other businesses not caught by the existing offence in section 458 of the Companies Act 1985.

3. The new offences are designed to catch behaviour that previously fell through gaps in the Theft Acts and could only be prosecuted as conspiracy to defraud. Indeed the Act is based on a Law Commission report (Cm 5560) which also recommended the abolition of the common law offence of conspiracy to defraud. The argument is that the offence is unfairly uncertain, and wide enough to have the potential to catch behaviour that should not be criminal. Furthermore it can seem anomalous that what is legal if performed by one person should be criminal if performed by many.

4. However, consultations showed a widespread view in favour of retention of common law conspiracy to defraud, and the Government decided to retain it for the meantime, but accepted the case for considering repeal in the longer term. Whether there is a continuing need for retention of the common law offence is one of the issues that will be addressed in the Home Office review of the operation of the Fraud Act 2006, which will take place 3 years after its implementation.

5. In 2003, 14,928 defendants were proceeded against in England and Wales for crimes of fraud; 1,018 of these were charged with the common law crime of conspiracy to defraud

of which 44% were found guilty (compared with 71% for the statutory fraud offences). The expectation now is that the common law offence will be used to a significantly lesser extent once the Fraud Act 2006 has come into force.

Issues to be considered in using the common law offence

6. In selecting charges in fraud cases, the prosecutor should first consider:
   - whether the behaviour could be prosecuted under statute—whether under the Fraud Act 2006 or another Act or as a statutory conspiracy; and
   - whether the available statutory charges adequately reflect the gravity of the offence.

7. Statutory conspiracy to commit a substantive offence should be charged if the alleged agreement satisfies the definition in section 1 of the Criminal Law Act 1977, provided that there is no wider dishonest objective that would be important to the presentation of the prosecution case in reflecting the gravity of the case.

8. Section 12 of the Criminal Justice Act 1987 provides that common law conspiracy to defraud may be charged even if the conduct agreed upon will involve the commission of a statutory offence. However, Lord Bingham said in *R v Rimmington* and *R v Goldstein* [(2005) UKHL 63]:

   "I would not go to the length of holding that conduct may never be lawfully prosecuted as a generally-expressed common law crime where it falls within the terms of a specific statutory provision, but good practice and respect for the primacy of statute do in my judgment require that conduct falling within the terms of a specific statutory provision should be prosecuted under that provision unless there is good reason for doing otherwise."

9. In the Attorney General's view the common law charge may still be appropriate in the type of cases set out in paragraphs 12–15, but in order to understand the circumstances under which conspiracy to defraud is used **prosecutors should make a record of the reasons for preferring that charge.**

Records of decisions

10. Where a charge of common law conspiracy to defraud is proposed the case lawyer must consider and set out in writing in the review note:
    - how much such a charge will add to the amount of evidence likely to be called both by the prosecution and the defence; and
    - the justification for using the charge, and why specific statutory offences are inadequate or otherwise inappropriate.

    Thereafter, and before charge, the use of this charge should be specifically approved by s supervising lawyer experienced in fraud cases. Equivalent procedures to ensure proper consideration of the charge and recording of the decision should be applied by all prosecuting authorities in their case review processes.

11. Information from these records will be collected retrospectively for the review to be conducted in 3 years. It will enable the identification of where and why the common law offence has been under. It could then also form the basis for any future work on whether, and if so how, to replace the common law or whether it can simply and safely be repealed. It is expected that in 3 years the Government will be able to review the situation in the light of the practical operation not only of the new fraud offences, but of other relevant changes. These include the Lord Chief Justice's protocol on the control and management of heavy fraud cases, and the sample count

provisions in the Domestic Violence, Crime and Victims Act 2004. Any actual or proposed changes to the law on assisting and encouraging crime in the light of the Law Commission's study of that issue *[Cm 6878, published in July 2006]* will also be taken into account.

A. CONDUCT THAT CAN MORE EFFECTIVELY BE PROSECUTED AS CONSPIRACY TO DEFRAUD

12. There may be cases where the interests of justice can only be served by presenting to a court an overall picture which cannot be achieved by charging a series of substantive offences or statutory conspiracies. Typically, such cases will involve some, but not necessarily all of the following:
    - evidence of several significant but different kinds of criminality;
    - several jurisdictions;
    - different types of victims, e.g. individuals, banks, web site administrators, credit card companies;
    - organised crime networks.

13. The proper presentation of such cases as statutory conspiracies could lead to:
    - large numbers of separate counts to reflect the different conspiracies;
    - severed trials for single or discrete groups of conspiracies;
    - evidence in one severed trial being deemed inadmissible in another.

14. If so, the consequences might be that no one court would receive a cohesive picture of the whole case which would allow sentencing on a proper basis. In contrast a single count of common law conspiracy to defraud might, in such circumstances, reflect the nature and extent of criminal conduct in a way that prosecuting the underlying statutory offences or conspiracies would fail to achieve.

B. CONDUCT THAT CAN ONLY BE PROSECUTED AS CONSPIRACY TO DEFRAUD

15. Examples of such conduct might include but are not restricted to agreements to the following courses of action:
    - The dishonest obtaining of land and other property which cannot be stolen such as intellectual property not protected by the Copyright, Designs and Patents Act 1988 and the Trademarks Act 1994, and other confidential information. The Fraud Act will bite where there is intent to make a gain or cause a loss through false representation, failure to disclose information where there is a legal obligation to do so, or the abuse of position;
    - Dishonestly infringing another's right; for example the dishonest exploitation of another's patent in the absence of a legal duty to disclose information about its existence;
    - Where it is intended that the final offence be committed by someone outside the conspiracy; and

- Cases where the accused cannot be proved to have had the necessary degree of knowledge of the substantive offence to be perpetrated;

HER MAJESTY'S ATTORNEY GENERAL

Dated this 9th day of January 2007

Attorney General's Chambers
9 Buckingham Gate
London SWIE 6JP

Criminal Justice Act 1993

An Act to make provision about the jurisdiction of courts in England and Wales in relation to certain offences of dishonesty and blackmail; to amend the law about drug trafficking offences and to implement provisions of the Community Council Directive No. 91/308/EEC; to amend Part VI of the Criminal Justice Act 1988; to make provision with respect to the financing of terrorism, the proceeds of terrorist-related activities and the investigation of terrorist activities; to amend Part I of the Criminal Justice Act 1991; to implement provisions of the Community Council Directive No. 89/592/EEC and to amend and restate the law about insider dealing in securities; to provide for certain offences created by the Banking Coordination (Second Council Directive) Regulations 1992 to be punishable in the same way as offences under sections 39, 40 and 41 of the Banking Act 1987 and to enable regulations implementing Article 15 of the Community Council Directive No. 89/646/EEC and Articles 3, 6 and 7 of the Community Council Directive No. 92/30/EEC to create offences punishable in that way; to make provision with respect to the penalty for causing death by dangerous driving or causing death by careless driving while under the influence of drink or drugs; to make it an offence to assist in or induce certain conduct which for the purposes of, or in connection with, the provisions of Community law is unlawful in another member State; to provide for the introduction of safeguards in connection with the return of persons under backing of warrants arrangements; to amend the Criminal Procedure (Scotland) Act 1975 and Part I of the Prisoners and Criminal Proceedings (Scotland) Act 1993; and for connected purposes. [27th July 1993]

BE IT ENACTED by the Queen's most Excellent Majesty, by and with the advice and consent of the Lords Spiritual and Temporal, and Commons, in this present Parliament assembled, and by the authority of the same, as follows:—

PART I
JURISDICTION

Offences to which this Part applies

1. —(1) This Part applies to two groups of offences—
    (a) any offence mentioned in subsection (2) (a 'Group A offence'); and
    (b) any offence mentioned in subsection (3) (a 'Group B offence').
(2) The Group A offences are—
    (a) an offence under any of the following provisions of the Theft Act 1968—section 1 (theft);

[...]¹
section 17 (false accounting);
section 19 (false statements by company directors, etc.);
[...]²
section 21 (blackmail);
section 22 (handling stolen goods);
[section 24A (retaining credits from dishonest sources, etc)]³
[...]⁴
[(bb) an offence under any of the following provisions of the Fraud Act 2006—
section 1 (fraud);
section 6 (possession etc. of articles for use in frauds);
section 7 (making or supplying articles for use in frauds);
section 9 (participating in fraudulent business carried on by sole trader etc.);
section 11 (obtaining services dishonestly).]⁵
(c) an offence under any of the following provisions of the Forgery and Counterfeiting Act 1981—
section 1 (forgery);
section 2 (copying a false instrument);
section 3 (using a false instrument);
section 4 (using a copy of a false instrument);
section 5 (offences which relate to money orders, share certificates, passports, etc.);
[section 14 (offences of counterfeiting notes and coins);
section 15 (offences of passing etc counterfeit notes and coins);
section 16 (offences involving the custody or control of counterfeit notes and coins);
section 17 (offences involving the making or custody or control of counterfeiting materials and implements);
section 20 (prohibition of importation of counterfeit notes and coins);
section 21 (prohibition of exportation of counterfeit notes and coins);]⁶
[(ca) an offence under section 25 of the Identity Cards Act 2006;]⁷
(d) the common law offence of cheating in relation to the public revenue.
(3) The Group B offences are—
(a) conspiracy to commit a Group A offence;
(b) conspiracy to defraud;
(c) attempting to commit a Group A offence;
(d) incitement to commit a Group A offence.
(4) The Secretary of State may by order amend subsection (2) or (3) by adding or removing any offence.
(5) The power to make such an order shall be exercisable by statutory instrument.
(6) No order shall be made under subsection (4) unless a draft of it has been laid before and approved by a resolution of each House of Parliament.

¹ Repealed by Fraud Act 2006. ² Repealed by Fraud Act 2006.
³ Inserted by Theft (Amendment) Act 1996. ⁴ Repealed by Fraud Act 2006.
⁵ Inserted by Fraud Act 2006. ⁶ Inserted by SI 2000/1878.
⁷ Inserted by Identity Cards Act 2006.

Jurisdiction in respect of Group A offences

2.— (1) For the purposes of this Part, 'relevant event', in relation to any Group A offence, means[(subject to subsection (1A))]⁸ any act or omission or other event (including any result of one or more acts or omissions) proof of which is required for conviction of the offence.

[(1A) In relation to an offence under section 1 of the Fraud Act 2006 (fraud), "relevant event" includes—
if the fraud involved an intention to make a gain and the gain occurred, that occurrence;
if the fraud involved an intention to cause a loss or to expose another to a risk of loss and the loss occurred, that occurrence.] ⁹

(2) For the purpose of determining whether or not a particular event is a relevant event in relation to a Group A offence, any question as to where it occurred is to be disregarded.

(3) A person may be guilty of a Group A offence if any of the events which are relevant events in relation to the offence occurred in England and Wales.

Questions immaterial to jurisdiction in the case of certain offences

3.— (1) A person may be guilty of a Group A or Group B offence whether or not—
(a) he was a British citizen at any material time;
(b) he was in England and Wales at any such time.

(2) On a charge of conspiracy to commit a Group A offence, or on a charge of conspiracy to defraud in England and Wales, the defendant may be guilty of the offence whether or not—
(a) he became a party to the conspiracy in England and Wales;
(b) any act or omission or other event in relation to the conspiracy occurred in England and Wales.

(3) On a charge of attempting to commit a Group A offence, the defendant may be guilty of the offence whether or not—
(a) the attempt was made in England and Wales;
(b) it had an effect in England and Wales.

(4) Subsection (1)(a) does not apply where jurisdiction is given to try the offence in question by an enactment which makes provision by reference to the nationality of the person charged.

(5) Subsection (2) does not apply in relation to any charge under the Criminal Law Act 1977 brought by virtue of section 1A of that Act.

(6) Subsection (3) does not apply in relation to any charge under the Criminal Attempts Act 1981 brought by virtue of section 1A of that Act.

Rules for determining certain jurisdictional questions relating to the location of events

4. In relation to a Group A or Group B offence—

---

⁸ Inserted by Fraud Act 2006.   ⁹ Inserted by Fraud Act 2006.

    (a) there is an obtaining of property in England and Wales if the property is either despatched from or received at a place in England and Wales; and

    (b) there is a communication in England and Wales of any information, instruction, request, demand or other matter if it is sent by any means—

        (i) from a place in England and Wales to a place elsewhere; or

        (ii) from a place elsewhere to a place in England and Wales.

Conspiracy, attempt and incitement

5. —...

(3) A person may be guilty of conspiracy to defraud if—

    (a) a party to the agreement constituting the conspiracy, or a party's agent, did anything in England and Wales in relation to the agreement before its formation, or

    (b) a party to it became a party in England and Wales (by joining it either in person or through an agent), or

    (c) a party to it, or a party's agent, did or omitted anything in England and Wales in pursuance of it,

    and the conspiracy would be triable in England and Wales but for the fraud which the parties to it had in view not being intended to take place in England and Wales.

(4) A person may be guilty of incitement to commit a Group A offence if the incitement—

    (a) takes place in England and Wales; and

    (b) would be triable in England and Wales but for what the person charged had in view not being an offence triable in England and Wales.

(5) Subsections (3) and (4) are subject to section 6.

Relevance of external law

6. —(1) A person is guilty of an offence triable

    [...][10] by virtue of section 5(3), only if the pursuit of the agreed course of conduct would at some stage involve—

    (a) an act or omission by one or more of the parties, or

    (b) the happening of some other event,

    constituting an offence under the law in force where the act, omission or other event was intended to take place.

(2) A person is guilty of an offence triable by virtue of section 1A of the Criminal Attempts Act 1981 , or by virtue of section 5(4), only if what he had in view would involve the commission of an offence under the law in force where the whole or any part of it was intended to take place.

(3) Conduct punishable under the law in force in any place is an offence under that law for the purposes of this section, however it is described in that law.

(4) Subject to subsection (6), a condition specified in subsection (1) or (2) shall be taken to be satisfied unless, not later than rules of court may provide, the defence serve on the prosecution a notice—

---

[10] Repealed by Criminal Justice (Terrorism and Conspiracy) Act 1998.

    (a) stating that, on the facts as alleged with respect to the relevant conduct, the condition is not in their opinion satisfied;

    (b) showing their grounds for that opinion; and

    (c) requiring the prosecution to show that it is satisfied.

(5) In subsection (4) 'the relevant conduct' means—

    (a) where the condition in subsection (1) is in question, the agreed course of conduct; and

    (b) where the condition in subsection (2) is in question, what the defendant had in view.

(6) The court, if it thinks fit, may permit the defence to require the prosecution to show that the condition is satisfied without the prior service of a notice under subsection (4).

(7) In the Crown Court, the question whether the condition is satisfied shall be decided by the judge alone.

(8) ...

Other Fraud Legislation

A. THEFT ACT 1968

CONTENTS

Definition of "Theft"

1 Basic definition of theft
2 "Dishonestly"
3 "Appropriates"
4 "Property"
5 "Belonging to another"
6 "With the intention of permanently depriving the other of it"

Theft, Robbery, Burglary, etc

7 Theft
8 Robbery
9 Burglary
10 Aggravated burglary
11 Removal of articles from places open to the public
12 Taking motor vehicle or other conveyance without authority
[12A Aggravated vehicle-taking]
13 Abstracting of electricity
14 Extension to thefts from mails outside England and Wales, and robbery etc on such
a theft

Fraud and Blackmail

[...]¹

17 False accounting
18 Liability of company officers for certain offences by company
19 False statements by company directors, etc
20 Suppression, etc of documents
21 Blackmail

Offences relating to goods stolen etc

22 Handling stolen goods
23 Advertising rewards for return of goods stolen or lost
24 Scope of offences relating to stolen goods
[24A Dishonestly retaining a wrongful credit]*

Possession of house breaking implements, etc

25 Going equipped for stealing, etc

Enforcement and procedure

26 Search for stolen goods
27 Evidence and procedure on charge of theft or handling stolen goods
28 ...
29 ...

General and consequential provisions

30 Husband and wife [30 Spouses and civil partners]
31 Effect on civil proceedings and rights
32 Effect on existing law and construction of references to offences
33 Miscellaneous and consequential amendments, and repeal

Supplementary

34 Interpretation
35 Commencement and transitional provisions
36 Short title, and general provisions as to Scotland and Northern Ireland

An Act to revise the law of England and Wales as to theft and similar or associated offences, and in connection therewith to make provision as to criminal proceedings by one party to a marriage against the other, and to make certain amendments extending beyond England and Wales in the Post Office Act 1953 and other enactments; and for other purposes connected therewith.   [26th July 1968]

BE IT ENACTED by the Queen's most Excellent Majesty, by and with the advice and consent of the Lords Spiritual and Temporal, and Commons, in this present Parliament assembled, and by the authority of the same, as follows:—

---

¹ Repealed by Fraud Act 2006.

Definition of 'theft'

Basic definition of theft

1. —(1) A person is guilty of theft if he dishonestly appropriates property belonging to another with the intention of permanently depriving the other of it; and 'thief' and 'steal' shall be construed accordingly.

(2) It is immaterial whether the appropriation is made with a view to gain, or is made for the thief's own benefit.

(3) The five following sections of this Act shall have effect as regards the interpretation and operation of this section (and, except as otherwise provided by this Act, shall apply only for purposes of this section).

'Dishonestly'

2. —(1) A person's appropriation of property belonging to another is not to be regarded as dishonest—

(a) if he appropriates the property in the belief that he has in law the right to deprive the other of it, on behalf of himself or of a third person; or

(b) if he appropriates the property in the belief that he would have the other's consent if the other knew of the appropriation and the circumstances of it; or

(c) (except where the property came to him as trustee or personal representative) if he appropriates the property in the belief that the person to whom the property belongs cannot be discovered by taking reasonable steps.

(2) A person's appropriation of property belonging to another may be dishonest notwithstanding that he is willing to pay for the property.

'Appropriates'

3. —(1) Any assumption by a person of the rights of an owner amounts to an appropriation, and this includes, where he has come by the property (innocently or not) without stealing it, any later assumption of a right to it by keeping or dealing with it as owner.

(2) Where property or a right or interest in property is or purports to be transferred for value to a person acting in good faith, no later assumption by him of rights which he believed himself to be acquiring shall, by reason of any defect in the transferor's title, amount to theft of the property.

'Property'

4. —(1) 'Property' includes money and all other property, real or personal, including things in action and other intangible property.

(2) A person cannot steal land, or things forming part of land and severed from it by him or by his directions, except in the following cases, that is to say—

(a) when he is a trustee or personal representative, or is authorised by power of attorney, or as liquidator of a company, or otherwise, to sell or dispose of land belonging to another, and he appropriates the land or anything forming part of it by dealing with it in breach of the confidence reposed in him; or

    (b) when he is not in possession of the land and appropriates anything forming part of the land by severing it or causing it to be severed, or after it has been severed; or

    (c) when, being in possession of the land under a tenancy, he appropriates the whole or part of any fixture or structure let to be used with the land.

For purposes of this subsection 'land' does not include incorporeal hereditaments; 'tenancy' means a tenancy for years or any less period and includes an agreement for such a tenancy, but a person who after the end of a tenancy remains in possession as statutory tenant or otherwise is to be treated as having possession under the tenancy, and 'let' shall be construed accordingly.

(3) A person who picks mushrooms growing wild on any land, or who picks flowers, fruit or foliage from a plant growing wild on any land, does not (although not in possession of the land) steal what he picks, unless he does it for reward or for sale or other commercial purpose.

For purposes of this subsection 'mushroom' includes any fungus, and 'plant' includes any shrub or tree.

(4) Wild creatures, tamed or untamed, shall be regarded as property; but a person cannot steal a wild creature not tamed nor ordinarily kept in captivity, or the carcase of any such creature, unless either it has been reduced into possession by or on behalf of another person and possession of it has not since been lost or abandoned, or another person is in course of reducing it into possession.

'Belonging to another'

5. —(1) Property shall be regarded as belonging to any person having possession or control of it, or having in it any proprietary right or interest (not being an equitable interest arising only from an agreement to transfer or grant an interest).

(2) Where property is subject to a trust, the persons to whom it belongs shall be regarded as including any person having a right to enforce the trust, and an intention to defeat the trust shall be regarded accordingly as an intention to deprive of the property any person having that right.

(3) Where a person receives property from or on account of another, and is under an obligation to the other to retain and deal with that property or its proceeds in a particular way, the property or proceeds shall be regarded (as against him) as belonging to the other.

(4) Where a person gets property by another's mistake, and is under an obligation to make restoration (in whole or in part) of the property or its proceeds or of the value thereof, then to the extent of that obligation the property or proceeds shall be regarded (as against him) as belonging to the person entitled to restoration, and an intention not to make restoration shall be regarded accordingly as an intention to deprive that person of the property or proceeds.

(5) Property of a corporation sole shall be regarded as belonging to the corporation notwithstanding a vacancy in the corporation.

'With the intention of permanently depriving the other of it'

6. —(1) A person appropriating property belonging to another without meaning the other permanently to lose the thing itself is nevertheless to be regarded as having the intention

of permanently depriving the other of it if his intention is to treat the thing as his own to dispose of regardless of the other's rights; and a borrowing or lending of it may amount to so treating it if, but only if, the borrowing or lending is for a period and in circumstances making it equivalent to an outright taking or disposal.

(2) Without prejudice to the generality of subsection (1) above, where a person, having possession or control (lawfully or not) of property belonging to another, parts with the property under a condition as to its return which he may not be able to perform, this (if done for purposes of his own and without the other's authority) amounts to treating the property as his own to dispose of regardless of the other's rights.

Theft, robbery, burglary, etc

Theft

7. A person guilty of theft shall on conviction on indictment be liable to imprisonment for a term not exceeding [seven years]²

Robbery

8. —(1) A person is guilty of robbery if he steals, and immediately before or at the time of doing so, and in order to do so, he uses force on any person or puts or seeks to put any person in fear of being then and there subjected to force.
(2) A person guilty of robbery, or of an assault with intent to rob, shall on conviction on indictment be liable to imprisonment for life.

Burglary

9. —(1) A person is guilty of burglary if—
   (a) he enters any building or part of a building as a trespasser and with intent to commit any such offence as is mentioned in subsection (2) below; or
   (b) having entered any building or part of a building as a trespasser he steals or attempts to steal anything in the building or that part of it or inflicts or attempts to inflict on any person therein any grievous bodily harm.
(2) The offences referred to in subsection (1)(a) above are offences of stealing anything in the building or part of a building in question, of inflicting on any person therein any grievous bodily harm [...]³ therein, and of doing unlawful damage to the building or anything therein.
[(3) A person guilty of burglary shall on conviction on indictment be liable to imprisonment for a term not exceeding—
   (a) where the offence was committed in respect of a building or part of a building which is a dwelling, fourteen years;
   (b) in any other case, ten years.
(4) References in subsections (1) and (2) above to a building, and the reference in subsection (3) above to a building which is a dwelling, shall apply also to an inhabited vehicle or vessel, and shall apply to any such vehicle or vessel at times when the person having a habitation in it is not there as well as at times when he is.]⁴

---

² Amended by Criminal Justice Act 1991.   ³ Repealed by Sexual Offences Act 2003.
⁴ Amended by Criminal Justice Act 1991.

Aggravated burglary

10. —(1) A person is guilty of aggravated burglary if he commits any burglary and at the time has with him any firearm or imitation firearm, any weapon of offence, or any explosive; and for this purpose—

    (a) 'firearm' includes an airgun or air pistol, and 'imitation firearm' means anything which has the appearance of being a firearm, whether capable of being discharged or not; and

    (b) 'weapon of offence' means any article made or adapted for use for causing injury to or incapacitating a person, or intended by the person having it with him for such use; and

    (c) 'explosive' means any article manufactured for the purpose of producing a practical effect by explosion, or intended by the person having it with him for that purpose.

(2) A person guilty of aggravated burglary shall on conviction on indictment be liable to imprisonment for life.

Removal of articles from places open to the public

11. —(1) Subject to subsections (2) and (3) below, where the public have access to a building in order to view the building or part of it, or a collection or part of a collection housed in it, any person who without lawful authority removes from the building or its grounds the whole or part of any article displayed or kept for display to the public in the building or that part of it or in its grounds shall be guilty of an offence.

For this purpose 'collection' includes a collection got together for a temporary purpose, but references in this section to a collection do not apply to a collection made or exhibited for the purpose of effecting sales or other commercial dealings.

(2) It is immaterial for purposes of subsection (1) above, that the public's access to a building is limited to a particular period or particular occasion; but where anything removed from a building or its grounds is there otherwise than as forming part of, or being on loan for exhibition with, a collection intended for permanent exhibition to the public, the person removing it does not thereby commit an offence under this section unless he removes it on a day when the public have access to the building as mentioned in subsection (1) above.

(3) A person does not commit an offence under this section if he believes that he has lawful authority for the removal of the thing in question or that he would have it if the person entitled to give it knew of the removal and the circumstances of it.

(4) A person guilty of an offence under this section shall, on conviction on indictment, be liable to imprisonment for a term not exceeding five years.

Taking motor vehicle or other conveyance without authority

12. —(1) Subject to subsections (5) and (6) below, a person shall be guilty of an offence if, without having the consent of the owner or other lawful authority, he takes any conveyance for his own or another's use or, knowing that any conveyance has been taken without such authority, drives it or allows himself to be carried in or on it.

(2) A person guilty of an offence under subsection (1) above shall ... [be liable on summary conviction to a fine not exceeding level 5 on the standard scale, to imprisonment for a term not exceeding six months, or to both.][5]

---

[5] Amended by Criminal Justice Act 1988.

[…]⁶

(4)   If on the trial of an indictment for theft the jury are not satisfied that the accused committed theft, but it is proved that the accused committed an offence under subsection (1) above, the jury may find him guilty of the offence under subsection (1)[and if he is found guilty of it, he shall be liable as he would have been liable under subsection (2) above on summary conviction.]⁷

[(4A) Proceedings for an offence under subsection (1) above (but not proceedings of a kind falling within subsection (4) above) in relation to a mechanically propelled vehicle—

(a) shall not be commenced after the end of the period of three years beginning with the day on which the offence was committed; but

(b) subject to that, may be commenced at any time within the period of six months beginning with the relevant day.

(4B)   In subsection (4A)(b) above "the relevant day" means—

(a) in the case of a prosecution for an offence under subsection (1) above by a public prosecutor, the day on which sufficient evidence to justify the proceedings came to the knowledge of any person responsible for deciding whether to commence any such prosecution;

(b) in the case of a prosecution for an offence under subsection (1) above which is commenced by a person other than a public prosecutor after the discontinuance of a prosecution falling within paragraph (a) above which relates to the same facts, the day on which sufficient evidence to justify the proceedings came to the knowledge of the person who has decided to commence the prosecution or (if later) the discontinuance of the other prosecution;

(c) in the case of any other prosecution for an offence under subsection (1) above, the day on which sufficient evidence to justify the proceedings came to the knowledge of the person who has decided to commence the prosecution.

(4C)   For the purposes of subsection (4A)(b) above a certificate of a person responsible for deciding whether to commence a prosecution of a kind mentioned in subsection (4B)(a) above as to the date on which such evidence as is mentioned in the certificate came to the knowledge of any person responsible for deciding whether to commence any such prosecution shall be conclusive evidence of that fact.]⁸

(5)   Subsection (1) above shall not apply in relation to pedal cycles; but, subject to subsection (6) below, a person who, without having the consent of the owner or other lawful authority, takes a pedal cycle for his own or another's use, or rides a pedal cycle knowing it to have been taken without such authority, shall on summary conviction be liable to a fine [level 3 on the standard scale.]⁹

(6)   A person does not commit an offence under this section by anything done in the belief that he has lawful authority to do it or that he would have the owner's consent if the owner knew of his doing it and the circumstances of it.

(7)   For purposes of this section—

---

⁶ Repealed by Police and Criminal Evidence Act 1984.
⁷ Inserted by Criminal Justice Act 1988.   ⁸ Inserted by Vehicles (Crime) Act 2001.
⁹ Inserted by the Criminal Justice Act 1982.

(a) 'conveyance' means any conveyance constructed or adapted for the carriage of a person or persons whether by land, water or air, except that it does not include a conveyance constructed or adapted for use only under the control of a person not carried in or on it, and 'drive' shall be construed accordingly; and

(b) 'owner', in relation to a conveyance which is the subject of a hiring agreement or hire-purchase agreement, means the person in possession of the conveyance under that agreement.

[Aggravated vehicle-taking

12A. —(1) Subject to subsection (3) below, a person is guilty of aggravated taking of a vehicle if—

(a) he commits an offence under section 12(1) above (in this section referred to as a "basic offence") in relation to a mechanically propelled vehicle; and

(b) it is proved that, at any time after the vehicle was unlawfully taken (whether by him or another) and before it was recovered, the vehicle was driven, or injury or damage was caused, in one or more of the circumstances set out in paragraphs (a) to (d) of subsection (2) below.

(2) The circumstances referred to in subsection (1)(b) above are—

(a) that the vehicle was driven dangerously on a road or other public place;

(b) that, owing to the driving of the vehicle, an accident occurred by which injury was caused to any person;

(c) that, owing to the driving of the vehicle, an accident occurred by which damage was caused to any property, other than the vehicle;

(d) that damage was caused to the vehicle.

(3) A person is not guilty of an offence under this section if he proves that, as regards any such proven driving, injury or damage as is referred to in subsection (1)(b) above, either—

(a) the driving, accident or damage referred to in subsection (2) above occurred before he committed the basic offence; or

(b) he was neither in nor on nor in the immediate vicinity of the vehicle when that driving, accident or damage occurred.

(4) A person guilty of an offence under this section shall be liable on conviction on indictment to imprisonment for a term not exceeding two years or, if it is proved that, in circumstances falling within subsection (2)(b) above, the accident caused the death of the person concerned, [fourteen years.][10]

(5) If a person who is charged with an offence under this section is found not guilty of that offence but it is proved that he committed a basic offence, he may be convicted of the basic offence.

(6) If by virtue of subsection (5) above a person is convicted of a basic offence before the Crown Court, that court shall have the same powers and duties as a magistrates' court would have had on convicting him of such an offence.

(7) For the purposes of this section a vehicle is driven dangerously if—

---

[10] Inserted by Criminal Justice 2003.

(a) it is driven in a way which falls far below what would be expected of a competent and careful driver; and

(b) it would be obvious to a competent and careful driver that driving the vehicle in that way would be dangerous.

(8) For the purposes of this section a vehicle is recovered when it is restored to its owner or to other lawful possession or custody; and in this subsection "owner" has the same meaning as in section 12 above.][11]

Abstracting of electricity

13. A person who dishonestly uses without due authority, or dishonestly causes to be wasted or diverted, any electricity shall on conviction on indictment be liable to imprisonment for a term not exceeding five years.

Extension to thefts from mails outside England and Wales, and robbery etc. on such a theft

14. —(1) Where a person—

(a) steals or attempts to steal any mail bag or postal packet in the course of transmission as such between places in different jurisdictions in the British postal area, or any of the contents of such a mail bag or postal packet; or

(b) in stealing or with intent to steal any such mail bag or postal packet or any of its contents, commits any robbery, attempted robbery or assault with intent to rob; then, notwithstanding that he does so outside England and Wales, he shall be guilty of committing or attempting to commit the offence against this Act as if he had done so in England or Wales, and he shall accordingly be liable to be prosecuted, tried and punished in England and Wales without proof that the offence was committed there.

(2) In subsection (1) above the reference to different jurisdictions in the British postal area is to be construed as referring to the several jurisdictions of England and Wales, of Scotland, of Northern Ireland, of the Isle of Man and of the Channel Islands.

[...][12]

Fraud and blackmail

Obtaining property by deception
15.—[...][13]

Obtaining a money transfer by deception
15A.—[...][14]

Section 15A: supplementary
15B.[...][15]

---

[11] Inserted by the Aggravated Vehicle-Taking Act 1992.
[12] Repealed by Postal Services Act 2000.   [13] Repealed by Fraud Act 2006.
[14] Repealed by Fraud Act 2006.   [15] Repealed by Fraud Act 2006.

Obtaining pecuniary advantage by deception

16.—[...][16]

False accounting

17. —(1) Where a person dishonestly, with a view to gain for himself or another or with intent to cause loss to another,—

(a) destroys, defaces, conceals or falsifies any account or any record or document made or required for any accounting purpose; or

(b) in furnishing information for any purpose produces or makes use of any account, or any such record or document as aforesaid, which to his knowledge is or may be misleading, false or deceptive in a material particular; he shall, on conviction on indictment, be liable to imprisonment for a term not exceeding seven years.

(2) For purposes of this section a person who makes or concurs in making in an account or other document an entry which is or may be misleading, false or deceptive in a material particular, or who omits or concurs in omitting a material particular from an account or other document, is to be treated as falsifying the account or document.

Liability of company officers for certain offences by company

18. —(1) Where an offence committed by a body corporate under section [...][17] 17 of this Act is proved to have been committed with the consent or connivance of any director, manager, secretary or other similar officer of the body corporate, or any person who was purporting to act in any such capacity, he as well as the body corporate shall be guilty of that offence, and shall be liable to be proceeded against and punished accordingly.

(2) Where the affairs of a body corporate are managed by its members, this section shall apply in relation to the acts and defaults of a member in connection with his functions of management as if he were a director of the body corporate.

False statements by company directors, etc

19. —(1) Where an officer of a body corporate or unincorporated association (or person purporting to act as such), with intent to deceive members or creditors of the body corporate or association about its affairs, publishes or concurs in publishing a written statement or account which to his knowledge is or may be misleading, false or deceptive in a material particular, he shall on conviction on indictment be liable to imprisonment for a term not exceeding seven years.

(2) For purposes of this section a person who has entered into a security for the benefit of a body corporate or association is to be treated as a creditor of it.

(3) Where the affairs of a body corporate or association are managed by its members, this section shall apply to any statement which a member publishes or concurs in publishing in connection with his functions of management as if he were an officer of the body corporate or association.

Suppression, etc. of documents

20. —(1) A person who dishonestly, with a view to gain for himself or another or with intent to cause loss to another, destroys, defaces or conceals any valuable security, any will or other testamentary document or any original document of or belonging to, or filed or

---

[16] Repealed by Fraud Act 2006.   [17] Repealed by Fraud Act 2006.

deposited in, any court of justice or any government department shall on conviction on indictment be liable to imprisonment for a term not exceeding seven years.

(2) [...][18]

(3) For purposes of this section [...][19] 'valuable security' means any document creating, transferring, surrendering or releasing any right to, in or over property, or authorising the payment of money or delivery of any property, or evidencing the creation, transfer, surrender or release of any such right, or the payment of money or delivery of any property, or the satisfaction of any obligation.

Blackmail

21. —(1) A person is guilty of blackmail if, with a view to gain for himself or another or with intent to cause loss to another, he makes any unwarranted demand with menaces; and for this purpose a demand with menaces is unwarranted unless the person making it does so in the belief—

(a) that he has reasonable grounds for making the demand; and

(b) that the use of the menaces is a proper means of reinforcing the demand.

(2) The nature of the act or omission demanded is immaterial, and it is also immaterial whether the menaces relate to action to be taken by the person making the demand.

(3) A person guilty of blackmail shall on conviction on indictment be liable to imprisonment for a term not exceeding fourteen years.

Offences relating to goods stolen etc

Handling stolen goods

22. —(1) A person handles stolen goods if (otherwise than in the course of the stealing) knowing or believing them to be stolen goods he dishonestly receives the goods, or dishonestly undertakes or assists in their retention, removal, disposal or realisation by or for the benefit of another person, or if he arranges to do so.

(2) A person guilty of handling stolen goods shall on conviction on indictment be liable to imprisonment for a term not exceeding fourteen years.

Advertising rewards for return of goods stolen or lost

23. Where any public advertisement of a reward for the return of any goods which have been stolen or lost uses any words to the effect that no questions will be asked, or that the person producing the goods will be safe from apprehension or inquiry, or that any money paid for the purchase of the goods or advanced by way of loan on them will be repaid, the person advertising the reward and any person who prints or publishes the advertisement shall on summary conviction be liable to a fine not exceeding [level 3 on the standard scale.][20]

Scope of offences relating to stolen goods

24. —(1) The provisions of this Act relating to goods which have been stolen shall apply whether the stealing occurred in England or Wales or elsewhere, and whether it occurred

---

[18] Repealed by Fraud Act 2006.   [19] Repealed by Fraud Act 2006.
[20] Inserted by Criminal Justice Act 1982.

before or after the commencement of this Act, provided that the stealing (if not an offence under this Act) amounted to an offence where and at the time when the goods were stolen; and references to stolen goods shall be construed accordingly.

(2) For purposes of those provisions references to stolen goods shall include, in addition to the goods originally stolen and parts of them (whether in their original state or not),—

   (a) any other goods which directly or indirectly represent or have at any time represented the stolen goods in the hands of the thief as being the proceeds of any disposal or realisation of the whole or part of the goods stolen or of goods so representing the stolen goods; and

   (b) any other goods which directly or indirectly represent or have at any time represented the stolen goods in the hands of a handler of the stolen goods or any part of them as being the proceeds of any disposal or realisation of the whole or part of the stolen goods handled by him or of goods so representing them.

(3) But no goods shall be regarded as having continued to be stolen goods after they have been restored to the person from whom they were stolen or to other lawful possession or custody, or after that person and any other person claiming through him have otherwise ceased as regards those goods to have any right to restitution in respect of the theft.

(4) For purposes of the provisions of this Act relating to goods which have been stolen (including subsections (1) to (3) above) goods obtained in England or Wales or elsewhere either by blackmail or[, subject to subsection (5) below, by fraud (within meaning of the Fraud Act 2006)][21] shall be regarded as stolen; and 'steal', 'theft' and 'thief' shall be construed accordingly.

[(5) Subsection (1) above applies in relation to goods obtained by fraud as if-

   (a) the reference to the commencement of this Act were a reference to the commencement of the Fraud Act 2006, and

   (b) the reference to an offence under this Act were a reference to an offence under section 1 of that Act.][22]

[Dishonestly retaining a wrongful credit]

[24A —(1) A person is guilty of an offence if–

   (a) a wrongful credit has been made to an account kept by him or in respect of which he has any right or interest;

   (b) he knows or believes that the credit is wrongful; and

   (c) he dishonestly fails to take such steps as are reasonable in the circumstances to secure that the credit is cancelled.

(2) References to a credit are to a credit of an amount of money.

[(2A) A credit to an account is wrongful to the extent it derives from—

   (a) theft;

   (b) blackmail;

   (c) fraud (contrary to section 1 of the Fraud Act 2006); or

   (d) stolen goods.][23]

---

[21] Inserted by Fraud Act 2006.   [22] Inserted by Fraud Act 2006.
[23] Inserted by Fraud Act 2006.

[...]24

(5) In determining whether a credit to an account is wrongful, it is immaterial (in particular) whether the account is overdrawn before or after the credit is made.

(6) A person guilty of an offence under this section shall be liable on conviction on indictment to imprisonment for a term not exceeding ten years.

(7) Subsection (8) below applies for purposes of provisions of this Act relating to stolen goods (including subsection [2A]25above).

(8) References to stolen goods include money which is dishonestly withdrawn from an account to which a wrongful credit has been made, but only to the extent that the money derives from the credit.

(9) ["Account" means an account kept with-
   (a) a bank;
   (b) a person carrying on a business which falls within subsection (10) below; or
   (c) an issuer of electronic money (as defined for the purposes of Part 2 of the Financial Services and Markets Act 2000).

(10) A business falls within this subsection if-
   (a) in the course of the business money received by way of deposit is lent to others; or
   (b) any other activity of the business is financed, wholly or to any material extent, out of the capital or of the interest on money received by way of deposit.

(11) References in subsection (10) above to a deposit must be read with-
   (a) section 22 of the Financial Services and Markets Act 2000;
   (b) any relevant order made under that section; and
   (c) Schedule 2 to that Act;
   but any restriction on the meaning of deposit which arises from the identity of the person making it is to be disregarded.

(12) For the purposes of subsection (10) above-

   (a) all the activities which a person carries on by way of business shall be regarded as a single business carried on by him; and

   (b) "money" includes money expressed in a currency other than sterling.]26

Possession of housebreaking implements, etc

Going equipped for stealing, etc

25. —(1) A person shall be guilty of an offence if, when not at his place of abode, he has with him any article for use in the course of or in connection with any [burglary or theft]27.

(2) A person guilty of an offence under this section shall on conviction on indictment be liable to imprisonment for a term not exceeding three years.

(3) Where a person is charged with an offence under this section, proof that he had with him any article made or adapted for use in committing a [burglary or theft]28 shall be evidence that he had it with him for such use.
   [...]29

---

24 Repealed by Fraud Act 2006.   25 Amended by Fraud Act 2006.
26 Inserted by Fraud Act 2006.   27 Amended by Fraud Act 2006.
28 Amended by Fraud Act 2006.
29 Repealed by Serious Organised Crime and Police Act 2005.

(5) For purposes of this section an offence under section 12(1) of this Act of taking a conveyance shall be treated as theft [...][30].

Enforcement and procedure

Search for stolen goods

26. —(1) If it is made to appear by information on oath before a justice of the peace that there is reasonable cause to believe that any person has in his custody or possession or on his premises any stolen goods, the justice may grant a warrant to search for and seize the same; but no warrant to search for stolen goods shall be addressed to a person other than a constable except under the authority of an enactment expressly so providing.

[...][31]

(3) Where under this section a person is authorised to search premises for stolen goods, he may enter and search the premises accordingly, and may seize any goods he believes to be stolen goods.

[...][32]

(5) This section is to be construed in accordance with section 24 of this Act; and in subsection (2) above the references to handling stolen goods shall include any corresponding offence committed before the commencement of this Act.

Evidence and procedure on charge of theft or handling stolen goods

27. —(1) Any number of persons may be charged in one indictment, with reference to the same theft, with having at different times or at the same time handled all or any of the stolen goods, and the persons so charged may be tried together.

(2) On the trial of two or more persons indicted for jointly handling any stolen goods the jury may find any of the accused guilty if the jury are satisfied that he handled all or any of the stolen goods, whether or not he did so jointly with the other accused or any of them.

(3) Where a person is being proceeded against for handling stolen goods (but not for any offence other than handling stolen goods), then at any stage of the proceedings, if evidence has been given of his having or arranging to have in his possession the goods the subject of the charge, or of his undertaking or assisting in, or arranging to undertake or assist in, their retention, removal, disposal or realisation, the following evidence shall be admissible for the purpose of proving that he knew or believed the goods to be stolen goods:—

(a) evidence that he has had in his possession, or has undertaken or assisted in the retention, removal, disposal or realisation of, stolen goods from any theft taking place not earlier than twelve months before the offence charged; and

(b) (provided that seven days' notice in writing has been given to him of the intention to prove the conviction) evidence that he has within the five years preceding the date of the offence charged been convicted of theft or of handling stolen goods.

---

[30] Repealed by Fraud Act 2006.
[31] Repealed by Police and Criminal Evidence Act 1984.
[32] Repealed by Criminal Justice Act 1972.

(4)	In any proceedings for the theft of anything in the course of transmission (whether by post or otherwise), or for handling stolen goods from such a theft, a statutory declaration made by any person that he despatched or received or failed to receive any goods or postal packet, or that any goods or postal packet when despatched or received by him were in a particular state or condition, shall be admissible as evidence of the facts stated in the declaration, subject to the following conditions:—

(a)	a statutory declaration shall only be admissible where and to the extent to which oral evidence to the like effect would have been admissible in the proceedings; and

(b)	a statutory declaration shall only be admissible if at least seven days before the hearing or trial a copy of it has been given to the person charged, and he has not, at least three days before the hearing or trial or within such further time as the court may in special circumstances allow, given the prosecutor written notice requiring the attendance at the hearing or trial of the person making the declaration.

[(4A)	Where the proceedings mentioned in subsection (4) above are proceedings before a magistrates' court inquiring into an offence as examining justices that subsection shall have effect with the omission of the words from "subject to the following conditions" to the end of the subsection.][33]

(5)	This section is to be construed in accordance with section 24 of this Act; and in subsection (3)(b) above the reference to handling stolen goods shall include any corresponding offence committed before the commencement of this Act.

28.—[…][34]
29.—[…][35]

General and consequential provisions

[Spouses and civil partners][36]

30. —(1) This Act shall apply in relation to the parties to a marriage, and to property belonging to the wife or husband whether or not by reason of an interest derived from the marriage, as it would apply if they were not married and any such interest subsisted independently of the marriage.

(2) Subject to subsection (4) below, a person shall have the same right to bring proceedings against that person's wife or husband for any offence (whether under this Act or otherwise) as if they were not married, and a person bringing any such proceedings shall be competent to give evidence for the prosecution at every stage of the proceedings. […][37]

(4) Proceedings shall not be instituted against a person for any offence of stealing or doing unlawful damage to property which at the time of the offence belongs to that person's wife or husband [or civil partner], or for any attempt, incitement or conspiracy to commit such an offence, unless the proceedings are instituted by or with the consent of the Director of Public Prosecutions:

---

[33] Inserted by Criminal Procedure and Investigations Act 1996 and to be repealed by Criminal Justice Act 2003.
[34] Repealed by Powers of Criminal Courts (Sentencing) Act 2000.
[35] Repealed by Courts Act 1971.	[36] Amended by Civil Partnership Act 2004.
[37] Repealed by Police and Criminal Evidence Act 1984.

Provided that—

(a) this subsection shall not apply to proceedings against a person for an offence—

    (i) if that person is charged with committing the offence jointly with the wife or husband [or civil partner]; or

    (ii) if by virtue of any judicial decree or order (wherever made) that person and the wife or husband are at the time of the offence under no obligation to cohabit; [or

    (iii) an order (wherever made) is in force providing for the separation of that person and his or her civil partner.]

[(5) Notwithstanding [section 6 of the Prosecution of Offences Act 1979] subsection (4) of this section shall apply—

(a) to an arrest (if without warrant) made by the wife or husband [or civil partner], and

(b) to a warrant of arrest issued on an information laid by the wife or husband [or civil partner].][38]

Effect on civil proceedings and rights

31. —(1) A person shall not be excused, by reason that to do so may incriminate that person or the wife or husband of that person of an offence under this Act—

(a) from answering any question put to that person in proceedings for the recovery or administration of any property, for the execution of any trust or for an account of any property or dealings with property; or

(b) from complying with any order made in any such proceedings;

but no statement or admission made by a person in answering a question put or complying with an order made as aforesaid shall, in proceedings for an offence under this Act, be admissible in evidence against that person or (unless they [married or became civil partners after the making of the statement or admission) against the spouse or civil partner][39] of that person.

(2) Notwithstanding any enactment to the contrary, where property has been stolen or obtained by fraud or other wrongful means, the title to that or any other property shall not be affected by reason only of the conviction of the offender.

Effect on existing law and construction of references to offences

32. —(1) The following offences are hereby abolished for all purposes not relating to offences committed before the commencement of this Act, that is to say—

(a) any offence at common law of larceny, robbery, burglary, receiving stolen property, obtaining property by threats, extortion by colour of office or franchise, false accounting by public officers, concealment of treasure trove and, except as regards offences relating to the public revenue, cheating; and

(b) any offence under an enactment mentioned in Part I of Schedule 3 to this Act, to the extent to which the offence depends on any section or part of a section included in column 3 of that Schedule;

---

[38] Section appears as amended or repealed by: Civil Partnership Act 2004; Criminal Jurisdiction Act 1975; and Prosecution of Offences Act 1979.

[39] Inserted by Civil Partnership Act 2004.

but so that the provisions in Schedule 1 to this Act (which preserve with modifications certain offences under the Larceny Act 1861 of taking or killing deer and taking or destroying fish) shall have effect as there set out.

(2) Except as regards offences committed before the commencement of this Act, and except in so far as the context otherwise requires,—

(a) references in any enactment passed before this Act to an offence abolished by this Act shall, subject to any express amendment or repeal made by this Act, have effect as references to the corresponding offence under this Act, and in any such enactment the expression 'receive' (when it relates to an offence of receiving) shall mean handle, and 'receiver' shall be construed accordingly; and

(b) without prejudice to paragraph (a) above, references in any enactment, whenever passed, to theft or stealing (including references to stolen goods), and references to robbery, blackmail, burglary, aggravated burglary or handling stolen goods, shall be construed in accordance with the provisions of this Act, including those of section 24.

Miscellaneous and consequential amendments, and repeal

33. —(1) [...]

...

(4) No amendment or repeal made by this Act in Schedule 1 to the Extradition Act 1870 or in the Schedule to the Extradition Act 1873 shall affect the operation of that Schedule by reference to the law of a British possession; but the repeal made in Schedule 1 to the Extradition Act 1870 shall extend throughout the United Kingdom.

Supplementary

Interpretation

34. —(1) Sections 4(1) and 5(1) of this Act shall apply generally for purposes of this Act as they apply for purposes of section 1.

(2) For purposes of this Act—

(a) 'gain' and 'loss' are to be construed as extending only to gain or loss in money or other property, but as extending to any such gain or loss whether temporary or permanent; and—

(i) 'gain' includes a gain by keeping what one has, as well as a gain by getting what one has not; and

(ii) 'loss' includes a loss by not getting what one might get, as well as a loss by parting with what one has;

(b) 'goods', except in so far as the context otherwise requires, includes money and every other description of property except land, and includes things severed from the land by stealing[; and

(c) "mail bag" and "postal packet" have the meanings given by section 125(1) of the Postal Services Act 2000.[40]

---

[40] Inserted by SI 2003/2908.

Commencement and transitional provisions

35. —(1) This Act shall come into force on the 1st January 1969 and, save as otherwise provided by this Act, shall have effect only in relation to offences wholly or partly committed on or after that date.

(2) [Section 27 of this Act and section 148 of the Powers of Criminal Courts (Sentencing) Act 2000][41] shall apply in relation to proceedings for an offence committed before the commencement of this Act as they would apply in relation to proceedings for a corresponding offence under this Act, and shall so apply in place of any corresponding enactment repealed by this Act.

(3) Subject to subsection (2) above, no repeal or amendment by this Act of any enactment relating to procedure or evidence, or to the jurisdiction or powers of any court, or to the effect of a conviction, shall affect the operation of the enactment in relation to offences committed before the commencement of this Act or to proceedings for any such offence.

Short title, and general provisions as to Scotland and Northern Ireland

36. —(1) This Act may be cited as the Theft Act 1968.

...

(3) This Act does not extend to Scotland or ... to Northern Ireland, except as regards any amendment or repeal which in accordance with section 33 above is to extend to Scotland or Northern Ireland.

SCHEDULES

Section 32.

SCHEDULE 1

OFFENCES OF TAKING, ETC. DEER OR FISH

...

Taking or destroying fish

2. —(1) Subject to subparagraph (2) below, a person who unlawfully takes or destroys, or attempts to take or destroy, any fish in water which is private property or in which there is any private right of fishery shall on summary conviction be liable to a fine not exceeding fifty pounds or, for an offence committed after a previous conviction of an offence under this subparagraph, to imprisonment for a term not exceeding three months or to a fine not exceeding one hundred pounds or to both.

(2) Subparagraph (1) above shall not apply to taking or destroying fish by angling in the daytime (that is to say, in the period beginning one hour before sunrise and ending one hour after sunset); but a person who by angling in the daytime unlawfully takes or destroys, or attempts to take or destroy, any fish in water which is private property or in

---

[41] Amended by Powers of Criminal Courts (Sentencing) Act 2000.

which there is any private right of fishery shall on summary conviction be liable to a fine not exceeding [level 1 on the standard scale.]

(3) The court by which a person is convicted of an offence under this paragraph may order the forfeiture of anything which, at the time of the offence, he had with him for use for taking or destroying fish.

(4) Any person may arrest without warrant anyone who is, or whom he, with reasonable cause, suspects to be, committing an offence under subparagraph (1) above, and may seize from any person who is, or whom he, with reasonable cause, suspects to be, committing any offence under this paragraph anything which on that person's conviction of the offence would be liable to be forfeited under subparagraph (3) above.

B. THEFT ACT 1978

An Act to replace section 16(2)(a) of the Theft Act 1968 with other provision against fraudulent conduct; and for connected purposes.   [20th July 1978]

BE IT ENACTED by the Queen's most Excellent Majesty, by and with the advice and consent of the Lords Spiritual and Temporal, and Commons, in this present Parliament assembled, and by the authority of the same, as follows:—

Obtaining services by deception

1.—[...]42

Evasion of liability by deception

2.—[...]43

Making off without payment

3. —(1) Subject to subsection (3) below, a person who, knowing that payment on the spot for any goods supplied or service done is required or expected from him, dishonestly makes off without having paid as required or expected and with intent to avoid payment of the amount due shall be guilty of an offence.

(2) For purposes of this section 'payment on the spot' includes payment at the time of collecting goods on which work has been done or in respect of which service has been provided.

(3) Subsection (1) above shall not apply where the supply of the goods or the doing of the service is contrary to law, or where the service done is such that payment is not legally enforceable.

(4) Any person may arrest without warrant anyone who is, or whom he, with reasonable cause, suspects to be, committing or attempting to commit an offence under this section.

Punishments

4. —(1) Offences under this Act shall be punishable either on conviction on indictment or on summary conviction.

(2) A person convicted on indictment shall be liable—

---

42 Repealed by Fraud Act 2006.   43 Repealed by Fraud Act 2006.

[...]⁴⁴

(b) for an offence under section 3 of this Act, to imprisonment for a term not exceeding two years.

(3) A person convicted summarily of any offence under this Act shall be liable—

(a) to imprisonment for a term not exceeding six months; or

(b) to a fine not exceeding the prescribed sum for the purposes of [section 32 of the Magistrates' Courts Act 1980]⁴⁵ (punishment on summary conviction of offences triable either way: 1,000 or other sum substituted by order under that Act), or to both.

Supplementary

5. —(1) [...]⁴⁶

(2) Sections 30(1) (husband and wife), 31(1) (effect on civil proceedings) and 34 (interpretation) of the Theft Act 1968, so far as they are applicable in relation to this Act, shall apply as they apply in relation to that Act.

...

Enactment of same provisions for Northern Ireland

6. An Order in Council under paragraph 1(1)(b) of Schedule 1 to the Northern Ireland Act 1974 (legislation for Northern Ireland in the interim period) which contains a statement that it operates only so as to make for Northern Ireland provision corresponding to this Act—

(a) shall not be subject to paragraph 1(4) and (5) of that Schedule (affirmative resolution of both Houses of Parliament); but

(b) shall be subject to annulment by resolution of either House.

Short title, commencement and extent

7. —(1) This Act may be cited as the Theft Act 1978.

(2) This Act shall come into force at the expiration of three months beginning with the date on which it is passed.

(3) This Act except section 5(3), shall not extend to Scotland; and except for that subsection, and subject also to section 6, it shall not extend to Northern Ireland.

C. FORGERY AND COUNTERFEITING ACT 1981 (SS 1–10)

An Act to make fresh provision for England and Wales and Northern Ireland with respect to forgery and kindred offences; to make fresh provision for Great Britain and Northern Ireland with respect to the counterfeiting of notes and coins and kindred offences; to amend the penalties for offences under section 63 of the Post Office Act 1953; and for connected purposes.   [27th July 1981]

---

⁴⁴ Repealed by Fraud Act 2006.   ⁴⁵ Amended by Magistrates' Court Act 1980.
⁴⁶ Repealed by Fraud Act 2006.

BE IT ENACTED by the Queen's most Excellent Majesty, by and with the advice and consent of the Lords Spiritual and Temporal, and Commons, in this present Parliament assembled, and by the authority of the same, as follows:—

PART I

FORGERY AND KINDRED OFFENCES

Offences

The offence of forgery

1. A person is guilty of forgery if he makes a false instrument, with the intention that he or another shall use it to induce somebody to accept it as genuine, and by reason of so accepting it to do or not to do some act to his own or any other person's prejudice.

The offence of copying a false instrument

2. It is an offence for a person to make a copy of an instrument which is, and which he knows or believes to be, a false instrument, with the intention that he or another shall use it to induce somebody to accept it as a copy of a genuine instrument, and by reason of so accepting it to do or not to do some act to his own or any other person's prejudice.

The offence of using a false instrument

3. It is an offence for a person to use an instrument which is, and which he knows or believes to be, false, with the intention of inducing somebody to accept it as genuine, and by reason of so accepting it to do or not to do some act to his own or any other person's prejudice.

The offence of using a copy of a false instrument

4. It is an offence for a person to use a copy of an instrument which is, and which he knows or believes to be, a false instrument, with the intention of inducing somebody to accept it as a copy of a genuine instrument, and by reason of so accepting it to do or not to do some act to his own or any other person's prejudice.

Offences relating to money orders share certificates passports, etc

5. —(1) It is an offence for a person to have in his custody or under his control an instrument to which this section applies which is, and which he knows or believes to be, false, with the intention that he or another shall use it to induce somebody to accept it as genuine, and by reason of so accepting it to do or not to do some act to his own or any other person's prejudice.

(2) It is an offence for a person to have in his custody or under his control, without lawful authority or excuse, an instrument to which this section applies which is, and which he knows or believes to be, false.

(3) It is an offence for a person to make or to have in his custody or under his control a machine or implement, or paper or any other material, which to his knowledge is or has been specially designed or adapted for the making of an instrument to which this section applies, with the intention that he or another shall make an instrument to which this

section applies which is false and that he or another shall use the instrument to induce somebody to accept it as genuine, and by reason of so accepting it to do or not to do some act to his own or any other person's prejudice.

(4) It is an offence for a person to make or to have in his custody or under his control any such machine, implement, paper or material, without lawful authority or excuse.

(5) The instruments to which this section applies are—

    (a)   money orders;

    (b)   postal orders;

    (c)   United Kingdom postage stamps;

    (d)   Inland Revenue stamps;

    (e)   share certificates;

    (f)   [...][47]

    (fa)   [...][48]

    (g)   cheques [and other bills of exchange];

    (h)   travellers' cheques;

    [(ha) bankers' drafts;

    (hb) promissory notes;][49]

    (j)   cheque cards;

    [(ja) debit cards;][50]

    (k)   credit cards;

    (l)   certified copies relating to an entry in a register of births, adoptions, marriages or deaths and issued by the Registrar General, the Registrar General for Northern Ireland, a registration officer or a person lawfully authorised to [issue certified copies relating to such entries][51]; and

    (m) certificates relating to entries in such registers.

(6) In subsection (5) (e) above 'share certificate' means an instrument entitling or evidencing the title of a person to a share or interest—

    (a) in any public stock, annuity, fund or debt of any government or state, including a state which forms part of another state; or

    (b) in any stock, fund or debt of a body (whether corporate or unincorporated) established in the United Kingdom or elsewhere.

[(7) An instrument is also an instrument to which this section applies if it is a monetary instrument specified for the purposes of this section by an order made by the Secretary of State.

(8) The power under subsection (7) above is exercisable by statutory instrument subject to annulment in pursuance of a resolution of either House of Parliament.][52]

    ...

---

[47] Repealed by Identity Cards Act 2006.

[48] Inserted by Asylum and Immigration Act 2004 and repealed by Identity Cards Act 2006.

[49] Inserted by Crime (International Co-operation) Act 2003.

[50] Inserted by Crime (International Co-operation) Act 2003.

[51] Inserted by Civil Partnership Act 2004.

[52] Inserted by Crim (International Co-operation) Act 2003.

Penalties etc

Penalties for offences under Part I

6.   —(1) A person guilty of an offence under this Part of this Act shall be liable on summary conviction—
   (a) to a fine not exceeding the statutory maximum; or
   (b) to imprisonment for a term not exceeding six months; or
   (c) to both.

(2) A person guilty of an offence to which this subsection applies shall be liable on conviction on indictment to imprisonment for a term not exceeding ten years.

(3) The offences to which subsection (2) above applies are offences under the following provisions of this Part of this Act—
   (a) section 1;
   (b) section 2;
   (c) section 3;
   (d) section 4;
   (e) section 5(1); and
   (f) section 5(3).

(4) A person guilty of an offence under section 5(2) or (4) above shall be liable on conviction on indictment to imprisonment for a term not exceeding two years.

...

Powers of search, forfeiture, etc

7.   —(1) If it appears to a justice of the peace, from information given him on oath, that there is reasonable cause to believe that a person has in his custody or under his control—
   (a) any thing which he or another has used, whether before or after the coming into force of this Act, or intends to use, for the making of any false instrument or copy of a false instrument, in contravention of section 1 or 2 above; or
   (b) any false instrument or copy of a false instrument which he or another has used, whether before or after the coming into force of this Act, or intends to use, in contravention of section 3 or 4 above; or
   (c) any thing custody or control of which without lawful authority or excuse is an offence under section 5 above, the justice may issue a warrant authorising a constable to search for and seize the object in question, and for that purpose to enter any premises specified in the warrant.

(2) A constable may at any time after the seizure of any object suspected of falling within paragraph (a), (b) or (c) of subsection (1) above (whether the seizure was effected by virtue of a warrant under that subsection or otherwise) apply to a magistrates' court for an order under this subsection with respect to the object; and the court, if it is satisfied both that the object in fact falls within any of those paragraphs and that it is conducive to the public interest to do so, may make such order as it thinks fit for the forfeiture of the object and its subsequent destruction or disposal.

(3) Subject to subsection (4) below, the court by or before which a person is convicted of an offence under this Part of this Act may order any object shown to the satisfaction of the

court to relate to the offence to be forfeited and either destroyed or dealt with in such other manner as the court may order.

(4) The court shall not order any object to be forfeited under subsection (2) or (3) above where a person claiming to be the owner of or otherwise interested in it applies to be heard by the court, unless an opportunity has been given to him to show cause why the order should not be made.

Interpretation of Part I

Meaning of 'instrument'

8. —(1) Subject to subsection (2) below, in this Part of this Act 'instrument' means—
    (a) any document, whether of a formal or informal character;
    (b) any stamp issued or sold by [a postal operator][53];
    (c) any Inland Revenue stamp; and
    (d) any disc, tape, sound track or other device on or in which information is recorded or stored by mechanical, electronic or other means.

(2) A currency note within the meaning of Part II of this Act is not an instrument for the purposes of this Part of this Act.

(3) A mark denoting payment of postage which [a postal operator authorises][54] to be used instead of an adhesive stamp is to be treated for the purposes of this Part of this Act as if it were a stamp issued by the [postal operator concerned.][55]

[(3A) In this section "postal operator" has the same meaning as in the Postal Services Act 2000.][56]

(4) In this Part of this Act 'Inland Revenue stamp' means a stamp as defined in section 27 of the Stamp Duties Management Act 1891.

Meaning of 'false' and 'making'

9. —(1) An instrument is false for the purposes of this Part of this Act—
    (a) if it purports to have been made in the form in which it is made by a person who did not in fact make it in that form; or
    (b) if it purports to have been made in the form in which it is made on the authority of a person who did not in fact authorise its making in that form; or
    (c) if it purports to have been made in the terms in which it is made by a person who did not in fact make it in those terms; or
    (d) if it purports to have been made in the terms in which it is made on the authority of a person who did not in fact authorise its making in those terms; or
    (e) if it purports to have been altered in any respect by a person who did not in fact alter it in that respect; or
    (f) if it purports to have been altered in any respect on the authority of a person who did not in fact authorise the alteration in that respect; or

---

[53] Substituted by SI 2001/1149.   [54] Substituted by SI 2001/1149.
[55] Substituted by SI 2001/1149.   [56] Substituted by SI 2001/1149.

(g) if it purports to have been made or altered on a date on which, or at a place at which, or otherwise in circumstances in which, it was not in fact made or altered; or

(h) if it purports to have been made or altered by an existing person but he did not in fact exist.

(2) A person is to be treated for the purposes of this Part of this Act as making a false instrument if he alters an instrument so as to make it false in any respect (whether or not it is false in some other respect apart from that alteration).

Meaning of 'prejudice' and 'induce'

10. —(1) Subject to subsections (2) and (4) below, for the purposes of this Part of this Act an act or omission intended to be induced is to a person's prejudice if, and only if, it is one which, if it occurs—

(a) will result—
    (i) in his temporary or permanent loss of property; or
    (ii) in his being deprived of an opportunity to earn remuneration or greater remuneration; or
    (iii) in his being deprived of an opportunity to gain a financial advantage otherwise than by way of remuneration; or

(b) will result in somebody being given an opportunity—
    (i) to earn remuneration or greater remuneration from him; or
    (ii) to gain a financial advantage from him otherwise than by way of remuneration; or

(c) will be the result of his having accepted a false instrument as genuine, or a copy of a false instrument as a copy of a genuine one, in connection with his performance of any duty.

(2) An act which a person has an enforceable duty to do and an omission to do an act which a person is not entitled to do shall be disregarded for the purposes of this Part of this Act.

(3) In this Part of this Act references to inducing somebody to accept a false instrument as genuine, or a copy of a false instrument as a copy of a genuine one, include references to inducing a machine to respond to the instrument or copy as if it were a genuine instrument or, as the case may be, a copy of a genuine one.

(4) Where subsection (3) above applies, the act or omission intended to be induced by the machine responding to the instrument or copy shall be treated as an act or omission to a person's prejudice.

(5) In this section 'loss' includes not getting what one might get as well as parting with what one has.

D. COPYRIGHT, DESIGNS AND PATENTS ACT 1988 (SS 107, 110, 198, 201, 202, 297, AND 300)

Criminal liability for making or dealing with infringing articles, &c

107. —(1) A person commits an offence who, without the licence of the copyright owner—

(a) makes for sale or hire, or

    (b) imports into the United Kingdom otherwise than for his private and domestic use, or

    (c) possesses in the course of a business with a view to committing any act infringing the copyright, or

    (d) in the course of a business—

        (i) sells or lets for hire, or

        (ii) offers or exposes for sale or hire, or

        (iii) exhibits in public, or

        (iv) distributes, or

    (e) distributes otherwise than in the course of a business to such an extent as to affect prejudicially the owner of the copyright, an article which is, and which he knows or has reason to believe is, an infringing copy of a copyright work.

(2) A person commits an offence who—

    (a) makes an article specifically designed or adapted for making copies of a particular copyright work, or

    (b) has such an article in his possession, knowing or having reason to believe that it is to be used to make infringing copies for sale or hire or for use in the course of a business.

[(2A) A person who infringes copyright in a work by communicating the work to the public—

    (a) in the course of a business, or

    (b) otherwise than in the course of a business to such an extent as to affect prejudicially the owner of the copyright,

commits an offence if he knows or has reason to believe that, by doing so, he is infringing copyright in that work.][57]

(3) Where copyright is infringed (otherwise than by reception of a [communication to the public][58])—

    (a) by the public performance of a literary, dramatic or musical work, or

    (b) by the playing or showing in public of a sound recording or film,

any person who caused the work to be so performed, played or shown is guilty of an offence if he knew or had reason to believe that copyright would be infringed.

(4) A person guilty of an offence under subsection (1)(a), (b), (d)(iv) or (e) is liable—

    (a) on summary conviction to imprisonment for a term not exceeding six months or a fine not exceeding the statutory maximum, or both;

    (b) on conviction on indictment to a fine or imprisonment for a term not exceeding [ten][59] years, or both.

[(4A) A person guilty of an offence under subsection (2A) is liable—

    (a) on summary conviction to imprisonment for a term not exceeding three months or a fine not exceeding the statutory maximum, or both;

    (b) on conviction on indictment to a fine or imprisonment for a term not exceeding two years, or both.][60]

---

[57] Inserted by SI 2003/2498.   [58] Substituted by SI 2003/2498.

[59] Amended by Copyright and Trade Marks (Offences and Enforcement) Act 2002.

[60] Inserted by SI 2003/2498.

(5) A person guilty of any other offence under this section is liable on summary conviction to imprisonment for a term not exceeding six months or a fine not exceeding level 5 on the standard scale, or both.

(6) Sections 104 to 106 (presumptions as to various matters connected with copyright) do not apply to proceedings for an offence under this section; but without prejudice to their application in proceedings for an order under section 108 below.

Offence by body corporate: liability of officers

110. —(1) Where an offence under section 107 committed by a body corporate is proved to have been committed with the consent or connivance of a director, manager, secretary or other similar officer of the body, or a person purporting to act in any such capacity, he as well as the body corporate is guilty of the offence and liable to be proceeded against and punished accordingly.

(2) In relation to a body corporate whose affairs are managed by its members 'director' means a member of the body corporate.

Criminal liability for making, dealing with or using illicit recordings

198. —(1) A person commits an offence who without sufficient consent—
   (a) makes for sale or hire, or
   (b) imports into the United Kingdom otherwise than for his private and domestic use, or
   (c) possesses in the course of a business with a view to committing any act infringing the rights conferred by this [Chapter][61], or
   (d) in the course of a business—
      (i) sells or lets for hire, or
      (ii) offers or exposes for sale or hire, or
      (iii) distributes, a recording which is, and which he knows or has reason to believe is, an illicit recording.

[(1A) A person who infringes a performer's making available right—
   (a) in the course of a business, or
   (b) otherwise than in the course of a business to such an extent as to affect prejudicially the owner of the making available right,
   commits an offence if he knows or has reason to believe that, by doing so, he is infringing the making available right in the recording.][62]

(2) A person commits an offence who causes a recording of a performance made without sufficient consent to be—
   (a) shown or played in public, or
   (b) [communicated to the public,][63]
   thereby infringing any of the rights conferred by this [Chapter][64], if he knows or has reason to believe that those rights are thereby infringed.

(3) In subsections (1) and (2) 'sufficient consent' means—
   (a) in the case of a qualifying performance, the consent of the performer, and
   (b) in the case of a non-qualifying performance subject to an exclusive recording contract—

---

[61] Inserted by SI 2006/18.   [62] Inserted by SI 2003/2498.
[63] Amended by SI 2003/2498.   [64] Inserted by SI 2006/18.

(i) for the purposes of subsection (1)(a) (making of recording), the consent of the performer or the person having recording rights, and

(ii) for the purposes of subsection (1)(b), (c) and (d) and subsection (2) (dealing with or using recording), the consent of the person having recording rights.

The references in this subsection to the person having recording rights are to the person having those rights at the time the consent is given or, if there is more than one such person, to all of them.

(4)   No offence is committed under subsection (1) or (2) by the commission of an act which by virtue of any provision of Schedule 2 may be done without infringing the rights conferred by this [Chapter.][65]

(5)   A person guilty of an offence under subsection (1)(a), (b) or (d)(iii) is liable—

(a) on summary conviction to imprisonment for a term not exceeding six months or a fine not exceeding the statutory maximum, or both;

(b) on conviction on indictment to a fine or imprisonment for a term not exceeding [ten][66] years, or both.

[(5A) A person guilty of an offence under subsection (1A) is liable—

(a) on summary conviction to imprisonment for a term not exceeding three months or a fine not exceeding the statutory maximum, or both;

(b) on conviction on indictment to a fine or imprisonment for a term not exceeding two years, or both.][67]

(6)   A person guilty of any other offence under this section is liable on summary conviction to a fine not exceeding level 5 on the standard scale or imprisonment for a term not exceeding six months, or both.

False representation of authority to give consent

201.   —(1) It is an offence for a person to represent falsely that he is authorised by any person to give consent for the purposes of this [Chapter][68] in relation to a performance, unless he believes on reasonable grounds that he is so authorised.

(2)   A person guilty of an offence under this section is liable on summary conviction to imprisonment for a term not exceeding six months or a fine not exceeding level 5 on the standard scale or both.

Offence by body corporate: liability of officers

202.   —(1) Where an offence under this Part committed by a body corporate is proved to have been committed with the consent or connivance of a director, manager, secretary or other similar officer of the body, or a person purporting to act in any such capacity, he as well as the body corporate is guilty of the offence and liable to be proceeded against and punished accordingly.

(2)   In relation to a body corporate whose affairs are managed by its members 'director' means a member of the body corporate.

---

[65] Inserted by SI 2006/18.
[66] Amended by Copyright and Trade Marks (Offences and Enforcement) Act 2002.
[67] Inserted by SI 2003/2498.   [68] Amended by SI 2006/18.

Offence of fraudulently receiving programme

297. —(1) A person who dishonestly receives a programme included in a broadcasting [...]⁶⁹ service provided from a place in the United Kingdom with intent to avoid payment of any charge applicable to the reception of the programme commits an offence and is liable on summary conviction to a fine not exceeding level 5 on the standard scale.

(2) Where an offence under this section committed by a body corporate is proved to have been committed with the consent or connivance of a director, manager, secretary or other similar officer of the body, or a person purporting to act in any such capacity, he as well as the body corporate is guilty of the offence and liable to be proceeded against and punished accordingly.

In relation to a body corporate whose affairs are managed by its members 'director' means a member of the body corporate.

Fraudulent application or use of trade mark an offence

300. In the Trade Marks Act 1938 the following sections are inserted before section 59, after the heading ''*Offences and restraint of use of Royal Arms*''—
    'Fraudulent application or use of trade mark an offence.

58A. —(1) It is an offence, subject to subsection (3) below, for a person—

    (a) to apply a mark identical to or nearly resembling a registered trade mark to goods, or to material used or intended to be used for labelling, packaging or advertising goods, or

    (b) to sell, let for hire, or offer or expose for sale or hire, or distribute—

        (i) goods bearing such a mark, or

        (ii) material bearing such a mark which is used or intended to be used for labelling, packaging or advertising goods, or

    (c) to use material bearing such a mark in the course of a business for labelling, packaging or advertising goods, or

    (d) to possess in the course of a business goods or material bearing such a mark with a view to doing any of the things mentioned in paragraphs (a) to (c),

    when he is not entitled to use the mark in relation to the goods in question and the goods are not connected in the course of trade with a person who is so entitled.

(2) It is also an offence, subject to subsection (3) below, for a person to possess in the course of a business goods or material bearing a mark identical to or nearly resembling a registered trade mark with a view to enabling or assisting another person to do any of the things mentioned in subsection (1)(a) to (c), knowing or having reason to believe that the other person is not entitled to use the mark in relation to the goods in question and that the goods are not connected in the course of trade with a person who is so entitled:

(3) A person commits an offence under subsection (1) or (2) only if—

---

⁶⁹ Repealed by repealed by SI 2003/2498.

     (a) he acts with a view to gain for himself or another, or with intent to cause loss to another, and

     (b) he intends that the goods in question should be accepted as connected in the course of trade with a person entitled to use the mark in question;

and it is a defence for a person charged with an offence under subsection (1) to show that he believed on reasonable grounds that he was entitled to use the mark in relation to the goods in question.

(4)   A person guilty of an offence under this section is liable—

     (a) on summary conviction to imprisonment for a term not exceeding six months or a fine not exceeding the statutory maximum, or both;

     (b) on conviction on indictment to a fine or imprisonment for a term not exceeding ten years, or both.

(5)   Where an offence under this section committed by a body corporate is proved to have been committed with the consent or connivance of a director, manager, secretary or other similar officer of the body, or a person purporting to act in any such capacity, he as well as the body corporate is guilty of the offence and liable to be proceeded against and punished accordingly.

In relation to a body corporate whose affairs are managed by its members 'director' means a member of the body corporate.

(6)   In this section 'business' includes 'a trade or profession.'

Delivery up of offending goods and material.

58B. —(1) The court by which a person is convicted of an offence under section 58A may, if satisfied that at the time of his arrest or charge he had in his possession, custody or control—

     (a) goods or material in respect of which the offence was committed, or

     (b) goods of the same description as those in respect of which the offence was committed, or material similar to that in respect of which the offence was committed, bearing a mark identical to or nearly resembling that in relation to which the offence was committed, order that the goods or material be delivered up to such person as the court may direct.

(2)   For this purpose a person shall be treated as charged with an offence—
     (a) in England, Wales and Northern Ireland, when he is orally charged or is served with a summons or indictment:
     (b) in Scotland, when he is cautioned, charged or served with a complaint or indictment.

(3)   An order may be made by the court of its own motion or on the application of the prosecutor (or, in Scotland, the Lord Advocate or procurator-fiscal), but shall not be made if it appears to the court unlikely that any order will be made under section 58C (order as to disposal of offending goods or material).

(4)   An appeal lies from an order made under this section by a magistrates' court—
     (a) in England and Wales, to the Crown Court, and
     (b) in Northern Ireland, to the county court:

and in Scotland, where an order has been made under this section, the person from whose possession, custody or control the goods or material have been removed may, without prejudice to any other form of appeal under any rule of law, appeal against that order in the same manner as against sentence.

(5) A person to whom goods or material are delivered up in pursuance of an order under this section shall retain it pending the making of an order under section 58C.

(6) Nothing in this section affects the powers of the court under section 43 of the Powers of Criminal Courts Act 1973, section 223 or 436 of the Criminal Procedure (Scotland) Act 1975 or Article 7 of the Criminal Justice (Northern Ireland) Order 1980 (general provisions as to forfeiture in criminal proceedings).

Order as to disposal of offending goods or material.

58C. —(1) Where goods or material have been delivered up in pursuance of an order under section 58B, an application may be made to the court for an order that they be destroyed or forfeited to such person as the court may think fit.

(2) Provision shall be made by rules of court as to the service of notice on persons having an interest in the goods or material, and any such person is entitled—

(a) to appear in proceedings for an order under this section, whether or not he was served with notice, and

(b) to appeal against any order made, whether or not he appeared;

and an order shall not take effect until the end of the period within which notice of an appeal may be given or, if before the end of that period notice of appeal is duly given, until the final determination or abandonment of the proceedings on the appeal.

(3) Where there is more than one person interested in goods or material, the court shall make such order as it thinks just.

(4) References in this section to a person having an interest in goods or material include any person in whose favour an order could be made under this section or under sections 114, 204 or 231 of the Copyright, Designs and Patents Act 1988 (which make similar provision in relation to infringement of copyright, rights in performances and design right).

(5) Proceedings for an order under this section may be brought—

(a) in a county court in England, Wales and Northern Ireland, provided the value of the goods or material in question does not exceed the county court limit for actions in tort, and

(b) in a sheriff court in Scotland;

but this shall not be construed as affecting the jurisdiction of the High Court or, in Scotland, the Court of Session.

Enforcement of section 58A.

58D. —(1) The functions of a local weights and measures authority include the enforcement in their area of section 58A.

(2) The following provisions of the Trade Descriptions Act 1968 apply in relation to the enforcement of that section as in relation to the enforcement of that Act—

section 27 (power to make test purchases),

section 28 (power to enter premises and inspect and seize goods and documents),

section 29 (obstruction of authorised officers), and

section 33 (compensation for loss, &c. of goods seized under s. 28).

(3) Subsection (1) above does not apply in relation to the enforcement of section 58A in Northern Ireland, but the functions of the Department of Economic Development include the enforcement of that section in Northern Ireland.

For that purpose the provisions of the Trade Descriptions Act 1968 specified in subsection (2) apply as if for the references to a local weights and measures authority and any officer of such an authority there were substituted references to that Department and any of its officers.

(4) Any enactment which authorises the disclosure of information for the purpose of facilitating the enforcement of the Trade Descriptions Act 1968 shall apply as if section 58A above were contained in that Act and as if the functions of any person in relation to the enforcement of that section were functions under that Act.'

E. COMPUTER MISUSE ACT 1990 (SS 1–3)

An Act to make provision for securing computer material against unauthorised access or modification; and for connected purposes. [29th June 1990]

BE IT ENACTED by the Queen's most Excellent Majesty, by and with the advice and consent of the Lords Spiritual and Temporal, and Commons, in this present Parliament assembled, and by the authority of the same, as follows:—

Computer misuse offences

Unauthorised access to computer material

1. —(1) A person is guilty of an offence if—
    (a) he causes a computer to perform any function with intent to secure access to any program or data held in any computer;
    (b) the access he intends to secure is unauthorised; and
    (c) he knows at the time when he causes the computer to perform the function that that is the case.
(2) The intent a person has to have to commit an offence under this section need not be directed at—
    (a) any particular program or data;
    (b) a program or data of any particular kind; or
    (c) a program or data held in any particular computer.
(3) A person guilty of an offence under this section shall be liable on summary conviction to imprisonment for a term not exceeding six months or to a fine not exceeding level 5 on the standard scale or to both.

Unauthorised access with intent to commit or facilitate commission of further offences

2.—(1) A person is guilty of an offence under this section if he commits an offence under section 1 above ('the unauthorised access offence') with intent—

(a) to commit an offence to which this section applies; or

(b) to facilitate the commission of such an offence (whether by himself or by any other person);

and the offence he intends to commit or facilitate is referred to below in this section as the further offence.

(2) This section applies to offences—

(a) for which the sentence is fixed by law; or

(b) for which a person of twenty-one years of age or over (not previously convicted) may be sentenced to imprisonment for a term of five years (or, in England and Wales, might be so sentenced but for the restrictions imposed by section 33 of the Magistrates' Courts Act 1980).

(3) It is immaterial for the purposes of this section whether the further offence is to be committed on the same occasion as the unauthorised access offence or on any future occasion.

(4) A person may be guilty of an offence under this section even though the facts are such that the commission of the further offence is impossible.

(5) A person guilty of an offence under this section shall be liable—

(a) on summary conviction, to imprisonment for a term not exceeding six months or to a fine not exceeding the statutory maximum or to both; and

(b) on conviction on indictment, to imprisonment for a term not exceeding five years or to a fine or to both.

Unauthorised modification of computer material

3.—(1) A person is guilty of an offence if—

(a) he does any act which causes an unauthorised modification of the contents of any computer; and

(b) at the time when he does the act he has the requisite intent and the requisite knowledge.

(2) For the purposes of subsection (1)(b) above the requisite intent is an intent to cause a modification of the contents of any computer and by so doing—

(a) to impair the operation of any computer;

(b) to prevent or hinder access to any program or data held in any computer; or

(c) to impair the operation of any such program or the reliability of any such data.

(3) The intent need not be directed at—

(a) any particular computer;

(b) any particular program or data or a program or data of any particular kind; or

(c) any particular modification or a modification of any particular kind.

(4) For the purposes of subsection (1)(b) above the requisite knowledge is knowledge that any modification he intends to cause is unauthorised.

(5) It is immaterial for the purposes of this section whether an unauthorised modification or any intended effect of it of a kind mentioned in subsection (2) above is, or is intended to be, permanent or merely temporary.

(6) For the purposes of the Criminal Damage Act 1971 a modification of the contents of a computer shall not be regarded as damaging any computer or computer storage medium unless its effect on that computer or computer storage medium impairs its physical condition.

(7) A person guilty of an offence under this section shall be liable—

(a) on summary conviction, to imprisonment for a term not exceeding six months or to a fine not exceeding the statutory maximum or to both; and

(b) on conviction on indictment, to imprisonment for a term not exceeding five years or to a fine or to both.

F. SOCIAL SECURITY ADMINISTRATION ACT 1992 (SS 111A–112)

[Dishonest representations for obtaining benefit etc][70]

[111A. —(1) If a person dishonestly—

(a) makes a false statement or representation [or][71];

(b) produces or furnishes, or causes or allows to be produced or furnished, any document or information which is false in a material particular;

...

with a view to obtaining any benefit or other payment or advantage under the [relevant][72] social security legislation (whether for himself or for some other person), he shall be guilty of an offence.

[(1A) A person shall be guilty of an offence if—

(a) there has been a change of circumstances affecting any entitlement of his to any benefit or other payment or advantage under any provision of the relevant social security legislation;

(b) the change is not a change that is excluded by regulations from the changes that are required to be notified;

(c) he knows that the change affects an entitlement of his to such a benefit or other payment or advantage; and

(d) he dishonestly fails to give a prompt notification of that change in the prescribed manner to the prescribed person.

(1B) A person shall be guilty of an offence if—

(a) there has been a change of circumstances affecting any entitlement of another person to any benefit or other payment or advantage under any provision of the relevant social security legislation;

---

[70] Inserted by Social Security Administration (Fraud) Act 1997.
[71] Inserted by Social Security Fraud Act 2001.
[72] Inserted by Child Support, Pensions and Social Security Act 2000.

(b) the change is not a change that is excluded by regulations from the changes that are required to be notified;

(c) he knows that the change affects an entitlement of that other person to such a benefit or other payment or advantage; and

(d) he dishonestly causes or allows that other person to fail to give a prompt notification of that change in the prescribed manner to the prescribed person.

(1C) This subsection applies where—

(a) there has been a change of circumstances affecting any entitlement of a person ('the claimant') to any benefit or other payment or advantage under any provision of the relevant social security legislation;

(b) the benefit, payment or advantage is one in respect of which there is another person ('the recipient') who for the time being has a right to receive payments to which the claimant has, or (but for the arrangements under which they are payable to the recipient) would have, an entitlement; and

(c) the change is not a change that is excluded by regulations from the changes that are required to be notified.

(1D) In a case where subsection (1C) above applies, the recipient is guilty of an offence if—

(a) he knows that the change affects an entitlement of the claimant to a benefit or other payment or advantage under a provision of the relevant social security legislation;

(b) the entitlement is one in respect of which he has a right to receive payments to which the claimant has, or (but for the arrangements under which they are payable to the recipient) would have, an entitlement; and

(c) he dishonestly fails to give a prompt notification of that change in the prescribed manner to the prescribed person.

(1E) In a case where that subsection applies, a person other than the recipient is guilty of an offence if—

(a) he knows that the change affects an entitlement of the claimant to a benefit or other payment or advantage under a provision of the relevant social security legislation;

(b) the entitlement is one in respect of which the recipient has a right to receive payments to which the claimant has, or (but for the arrangements under which they are payable to the recipient) would have, an entitlement; and

(c) he dishonestly causes or allows the recipient to fail to give a prompt notification of that change in the prescribed manner to the prescribed person.

(1F) In any case where subsection (1C) above applies but the right of the recipient is confined to a right, by reason of his being a person to whom the claimant is required to make payments in respect of a dwelling, to receive payments of housing benefit—

(a) a person shall not be guilty of an offence under subsection (1D) or (1E) above unless the change is one relating to one or both of the following—

(i) the claimant's occupation of that dwelling;

(ii) the claimant's liability to make payments in respect of that dwelling;

but

(b) subsections (1D)(a) and (1E)(a) above shall each have effect as if after knows there were inserted or could reasonably be expected to know.

(1G) For the purposes of subsections (1A) to (1E) above a notification of a change is prompt if, and only if, it is given as soon as reasonably practicable after the change occurs.][73]

...

(3) A person guilty of an offence under this section shall be liable—

(a) on summary conviction, to imprisonment for a term not exceeding six months, or to a fine not exceeding the statutory maximum, or to both; or

(b) on conviction on indictment, to imprisonment for a term not exceeding seven years, or to a fine, or to both.

(4) In the application of this section to Scotland, in [subsections (1) to (1E)][74] for dishonestly substitute knowingly.]

False representations for obtaining benefit etc

112. —(1) If a person for the purpose of obtaining any benefit or other payment under the [relevant][75] [social security legislation][76] whether for himself or some other person, or for any other purpose connected with that legislation—

(a) makes a statement or representation which he knows to be false; or

(b) produces or furnishes, or knowingly causes or knowingly allows to be produced or furnished, any document or information which he knows to be false in a material particular, he shall be guilty of an offence.

[(1A) A person shall be guilty of an offence if—

(a) there has been a change of circumstances affecting any entitlement of his to any benefit or other payment or advantage under any provision of the relevant social security legislation;

(b) the change is not a change that is excluded by regulations from the changes that are required to be notified;

(c) he knows that the change affects an entitlement of his to such a benefit or other payment or advantage; and

(d) he fails to give a prompt notification of that change in the prescribed manner to the prescribed person.

(1B) A person is guilty of an offence under this section if—

(a) there has been a change of circumstances affecting any entitlement of another person to any benefit or other payment or advantage under any provision of the relevant social security legislation;

---

73 Inserted by Social Security Fraud Act 2001.
74 Inserted by Social Security Fraud Act 2001.
75 Inserted by Child Support, Pensions and Social Security Act 2000.
76 Inserted by Social Security Administration (Fraud) Act 1997.

(b) the change is not a change that is excluded by regulations from the changes that are required to be notified;

(c) he knows that the change affects an entitlement of that other person to such a benefit or other payment or advantage; and

(d) he causes or allows that other person to fail to give a prompt notification of that change in the prescribed manner to the prescribed person.

(1C) In a case where subsection (1C) of section 111A above applies, the recipient is guilty of an offence if—

(a) he knows that the change affects an entitlement of the claimant to a benefit or other payment or advantage under a provision of the relevant social security legislation;

(b) the entitlement is one in respect of which he has a right to receive payments to which the claimant has, or (but for the arrangements under which they are payable to the recipient) would have, an entitlement; and

(c) he fails to give a prompt notification of that change in the prescribed manner to the prescribed person.

(1D) In a case where that subsection applies, a person other than the recipient is guilty of an offence if—

(a) he knows that the change affects an entitlement of the claimant to a benefit or other payment or advantage under a provision of the relevant social security legislation;

(b) the entitlement is one in respect of which the recipient has a right to receive payments to which the claimant has, or (but for the arrangements under which they are payable to the recipient) would have, an entitlement; and

(c) he causes or allows the recipient to fail to give a prompt notification of that change in the prescribed manner to the prescribed person.

(1E) Subsection (1F) of section 111A above applies in relation to subsections (1C) and (1D) above as it applies in relation to subsections (1D) and (1E) of that section.

(1F) For the purposes of subsections (1A) to (1D) above a notification of a change is prompt if, and only if, it is given as soon as reasonably practicable after the change occurs.][77]

(2) A person guilty of an offence under [this section][78] shall be liable on summary conviction to a fine not exceeding level 5 on the standard scale, or to imprisonment for a term not exceeding 3 months [51 weeks][79], or to both.

...

G. CRIMINAL JUSTICE ACT 1993 (S 52)

52. —(1) An individual who has information as an insider is guilty of insider dealing if, in the circumstances mentioned in subsection (3), he deals in securities that are price-affected securities in relation to the information.

---

[77] Inserted by Social Security Fraud Act 2001.
[78] Amended by Social Security Administration (Fraud) Act 1997.
[79] Amended by Criminal Justice Act 2003.

(2) An individual who has information as an insider is also guilty of insider dealing if—

    (a) he encourages another person to deal in securities that are (whether or not that other knows it) price-affected securities in relation to the information, knowing or having reasonable cause to believe that the dealing would take place in the circumstances mentioned in subsection (3); or

    (b) he discloses the information, otherwise than in the proper performance of the functions of his employment, office or profession, to another person.

(3) The circumstances referred to above are that the acquisition or disposal in question occurs on a regulated market, or that the person dealing relies on a professional intermediary or is himself acting as a professional intermediary.

(4) This section has effect subject to section 53.

H. TRADE MARKS ACT 1994 (S 92)

Unauthorised use of trade mark, &c. in relation to goods

92. —(1) A person commits an offence who with a view to gain for himself or another, or with intent to cause loss to another, and without the consent of the proprietor—

    (a) applies to goods or their packaging a sign identical to, or likely to be mistaken for, a registered trade mark, or

    (b) sells or lets for hire, offers or exposes for sale or hire or distributes goods which bear, or the packaging of which bears, such a sign, or

    (c) has in his possession, custody or control in the course of a business any such goods with a view to the doing of anything, by himself or another, which would be an offence under paragraph (b).

(2) A person commits an offence who with a view to gain for himself or another, or with intent to cause loss to another, and without the consent of the proprietor—

    (a) applies a sign identical to, or likely to be mistaken for, a registered trade mark to material intended to be used—

        (i) for labelling or packaging goods,

        (ii) as a business paper in relation to goods, or

        (iii) for advertising goods, or

    (b) uses in the course of a business material bearing such a sign for labelling or packaging goods, as a business paper in relation to goods, or for advertising goods, or

    (c) has in his possession, custody or control in the course of a business any such material with a view to the doing of anything, by himself or another, which would be an offence under paragraph (b).

(3) A person commits an offence who with a view to gain for himself or another, or with intent to cause loss to another, and without the consent of the proprietor—

    (a) makes an article specifically designed or adapted for making copies of a sign identical to, or likely to be mistaken for, a registered trade mark, or

    (b) has such an article in his possession, custody or control in the course of a business, knowing or having reason to believe that it has been, or is to be, used to produce goods, or material for labelling or packaging goods, as a business paper in relation to goods, or for advertising goods.

(4) A person does not commit an offence under this section unless—

(a) the goods are goods in respect of which the trade mark is registered, or

(b) the trade mark has a reputation in the United Kingdom and the use of the sign takes or would take unfair advantage of, or is or would be detrimental to, the distinctive character or the repute of the trade mark.

(5) It is a defence for a person charged with an offence under this section to show that he believed on reasonable grounds that the use of the sign in the manner in which it was used, or was to be used, was not an infringement of the registered trade mark.

(6) A person guilty of an offence under this section is liable—

(a) on summary conviction to imprisonment for a term not exceeding six months or a fine not exceeding the statutory maximum, or both;

(b) on conviction on indictment to a fine or imprisonment for a term not exceeding ten years, or both.

I. VALUE ADDED TAX ACT 1994 (S 72)

72. —(1) If any person is knowingly concerned in, or in the taking of steps with a view to, the fraudulent evasion of VAT by him or any other person, he shall be liable—

(a) on summary conviction, to a penalty of the statutory maximum or of three times the amount of the VAT,
whichever is the greater, or to imprisonment for a term not exceeding 6 months or to both; or

(b) on conviction on indictment, to a penalty of any amount or to imprisonment for a term not exceeding 7 years or to both.

(2) Any reference in subsection (1) above or subsection (8) below to the evasion of VAT includes a reference to the obtaining of—

(a) the payment of a VAT credit; or

(b) a refund under section 35, 36 or 40 of this Act or section 22 of the 1983 Act: or

(c) a refund under any regulations made by virtue of section 13(5); or

(d) a repayment under section 39;
and any reference in those subsections to the amount of the VAT shall be construed—

(i) in relation to VAT itself or a VAT credit, as a reference to the aggregate of the amount (if any) falsely claimed by way of credit for input tax and the amount (if any) by which output tax was falsely understated, and

(ii) in relation to a refund or repayment falling within paragraph (b), (c) or (d) above, as a reference to the amount falsely claimed by way of refund or repayment.

(3) If any person—

(a) with intent to deceive produces, furnishes or sends for the purposes of this Act or otherwise makes use for those purposes of any document which is false in a material particular; or

(b) in furnishing any information for the purposes of this Act makes any statement which he knows to be false in a material particular or recklessly makes a statement which is false in a material particular,

he shall be liable—

    (i) on summary conviction, to a penalty of the statutory maximum or, where subsection (4) or (5) below applies, to the alternative penalty specified in that subsection if it is greater, or to imprisonment for a term not exceeding 6 months or to both; or

    (ii) on conviction on indictment, to a penalty of any amount or to imprisonment for a term not exceeding 7 years or to both.

(4) In any case where—

    (a) the document referred to in subsection (3)(a) above is a return required under this Act, or

    (b) the information referred to in subsection (3)(b) above is contained in or otherwise relevant to such a return,

the alternative penalty referred to in subsection (3)(i) above is a penalty equal to three times the aggregate of the amount (if any) falsely claimed by way of credit for input tax and the amount (if any) by which output tax was falsely understated.

(5) In any case where—

    (a) the document referred to in subsection (3)(a) above is a claim for a refund under section 35, 36 or 40 of this Act or section 22 of the 1983 Act, for a refund under any regulations made by virtue of section 13(5) or for a repayment under section 39, or

    (b) the information referred to in subsection (3)(b) above is contained in or otherwise relevant to such a claim,

the alternative penalty referred to in subsection (3)(i) above is a penalty equal to 3 times the amount falsely claimed.

(6) The reference in subsection (3)(a) above to furnishing, sending or otherwise making use of a document which is false in a material particular, with intent to deceive, includes a reference to furnishing, sending or otherwise making use of such a document, with intent to secure that a machine will respond to the document as if it were a true document.

(7) Any reference in subsection (3)(a) or (6) above to producing, furnishing or sending a document includes a reference to causing a document to be produced, furnished or sent.

(8) Where a person's conduct during any specified period must have involved the commission by him of one or more offences under the preceding provisions of this section, then, whether or not the particulars of that offence or those offences are known, he shall, by virtue of this subsection, be guilty of an offence and liable—

    (a) on summary conviction, to a penalty of the statutory maximum or, if greater, 3 times the amount of any VAT that was or was intended to be evaded by his conduct, or to imprisonment for a term not exceeding 6 months or to both, or

    (b) on conviction on indictment to a penalty of any amount or to imprisonment for a term not exceeding 7 years or to both.

(9) Where an authorised person has reasonable grounds for suspecting that an offence has

been committed under the preceding provisions of this section, he may arrest anyone whom he has reasonable grounds for suspecting to be guilty of the offence.

(10) If any person acquires possession of or deals with any goods, or accepts the supply of any services, having reason to believe that VAT on the supply of the goods or services, on the acquisition of the goods from another member State or on the importation of the goods from a place outside the member States has been or will be evaded, he shall be liable on summary conviction to a penalty of level 5 on the standard scale or three times the amount of the VAT, whichever is the greater.

(11) If any person supplies [or is supplied with][80] goods or services in contravention of paragraph 4(2) of Schedule 11, he shall be liable on summary conviction to a penalty of level 5 on the standard scale.

(12) Subject to subsection (13) below, sections 145 to 155 of the Management Act (proceedings for offences, mitigation of penalties and certain other matters) shall apply in relation to offences under this Act (which include any act or omission in respect of which a penalty is imposed) and penalties imposed under this Act as they apply in relation to offences and penalties under the customs and excise Acts as defined in that Act; and accordingly in section 154(2) as it applies by virtue of this subsection the reference to duty shall be construed as a reference to VAT.

(13) In subsection (12) above the references to penalties do not include references to penalties under sections 60 to 70.

J. FINANCIAL SERVICES AND MARKETS ACT 2000 (S 397)

397. —(1) This subsection applies to a person who—

    (a) makes a statement, promise or forecast which he knows to be misleading, false or deceptive in a material particular;

    (b) dishonestly conceals any material facts whether in connection with a statement, promise or forecast made by him or otherwise; or

    (c) recklessly makes (dishonestly or otherwise) a statement, promise or forecast which is misleading, false or deceptive in a material particular.

(2) A person to whom subsection (1) applies is guilty of an offence if he makes the statement, promise or forecast or conceals the facts for the purpose of inducing, or is reckless as to whether it may induce, another person (whether or not the person to whom the statement, promise or forecast is made)—

    (a) to enter or offer to enter into, or to refrain from entering or offering to enter into, a relevant agreement; or

    (b) to exercise, or refrain from exercising, any rights conferred by a relevant investment.

(3) Any person who does any act or engages in any course of conduct which creates a false or misleading impression as to the market in or the price or value of any relevant investments is guilty of an offence if he does so for the purpose of creating that impression and of thereby inducing another person to acquire, dispose of, subscribe for

---

[80] Inserted by Finance Act 2003.

or underwrite those investments or to refrain from doing so or to exercise, or refrain from exercising, any rights conferred by those investments.

(4) In proceedings for an offence under subsection (2) brought against a person to whom subsection (1) applies as a result of paragraph (a) of that subsection, it is a defence for him to show that the statement, promise or forecast was made in conformity with [—

    (a) price stabilising rules;

    (b) control of information rules; or

    (c) the relevant provisions of Commission Regulation (EC) No 2273/2003 of 22 December 2003 implementing Directive 2003/6/EC of the European Parliament and of the Council as regards exemptions for buy-back programmes and stabilisation of financial instruments.][81]

(5) In proceedings brought against any person for an offence under subsection (3) it is a defence for him to show—
    (a) that he reasonably believed that his act or conduct would not create an impression that was false or misleading as to the matters mentioned in that subsection;
    (b) that he acted or engaged in the conduct—

        (i) for the purpose of stabilising the price of investments; and

        (ii) in conformity with price stabilising rules; ...

    (c) that he acted or engaged in the conduct in conformity with control of information rules[; or
    (d) that he acted or engaged in the conduct in conformity with the relevant provisions of Commission Regulation (EC) No 2273/2003 of 22 December 2003 implementing Directive 2003/6/EC of the European Parliament and of the Council as regards exemptions for buy-back programmes and stabilisation of financial instruments.][82]

(6) Subsections (1) and (2) do not apply unless—

    (a) the statement, promise or forecast is made in or from, or the facts are concealed in or from, the United Kingdom or arrangements are made in or from the United Kingdom for the statement, promise or forecast to be made or the facts to be concealed;

    (b) the person on whom the inducement is intended to or may have effect is in the United Kingdom; or

    (c) the agreement is or would be entered into or the rights are or would be exercised in the United Kingdom.

(7) Subsection (3) does not apply unless—
    (a) the act is done, or the course of conduct is engaged in, in the United Kingdom; or
    (b) the false or misleading impression is created there.

(8) A person guilty of an offence under this section is liable—

    (a) on summary conviction, to imprisonment for a term not exceeding six months or a fine not exceeding the statutory maximum, or both;

    (b) on conviction on indictment, to imprisonment for a term not exceeding seven years or a fine, or both.

---

[81] Amended by SI 2005/381.   [82] Inserted by SI 2005/381.

(9) 'Relevant agreement' means an agreement—

    (a) the entering into or performance of which by either party constitutes an activity of a specified kind or one which falls within a specified class of activity; and

    (b) which relates to a relevant investment.

(10) 'Relevant investment' means an investment of a specified kind or one which falls within a prescribed class of investment.

(11) Schedule 2 (except paragraphs 25 and 26) applies for the purposes of subsections (9) and (10) with references to section 22 being read as references to each of those subsections.

(12) Nothing in Schedule 2, as applied by subsection (11), limits the power conferred by subsection (9) or (10).

(13) 'Investment' includes any asset, right or interest.

(14) 'Specified' means specified in an order made by the Treasury.

K. PROCEEDS OF CRIME ACT 2002 (SS 327–340)

327 Concealing etc

(1) A person commits an offence if he—

    (a) conceals criminal property;

    (b) disguises criminal property;

    (c) converts criminal property;

    (d) transfers criminal property;

    (e) removes criminal property from England and Wales or from Scotland or from Northern Ireland.

(2) But a person does not commit such an offence if—

    (a) he makes an authorised disclosure under section 338 and (if the disclosure is made before he does the act mentioned in subsection (1)) he has the appropriate consent;

    (b) he intended to make such a disclosure but had a reasonable excuse for not doing so;

    (c) the act he does is done in carrying out a function he has relating to the enforcement of any provision of this Act or of any other enactment relating to criminal conduct or benefit from criminal conduct.

[(2A) Nor does a person commit an offence under subsection (1) if—

    (a) he knows, or believes on reasonable grounds, that the relevant criminal conduct occurred in a particular country or territory outside the United Kingdom, and

    (b) the relevant criminal conduct—

        (i) was not, at the time it occurred, unlawful under the criminal law then applying in that country or territory, and

        (ii) is not of a description prescribed by an order made by the Secretary of State.

(2B) In subsection (2A) "the relevant criminal conduct" is the criminal conduct by reference to which the property concerned is criminal property.

(2C) A deposit-taking body that does an act mentioned in paragraph (c) or (d) of subsection (1) does not commit an offence under that subsection if—

    (a) it does the act in operating an account maintained with it, and

    (b) the value of the criminal property concerned is less than the threshold amount determined under section 339A for the act.][83]

(3) Concealing or disguising criminal property includes concealing or disguising its nature, source, location, disposition, movement or ownership or any rights with respect to it.

328 Arrangements

(1) A person commits an offence if he enters into or becomes concerned in an arrangement which he knows or suspects facilitates (by whatever means) the acquisition, retention, use or control of criminal property by or on behalf of another person.

(2) But a person does not commit such an offence if—

    (a) he makes an authorised disclosure under section 338 and (if the disclosure is made before he does the act mentioned in subsection (1)) he has the appropriate consent;

    (b) he intended to make such a disclosure but had a reasonable excuse for not doing so;

    (c) the act he does is done in carrying out a function he has relating to the enforcement of any provision of this Act or of any other enactment relating to criminal conduct or benefit from criminal conduct.

[(3) Nor does a person commit an offence under subsection (1) if—

    (a) he knows, or believes on reasonable grounds, that the relevant criminal conduct occurred in a particular country or territory outside the United Kingdom, and

    (b) the relevant criminal conduct—

        (i) was not, at the time it occurred, unlawful under the criminal law then applying in that country or territory, and

        (ii) is not of a description prescribed by an order made by the Secretary of State.

(4) In subsection (3) "the relevant criminal conduct" is the criminal conduct by reference to which the property concerned is criminal property.

(5) A deposit-taking body that does an act mentioned in subsection (1) does not commit an offence under that subsection if—

    (a) it does the act in operating an account maintained with it, and

    (b) the arrangement facilitates the acquisition, retention, use or control of criminal property of a value that is less than the threshold amount determined under section 339A for the act.][84]

329 Acquisition, use and possession

(1)   A person commits an offence if he—

---

[83] Inserted by Serious Organised Crime and Police Act 2005.
[84] Inserted by Serious Organised Crime and Police Act 2005.

(a) acquires criminal property;

(b) uses criminal property;

(c) has possession of criminal property.

(2) But a person does not commit such an offence if—

(a) he makes an authorised disclosure under section 338 and (if the disclosure is made before he does the act mentioned in subsection (1)) he has the appropriate consent;

(b) he intended to make such a disclosure but had a reasonable excuse for not doing so;

(c) he acquired or used or had possession of the property for adequate consideration;

(d) the act he does is done in carrying out a function he has relating to the enforcement of any provision of this Act or of any other enactment relating to criminal conduct or benefit from criminal conduct.

[(2A) Nor does a person commit an offence under subsection (1) if—

(a) he knows, or believes on reasonable grounds, that the relevant criminal conduct occurred in a particular country or territory outside the United Kingdom, and

(b) the relevant criminal conduct—
   (i) was not, at the time it occurred, unlawful under the criminal law then applying in that country or territory, and
   (ii) is not of a description prescribed by an order made by the Secretary of State.

(2B) In subsection (2A) "the relevant criminal conduct" is the criminal conduct by reference to which the property concerned is criminal property.

(2C) A deposit-taking body that does an act mentioned in subsection (1) does not commit an offence under that subsection if—

(a) it does the act in operating an account maintained with it, and

(b) the value of the criminal property concerned is less than the threshold amount determined under section 339A for the act.]⁸⁵

(3) For the purposes of this section—

(a) a person acquires property for inadequate consideration if the value of the consideration is significantly less than the value of the property;

(b) a person uses or has possession of property for inadequate consideration if the value of the consideration is significantly less than the value of the use or possession;

(c) the provision by a person of goods or services which he knows or suspects may help another to carry out criminal conduct is not consideration.

330 Failure to disclose: regulated sector

(1) A person commits an offence [if the conditions in subsections (2) to (4) are satisfied.⁸⁶

(2) The first condition is that he—

---

⁸⁵ Inserted by Serious Organised Crime and Police Act 2005.
⁸⁶ Amended by Serious Organised Crime and Police Act 2005.

(a) knows or suspects, or

(b) has reasonable grounds for knowing or suspecting,
that another person is engaged in money laundering.

(3) The second condition is that the information or other matter—

(a) on which his knowledge or suspicion is based, or

(b) which gives reasonable grounds for such knowledge or suspicion,
came to him in the course of a business in the regulated sector.

[(3A) The third condition is—

(a) that he can identify the other person mentioned in subsection (2) or the whereabouts of any of the laundered property, or

(b) that he believes, or it is reasonable to expect him to believe, that the information
or other matter mentioned in subsection (3) will or may assist in identifying that
other person or the whereabouts of any of the laundered property.

(4) The fourth condition is that he does not make the required disclosure to—

(a) a nominated officer, or

(b) a person authorised for the purposes of this Part by the Director General of the
Serious Organised Crime Agency,
as soon as is practicable after the information or other matter mentioned in
subsection

(3) comes to him.

(5) The required disclosure is a disclosure of—
(a) the identity of the other person mentioned in subsection (2), if he knows it,
(b) the whereabouts of the laundered property, so far as he knows it, and
(c) the information or other matter mentioned in subsection (3).

(5A) The laundered property is the property forming the subject-matter of the money
laundering that he knows or suspects, or has reasonable grounds for knowing or
suspecting, that other person to be engaged in.

(6) But he does not commit an offence under this section if—

(a) he has a reasonable excuse for not making the required disclosure,

(b) he is a professional legal adviser [or other relevant professional adviser][87] and—

(i) if he knows either of the things mentioned in subsection (5)(a)and (b), he
knows the thing because of information or other matter that came to him in
privileged circumstances, or

(ii) the information or other matter mentioned in subsection (3) came to him in
privileged circumstances, or

(c) subsection (7) [or (7B)][88] applies to him.][89]

(7) This subsection applies to a person if—

(a) he does not know or suspect that another person is engaged in money laundering, and

---

[87] Inserted by SI 2006/308.   [88] Inserted by SI 2006/308.
[89] Amended by Serious Organised Crime and Police Act 2005.

(b) he has not been provided by his employer with such training as is specified by the Secretary of State by order for the purposes of this section.

[(7A) Nor does a person commit an offence under this section if—

(a) he knows, or believes on reasonable grounds, that the money laundering is occurring in a particular country or territory outside the United Kingdom, and

(b) the money laundering—

(i) is not unlawful under the criminal law applying in that country or territory, and

(ii) is not of a description prescribed in an order made by the Secretary of State.]⁹⁰

[(7B) This subsection applies to a person if—

(a) he is employed by, or is in partnership with, a professional legal adviser or a relevant professional adviser to provide the adviser with assistance or support,

(b) the information or other matter mentioned in subsection (3) comes to the person in connection with the provision of such assistance or support, and

(c) the information or other matter came to the adviser in privileged circumstances.]⁹¹

(8) In deciding whether a person committed an offence under this section the court must consider whether he followed any relevant guidance which was at the time concerned—

(a) issued by a supervisory authority or any other appropriate body,

(b) approved by the Treasury, and

(c) published in a manner it approved as appropriate in its opinion to bring the guidance to the attention of persons likely to be affected by it.

(9) A disclosure to a nominated officer is a disclosure which—

(a) is made to a person nominated by the alleged offender's employer to receive disclosures under this section, and

(b) is made in the course of the alleged offender's employment [...]⁹²

[(9A) But a disclosure which satisfies paragraphs (a) and (b) of subsection (9) is not to be taken as a disclosure to a nominated officer if the person making the disclosure—

(a) is a professional legal adviser [or other relevant professional adviser]⁹³,

(b) makes it for the purpose of obtaining advice about making a disclosure under this section, and

(c) does not intend it to be a disclosure under this section.]⁹⁴

(10) Information or other matter comes to a professional legal adviser [or other relevant professional adviser]⁹⁵ in privileged circumstances if it is communicated or given to him—

---

⁹⁰ Inserted by Serious Organised Crime and Police Act 2005.
⁹¹ Inserted by SI 2006/308.
⁹² Repealed by Serious Organised Crime and Police Act 2005.
⁹³ Inserted by SI 2006/308.
⁹⁴ Inserted by Serious Organised Crime and Police Act 2005.
⁹⁵ Inserted by SI 2006/308.

(a) by (or by a representative of) a client of his in connection with the giving by the adviser of legal advice to the client,

(b) by (or by a representative of) a person seeking legal advice from the adviser, or

(c) by a person in connection with legal proceedings or contemplated legal proceedings.

(11) But subsection (10) does not apply to information or other matter which is communicated or given with the intention of furthering a criminal purpose.

(12) Schedule 9 has effect for the purpose of determining what is—
(a) a business in the regulated sector;
(b) a supervisory authority.

(13) An appropriate body is any body which regulates or is representative of any trade, profession, business or employment carried on by the alleged offender.

[(14) A relevant professional adviser is an accountant, auditor or tax adviser who is a member of a professional body which is established for accountants, auditors or tax advisers (as the case may be) and which makes provision for—

(a) testing the competence of those seeking admission to membership of such a body as a condition for such admission; and

(b) imposing and maintaining professional and ethical standards for its members, as well as imposing sanctions for non-compliance with those standards.][96]

331 Failure to disclose: nominated officers in the regulated sector

(1) A person nominated to receive disclosures under section 330 commits an offence if the conditions in subsections (2) to (4) are satisfied.

(2) The first condition is that he—
(a) knows or suspects, or
(b) has reasonable grounds for knowing or suspecting,
that another person is engaged in money laundering.

(3) The second condition is that the information or other matter—
(a) on which his knowledge or suspicion is based, or
(b) which gives reasonable grounds for such knowledge or suspicion,
came to him in consequence of a disclosure made under section 330.

[(3A) The third condition is—

(a) that he knows the identity of the other person mentioned in subsection (2), or the whereabouts of any of the laundered property, in consequence of a disclosure made under section 330,

(b) that that other person, or the whereabouts of any of the laundered property, can be identified from the information or other matter mentioned in subsection (3), or

(c) that he believes, or it is reasonable to expect him to believe, that the information or other matter will or may assist in identifying that other person or the whereabouts of any of the laundered property.

(4) The fourth condition is that he does not make the required disclosure to a person authorised for the purposes of this Part by the Director General of the Serious

---

[96] Inserted by SI 2006/308.

Organised Crime Agency as soon as is practicable after the information or other matter mentioned in subsection (3) comes to him.

(5) The required disclosure is a disclosure of—

(a) the identity of the other person mentioned in subsection (2), if disclosed to him under section 330,

(b) the whereabouts of the laundered property, so far as disclosed to him under section 330, and

(c) the information or other matter mentioned in subsection (3).

(5A) The laundered property is the property forming the subject-matter of the money laundering that he knows or suspects, or has reasonable grounds for knowing or suspecting, that other person to be engaged in.

(6) But he does not commit an offence under this section if he has a reasonable excuse for not making the required disclosure.

(6A) Nor does a person commit an offence under this section if—

(a) he knows, or believes on reasonable grounds, that the money laundering is occurring in a particular country or territory outside the United Kingdom, and

(b) the money laundering—

(i) is not unlawful under the criminal law applying in that country or territory, and

(ii) is not of a description prescribed in an order made by the Secretary of State.][97]

(7) In deciding whether a person committed an offence under this section the court must consider whether he followed any relevant guidance which was at the time concerned—

(a) issued by a supervisory authority or any other appropriate body,

(b) approved by the Treasury, and

(c) published in a manner it approved as appropriate in its opinion to bring the guidance to the attention of persons likely to be affected by it.

(8) Schedule 9 has effect for the purpose of determining what is a supervisory authority.

(9) An appropriate body is a body which regulates or is representative of a trade, profession, business or employment.

332 Failure to disclose: other nominated officers

(1) A person nominated to receive disclosures under section 337 or 338 commits an offence if the conditions in subsections (2) to (4) are satisfied.

(2) The first condition is that he knows or suspects that another person is engaged in money laundering.

(3) The second condition is that the information or other matter on which his knowledge or suspicion is based came to him in consequence of a disclosure made under [the applicable section.][98]

[(3A) The third condition is—

---

[97] Amended by Serious Organised Crime and Police Act 2005.
[98] Amended by Serious Organised Crime and Police Act 2005.

(a) that he knows the identity of the other person mentioned in subsection (2), or the whereabouts of any of the laundered property, in consequence of a disclosure made under the applicable section,

(b) that that other person, or the whereabouts of any of the laundered property, can be identified from the information or other matter mentioned in subsection (3), or

(c) that he believes, or it is reasonable to expect him to believe, that the information or other matter will or may assist in identifying that other person or the whereabouts of any of the laundered property.

(4) The fourth condition is that he does not make the required disclosure to a person authorised for the purposes of this Part by the Director General of the Serious Organised Crime Agency as soon as is practicable after the information or other matter mentioned in subsection (3) comes to him.

(5) The required disclosure is a disclosure of—

(a) the identity of the other person mentioned in subsection (2), if disclosed to him under the applicable section,

(b) the whereabouts of the laundered property, so far as disclosed to him under the applicable section, and

(c) the information or other matter mentioned in subsection (3).

(5A) The laundered property is the property forming the subject-matter of the money laundering that he knows or suspects that other person to be engaged in.

(5B) The applicable section is section 337 or, as the case may be, section 338.

(6) But he does not commit an offence under this section if he has a reasonable excuse for not making the required disclosure.

(7) Nor does a person commit an offence under this section if—

(a) he knows, or believes on reasonable grounds, that the money laundering is occurring in a particular country or territory outside the United Kingdom, and

(b) the money laundering—
    (i) is not unlawful under the criminal law applying in that country or territory, and
    (ii) is not of a description prescribed in an order made by the Secretary of State.][99]

333 Tipping off

(1) A person commits an offence if—

(a) he knows or suspects that a disclosure falling within section 337 or 338 has been made, and

(b) he makes a disclosure which is likely to prejudice any investigation which might be conducted following the disclosure referred to in paragraph (a).

(2) But a person does not commit an offence under subsection (1) if—

(a) he did not know or suspect that the disclosure was likely to be prejudicial as mentioned in subsection (1);

---

[99] Amended by Serious Organised Crime and Police Act 2005.

(b) the disclosure is made in carrying out a function he has relating to the enforcement of any provision of this Act or of any other enactment relating to criminal conduct or benefit from criminal conduct;

(c) he is a professional legal adviser and the disclosure falls within subsection (3).

(3) A disclosure falls within this subsection if it is a disclosure—

(a) to (or to a representative of) a client of the professional legal adviser in connection with the giving by the adviser of legal advice to the client, or

(b) to any person in connection with legal proceedings or contemplated legal proceedings.

(4) But a disclosure does not fall within subsection (3) if it is made with the intention of furthering a criminal purpose.

334 Penalties

(1) A person guilty of an offence under section 327, 328 or 329 is liable—

(a) on summary conviction, to imprisonment for a term not exceeding six months or to a fine not exceeding the statutory maximum or to both, or

(b) on conviction on indictment, to imprisonment for a term not exceeding 14 years or to a fine or to both.

(2) A person guilty of an offence under section 330, 331, 332 or 333 is liable—

(a) on summary conviction, to imprisonment for a term not exceeding six months or to a fine not exceeding the statutory maximum or to both, or

(b) on conviction on indictment, to imprisonment for a term not exceeding five years or to a fine or to both.

[(3) A person guilty of an offence under section 339(1A) is liable on summary conviction to a fine not exceeding level 5 on the standard scale.][100]

335 Appropriate consent

(1) The appropriate consent is—

(a) the consent of a nominated officer to do a prohibited act if an authorised disclosure is made to the nominated officer;

(b) the consent of a constable to do a prohibited act if an authorised disclosure is made to a constable;

(c) the consent of a customs officer to do a prohibited act if an authorised disclosure is made to a customs officer.

(2) A person must be treated as having the appropriate consent if—

(a) he makes an authorised disclosure to a constable or a customs officer, and

(b) the condition in subsection (3) or the condition in subsection (4) is satisfied.

(3) The condition is that before the end of the notice period he does not receive notice from a constable or customs officer that consent to the doing of the act is refused.

(4) The condition is that—

(a) before the end of the notice period he receives notice from a constable or customs officer that consent to the doing of the act is refused, and

(b) the moratorium period has expired.

---

[100] Inserted by Serious Organised Crime and Police Act 2005.

(5) The notice period is the period of seven working days starting with the first working day after the person makes the disclosure.

(6) The moratorium period is the period of 31 days starting with the day on which the person receives notice that consent to the doing of the act is refused.

(7) A working day is a day other than a Saturday, a Sunday, Christmas Day, Good Friday or a day which is a bank holiday under the Banking and Financial Dealings Act 1971 (c. 80) in the part of the United Kingdom in which the person is when he makes the disclosure.

(8) References to a prohibited act are to an act mentioned in section 327(1), 328(1) or 329(1) (as the case may be).

(9) A nominated officer is a person nominated to receive disclosures under section 338.

(10) Subsections (1) to (4) apply for the purposes of this Part.

336 Nominated officer: consent

(1) A nominated officer must not give the appropriate consent to the doing of a prohibited act unless the condition in subsection (2), the condition in subsection (3) or the condition in subsection (4) is satisfied.

(2) The condition is that—

    (a) he makes a disclosure that property is criminal property to a person authorised for the purposes of this Part by the Director General of the [Serious Organised Crime Agency][101], and

    (b) such a person gives consent to the doing of the act.

(3) The condition is that—

    (a) he makes a disclosure that property is criminal property to a person authorised for the purposes of this Part by the Director General of the [Serious Organised Crime Agency][102], and

    (b) before the end of the notice period he does not receive notice from such a person that consent to the doing of the act is refused.

(4) The condition is that—

    (a) he makes a disclosure that property is criminal property to a person authorised for the purposes of this Part by the Director General of the [Serious Organised Crime Agency][103],

    (b) before the end of the notice period he receives notice from such a person that consent to the doing of the act is refused, and

    (c) the moratorium period has expired.

(5) A person who is a nominated officer commits an offence if—

    (a) he gives consent to a prohibited act in circumstances where none of the conditions in subsections (2), (3) and (4) is satisfied, and

    (b) he knows or suspects that the act is a prohibited act.

(6) A person guilty of such an offence is liable—

---

[101] Amended by Serious Organised Crime and Police Act 2005.
[102] Amended by Serious Organised Crime and Police Act 2005.
[103] Amended by Serious Organised Crime and Police Act 2005.

(a) on summary conviction, to imprisonment for a term not exceeding six months or to a fine not exceeding the statutory maximum or to both, or

(b) on conviction on indictment, to imprisonment for a term not exceeding five years or to a fine or to both.

(7) The notice period is the period of seven working days starting with the first working day after the nominated officer makes the disclosure.

(8) The moratorium period is the period of 31 days starting with the day on which the nominated officer is given notice that consent to the doing of the act is refused.

(9) A working day is a day other than a Saturday, a Sunday, Christmas Day, Good Friday or a day which is a bank holiday under the Banking and Financial Dealings Act 1971 (c. 80) in the part of the United Kingdom in which the nominated officer is when he gives the appropriate consent.

(10) References to a prohibited act are to an act mentioned in section 327(1), 328(1) or 329(1) (as the case may be).

(11) A nominated officer is a person nominated to receive disclosures under section 338.

337 Protected disclosures

(1) A disclosure which satisfies the following three conditions is not to be taken to breach any restriction on the disclosure of information (however imposed).

(2) The first condition is that the information or other matter disclosed came to the person making the disclosure (the discloser) in the course of his trade, profession, business or employment.

(3) The second condition is that the information or other matter—

(a) causes the discloser to know or suspect, or

(b) gives him reasonable grounds for knowing or suspecting, that another person is engaged in money laundering.

(4) The third condition is that the disclosure is made to a constable, a customs officer or a nominated officer as soon as is practicable after the information or other matter comes to the discloser.

[(4A) Where a disclosure consists of a disclosure protected under subsection (1) and a disclosure of either or both of—

(a) the identity of the other person mentioned in subsection (3), and

(b) the whereabouts of property forming the subject-matter of the money laundering that the discloser knows or suspects, or has reasonable grounds for knowing or suspecting, that other person to be engaged in,

the disclosure of the thing mentioned in paragraph (a) or (b) (as well as the disclosure protected under subsection (1) is not to be taken to breach any restriction on the disclosure of information (however imposed).]

(5) A disclosure to a nominated officer is a disclosure which—

(a) is made to a person nominated by the discloser's employer to receive disclosures under [section 330 or][104] this section, and

(b) is made in the course of the discloser's employment [...][105]

---

[104] Amended by Serious Organised Crime and Police Act 2005.
[105] Repealed by Serious Organised Crime and Police Act 2005.

338 Authorised disclosures

(1)   For the purposes of this Part a disclosure is authorised if—

    (a) it is a disclosure to a constable, a customs officer or a nominated officer by the alleged offender that property is criminal property,

    (b) [...][106] and

    (c) the first[, second or third][107] condition set out below is satisfied.

(2)   The first condition is that the disclosure is made before the alleged offender does the prohibited act.

[(2A) The second condition is that—

    (a) the disclosure is made while the alleged offender is doing the prohibited act,

    (b) he began to do the act at a time when, because he did not then know or suspect that the property constituted or represented a person's benefit from criminal conduct, the act was not a prohibited act, and

    (c) the disclosure is made on his own initiative and as soon as is practicable after he first knows or suspects that the property constitutes or represents a person's benefit from criminal conduct.][108]

(3)   The [third][109] condition is that—

    (a) the disclosure is made after the alleged offender does the prohibited act,

    (b) there is a good reason for his failure to make the disclosure before he did the act, and

    (c) the disclosure is made on his own initiative and as soon as it is practicable for him to make it.

(4)   An authorised disclosure is not to be taken to breach any restriction on the disclosure of information (however imposed).

(5)   A disclosure to a nominated officer is a disclosure which—

    (a) is made to a person nominated by the alleged offender's employer to receive authorised disclosures, and

    (b) is made in the course of the alleged offender's employment [...][110]

(6)   References to the prohibited act are to an act mentioned in section 327(1), 328(1) or 329(1) (as the case may be).

339 Form and manner of disclosures

(1)   The Secretary of State may by order prescribe the form and manner in which a disclosure under section 330, 331, 332 or 338 must be made.

[(1A) A person commits an offence if he makes a disclosure under section 330, 331, 332 or 338 otherwise than in the form prescribed under subsection (1) or otherwise than in the manner so prescribed.

(1B) But a person does not commit an offence under subsection (1A) if he has a reasonable excuse for making the disclosure otherwise than in the form prescribed under subsection (1) or (as the case may be) otherwise than in the manner so prescribed.

---

[106] Repealed by Serious Organised Crime and Police Act 2005.
[107] Amended by Serious Organised Crime and Police Act 2005.
[108] Inserted by Serious Organised Crime and Police Act 2005.
[109] Amended by Serious Organised Crime and Police Act 2005.
[110] Repealed by Serious Organised Crime and Police Act 2005.

(2)   The power under subsection (1) to prescribe the form in which a disclosure must be made includes power to provide for the form to include a request to a person making a disclosure that the person provide information specified or described in the form if he has not provided it in making the disclosure.

(3)   Where under subsection (2) a request is included in a form prescribed under subsection (1), the form must—

(a) state that there is no obligation to comply with the request, and

(b) explain the protection conferred by subsection (4) on a person who complies with the request.][111]

(4)   A disclosure made in pursuance of a request under subsection (2) is not to be taken to breach any restriction on the disclosure of information (however imposed). [...][112]

(7)   Subsection (2) does not apply to a disclosure made to a nominated officer.

[339A Threshold amounts

(1) This section applies for the purposes of sections 327(2C), 328(5) and 329(2C).

(2) The threshold amount for acts done by a deposit-taking body in operating an account is £250 unless a higher amount is specified under the following provisions of this section (in which event it is that higher amount).

(3) An officer of Revenue and Customs, or a constable, may specify the threshold amount for acts done by a deposit-taking body in operating an account—

(a) when he gives consent, or gives notice refusing consent, to the deposit-taking body's doing of an act mentioned in section 327(1), 328(1) or 329(1) in opening, or operating, the account or a related account, or

(b) on a request from the deposit-taking body.

(4) Where the threshold amount for acts done in operating an account is specified under subsection (3) or this subsection, an officer of Revenue and Customs, or a constable, may vary the amount (whether on a request from the deposit-taking body or otherwise) by specifying a different amount.

(5) Different threshold amounts may be specified under subsections (3) and (4) for different acts done in operating the same account.

(6) The amount specified under subsection (3) or (4) as the threshold amount for acts done in operating an account must, when specified, not be less than the amount specified in subsection (2).

(7) The Secretary of State may by order vary the amount for the time being specified in subsection (2).

(8) For the purposes of this section, an account is related to another if each is maintained with the same deposit-taking body and there is a person who, in relation to each account, is the person or one of the persons entitled to instruct the body as respects the operation of the account.][113]

---

[111] Amended by Serious Organised Crime and Police Act 2005.
[112] Repealed by Serious Organised Crime and Police Act 2005.
[113] Inserted by Serious Organised Crime and Police Act 2005.

340 Interpretation

(1) This section applies for the purposes of this Part.

(2) Criminal conduct is conduct which—
- (a) constitutes an offence in any part of the United Kingdom, or
- (b) would constitute an offence in any part of the United Kingdom if it occurred there.

(3) Property is criminal property if—
- (a) it constitutes a person's benefit from criminal conduct or it represents such a benefit (in whole or part and whether directly or indirectly), and
- (b) the alleged offender knows or suspects that it constitutes or represents such a benefit.

(4) It is immaterial—
- (a) who carried out the conduct;
- (b) who benefited from it;
- (c) whether the conduct occurred before or after the passing of this Act.

(5) A person benefits from conduct if he obtains property as a result of or in connection with the conduct.

(6) If a person obtains a pecuniary advantage as a result of or in connection with conduct, he is to be taken to obtain as a result of or in connection with the conduct a sum of money equal to the value of the pecuniary advantage.

(7) References to property or a pecuniary advantage obtained in connection with conduct include references to property or a pecuniary advantage obtained in both that connection and some other.

(8) If a person benefits from conduct his benefit is the property obtained as a result of or in connection with the conduct.

(9) Property is all property wherever situated and includes—
- (a) money;
- (b) all forms of property, real or personal, heritable or moveable;
- (c) things in action and other intangible or incorporeal property.

(10) The following rules apply in relation to property—
- (a) property is obtained by a person if he obtains an interest in it;
- (b) references to an interest, in relation to land in England and Wales or Northern Ireland, are to any legal estate or equitable interest or power;
- (c) references to an interest, in relation to land in Scotland, are to any estate, interest, servitude or other heritable right in or over land, including a heritable security;
- (d) references to an interest, in relation to property other than land, include references to a right (including a right to possession).

(11) Money laundering is an act which—
- (a) constitutes an offence under section 327, 328 or 329,
- (b) constitutes an attempt, conspiracy or incitement to commit an offence specified in paragraph (a),
- (c) constitutes aiding, abetting, counselling or procuring the commission of an offence specified in paragraph (a), or
- (d) would constitute an offence specified in paragraph (a), (b) or (c) if done in the United Kingdom.

(12) For the purposes of a disclosure to a nominated officer—

    (a) references to a person's employer include any body, association or organisation (including a voluntary organisation) in connection with whose activities the person exercises a function (whether or not for gain or reward), and

    (b) references to employment must be construed accordingly.

(13) References to a constable include references to a person authorised for the purposes of this Part by the Director General of the [Serious Organised Crime Agency.][114]

[(14) "Deposit-taking body" means—

    (a) a business which engages in the activity of accepting deposits, or

    (b) the National Savings Bank.][115]

---

[114] Amended by Serious Organised Crime and Police Act 2005.
[115] Inserted by Serious Organised Crime and Police Act 2005.

Criminal Procedure Rules on Case Management (Parts 1 and 3)

PART 1
THE OVERRIDING OBJECTIVE

Contents of this Part

rule 1.1 The overriding objective
rule 1.2 The duty of the participants in a criminal case
rule 1.3 The application by the court of the overriding objective

1.1 The overriding objective

(1) The overriding objective of this new code is that criminal cases be dealt with justly.
(2) Dealing with a criminal case justly includes—
    (a) acquitting the innocent and convicting the guilty;
    (b) dealing with the prosecution and the defence fairly;
    (c) recognising the rights of a defendant, particularly those under Article 6 of the European Convention on Human Rights;
    (d) respecting the interests of witnesses, victims and jurors and keeping them informed of the progress of the case;
    (e) dealing with the case efficiently and expeditiously;
    (f) ensuring that appropriate information is available to the court when bail and sentence are considered; and
    (g) dealing with the case in ways that take into account—
        (i)   the gravity of the offence alleged,
        (ii) the complexity of what is in issue,
        (iii) the severity of the consequences for the defendant and others affected, and
        (iv) the needs of other cases.

1.2 The duty of the participants in a criminal case

(1) Each participant, in the conduct of each case, must—

    (a) prepare and conduct the case in accordance with the overriding objective;

    (b) comply with these Rules, practice directions and directions made by the court; and

    (c) at once inform the court and all parties of any significant failure (whether or not that participant is responsible for that failure) to take any procedural step required by these Rules, any practice direction or any direction of the court. A failure is significant if it might hinder the court in furthering the overriding objective.

(2) Anyone involved in any way with a criminal case is a participant in its conduct for the purposes of this rule.

1.3 The application by the court of the overriding objective

The court must further the overriding objective in particular when—

(a) exercising any power given to it by legislation (including these Rules);
(b) applying any practice direction; or
(c) interpreting any rule or practice direction.

PART 3
CASE MANAGEMENT

Contents of this Part

rule 3.1   The scope of this Part
rule 3.2   The duty of the court
rule 3.3   The duty of the parties
rule 3.4   Case progression officers and their duties
rule 3.5   The court's case management powers
rule 3.6   Application to vary a direction
rule 3.7   Agreement to vary a time limit fixed by a direction
rule 3.8   Case preparation and progression
rule 3.9   Readiness for trial or appeal
rule 3.10 Conduct of a trial or an appeal
rule 3.11 Case management forms and records

3.1 The scope of this Part

This Part applies to the management of each case in a magistrates' court and in the Crown Court (including an appeal to the Crown Court) until the conclusion of that case.

[Note. Rules that apply to procedure in the Court of Appeal are in Parts 65 to 73 of these Rules.]

3.2 The duty of the court

(1) The court must further the overriding objective by actively managing the case.
(2) Active case management includes—
    (a) the early identification of the real issues;
    (b) the early identification of the needs of witnesses;
    (c) achieving certainty as to what must be done, by whom, and when, in particular by the early setting of a timetable for the progress of the case;
    (d) monitoring the progress of the case and compliance with directions;
    (e) ensuring that evidence, whether disputed or not, is presented in the shortest and clearest way;
    (f) discouraging delay, dealing with as many aspects of the case as possible on the same occasion, and avoiding unnecessary hearings;
    (g) encouraging the participants to co-operate in the progression of the case; and
    (h) making use of technology.
(3) The court must actively manage the case by giving any direction appropriate to the needs of that case as early as possible.

3.3 The duty of the parties

Each party must—

(a) actively assist the court in fulfilling its duty under rule 3.2, without or if necessary with a direction; and

(b) apply for a direction if needed to further the overriding objective.

3.4 Case progression officers and their duties

(1) At the beginning of the case each party must, unless the court otherwise directs—
    (a) nominate an individual responsible for progressing that case; and
    (b) tell other parties and the court who he is and how to contact him.

(2) In fulfilling its duty under rule 3.2, the court must where appropriate—
    (a) nominate a court officer responsible for progressing the case; and
    (b) make sure the parties know who he is and how to contact him.

(3) In this Part a person nominated under this rule is called a case progression officer.

(4) A case progression officer must—

    (a) monitor compliance with directions;

    (b) make sure that the court is kept informed of events that may affect the progress of that case;

    (c) make sure that he can be contacted promptly about the case during ordinary business hours;

    (d) act promptly and reasonably in response to communications about the case; and

    (e) if he will be unavailable, appoint a substitute to fulfil his duties and inform the other case progression officers.

3.5 The court's case management powers

(1) In fulfilling its duty under rule 3.2 the court may give any direction and take any step actively to manage a case unless that direction or step would be inconsistent with legislation, including these Rules.

(2) In particular, the court may—
    (a) nominate a judge, magistrate, justices' clerk or assistant to a justices' clerk to manage the case;
    (b) give a direction on its own initiative or on application by a party;
    (c) ask or allow a party to propose a direction;
    (d) for the purpose of giving directions, receive applications and representations by letter, by telephone or by any other means of electronic communication, and conduct a hearing by such means;
    (e) give a direction without a hearing;
    (f) fix, postpone, bring forward, extend or cancel a hearing;
    (g) shorten or extend (even after it has expired) a time limit fixed by a direction;
    (h) require that issues in the case should be determined separately, and decide in what order they will be determined; and
    (i) specify the consequences of failing to comply with a direction.

(3) A magistrates' court may give a direction that will apply in the Crown Court if the case is to continue there.

(4) The Crown Court may give a direction that will apply in a magistrates' court if the case is to continue there.

(5) Any power to give a direction under this Part includes a power to vary or revoke that direction.

[Note. Depending upon the nature of a case and the stage that it has reached, its progress may be affected by other Criminal Procedure Rules and by other legislation. The note at the end of this Part lists other rules and legislation that may apply.]

3.6 Application to vary a direction

(1) A party may apply to vary a direction if—
   (a) the court gave it without a hearing;
   (b) the court gave it at a hearing in his absence; or
   (c) circumstances have changed.
(2) A party who applies to vary a direction must—

   (a) apply as soon as practicable after he becomes aware of the grounds for doing so; and

   (b) give as much notice to the other parties as the nature and urgency of his application permits.

3.7 Agreement to vary a time limit fixed by a direction

(1) The parties may agree to vary a time limit fixed by a direction, but only if—
   (a) the variation will not—
      (i) affect the date of any hearing that has been fixed, or
      (ii) significantly affect the progress of the case in any other way;
   (b) the court has not prohibited variation by agreement; and
   (c) the court's case progression officer is promptly informed.
(2) The court's case progression officer must refer the agreement to the court if he doubts the condition in paragraph (1)(a) is satisfied.

3.8 Case preparation and progression

(1) At every hearing, if a case cannot be concluded there and then the court must give directions so that it can be concluded at the next hearing or as soon as possible after that.
(2) At every hearing the court must, where relevant—
   (a) if the defendant is absent, decide whether to proceed nonetheless;
   (b) take the defendant's plea (unless already done) or if no plea can be taken then find out whether the defendant is likely to plead guilty or not guilty;
   (c) set, follow or revise a timetable for the progress of the case, which may include a timetable for any hearing including the trial or (in the Crown Court) the appeal;
   (d) in giving directions, ensure continuity in relation to the court and to the parties' representatives where that is appropriate and practicable; and
   (e) where a direction has not been complied with, find out why, identify who was responsible, and take appropriate action.

3.9 Readiness for trial or appeal

(1) This rule applies to a party's preparation for trial or (in the Crown Court) appeal, and in this rule and rule 3.10 trial includes any hearing at which evidence will be introduced.
(2) In fulfilling his duty under rule 3.3, each party must—
   (a) comply with directions given by the court;

(b) take every reasonable step to make sure his witnesses will attend when they are needed;

(c) make appropriate arrangements to present any written or other material; and

(d) promptly inform the court and the other parties of anything that may—

    (i) affect the date or duration of the trial or appeal, or

    (ii) significantly affect the progress of the case in any other way.

(3) The court may require a party to give a certificate of readiness.

3.10 Conduct of a trial or an appeal

In order to manage the trial or (in the Crown Court) appeal, the court may require a party to identify—

(a) which witnesses he intends to give oral evidence;

(b) the order in which he intends those witnesses to give their evidence;

(c) whether he requires an order compelling the attendance of a witness;

(d) what arrangements, if any, he proposes to facilitate the giving of evidence by a witness;

(e) what arrangements, if any, he proposes to facilitate the participation of any other person, including the defendant;

(f) what written evidence he intends to introduce;

(g) what other material, if any, he intends to make available to the court in the presentation of the case;

(h) whether he intends to raise any point of law that could affect the conduct of the trial or appeal; and

(i) what timetable he proposes and expects to follow.

3.11 Case management forms and records

(1) The case management forms set out in the Practice Direction must be used, and where there is no form then no specific formality is required.

(2) The court must make available to the parties a record of directions given.

Note. Case management may be affected by the following other rules and legislation:

Criminal Procedure Rules
> *Parts 10.4 and 27.2: reminders of right to object to written evidence being read at trial*
> *Part 12.2: time for first appearance of accused sent for trial*
> *Part 13: dismissal of charges sent or transferred to the Crown Court*
> *Part 14: the indictment*
> *Part 15: preparatory hearings in serious fraud and other complex or lengthy cases*
> *Parts 21–26: the rules that deal with disclosure*
> *Parts 27–36: the rules that deal with evidence*
> *Part 37: summary trial*
> *Part 38: trial of children and young persons*
> *Part 39: trial on indictment*

Regulations
> *Prosecution of Offences (Custody Time Limits) Regulations 1987*
> *Criminal Justice Act 1987 (Notice of Transfer) Regulations 1988*
> *Criminal Justice Act 1991 (Notice of Transfer) Regulations 1992*

Criminal Procedure and Investigations Act 1996 (Defence Disclosure Time Limits) Regulations 1997

Crime and Disorder Act 1998 (Service of Prosecution Evidence) Regulations 2000

Provisions of Acts of Parliament

Sections 5, 10 and 18, Magistrates' Courts Act 1980: powers to adjourn hearings

Sections 128 and 129, Magistrates' Courts Act 1980: remand in custody by magistrates' courts

Part 1, Criminal Procedure and Investigations Act 1996: disclosure

Schedule 2, Criminal Procedure and Investigations Act 1996: use of witness statements at trial

Section 2, Administration of Justice (Miscellaneous Provisions) Act 1933: procedural conditions for trial in the Crown Court

Section 6, Magistrates' Courts Act 1980: committal for trial

Section 4, Criminal Justice Act 1987: section 53, Criminal Justice Act 1991: section 51, Crime and Disorder Act 1998: other procedures by which a case reaches the Crown Court

Section 7, Criminal Justice Act 1987; Parts III and IV, Criminal Procedure and Investigations Act 1996: pre-trial and preparatory hearings in the Crown Court

Section 9, Criminal Justice Act 1967: proof by written witness statement]

Preparatory Hearings

A. CRIMINAL JUSTICE ACT 1987

Power to order preparatory hearing

7.— (1) Where it appears to a judge of the Crown Court that the evidence on an indictment reveals a case of fraud of such seriousness [or][1] complexity that substantial benefits are likely to accrue from a hearing (in this Act referred to as a 'preparatory hearing') before the [time the][2] jury are sworn, for the purpose of—

[(a) identifying issues which are likely to be material to the determinations and findings which are likely to be required during the trial, (b) if there is to be a jury, assisting their comprehension of those issues and expediting the proceedings before them, (c) determining an application to which section 45 of the Criminal Justice Act 2003 applies,][3]

(d) assisting the judge's management of the trial, [or

(e) considering questions as to the severance or joinder of charges,][4] he may order that such a hearing shall be held.

(2) A judge may make an order under subsection (1) above on the application either of the prosecution or of the person indicted or, if the indictment charges a number of persons, any of them, or of his own motion.

[(2A) The reference in subsection (1) above to the time when the jury are sworn includes the time when the jury would be sworn but for the making of an order under Part 7 of the Criminal Justice Act 2003.][5]

...

The preparatory hearing.

9.— (1) At the preparatory hearing the judge may exercise any of the powers specified in this section.

(2) The judge may adjourn a preparatory hearing from time to time.

---

[1] Amended by Criminal Justice and Public Order Act 1994.
[2] Inserted by Criminal Justice Act 2003.
[3] Amended by Criminal Justice Act 2003.
[4] Inserted by Criminal Justice Act 2003.
[5] Inserted by Criminal Justice Act 2003.

(3) He may determine—

(a) [...]⁶

[(aa) a question arising under section 6 of the Criminal Justice Act 1993 (relevance of external law to certain charges of conspiracy, attempt and incitement);]⁷

(b) any question as to the admissibility of evidence; and

(c) any other question of law relating to the case [; and

(d) any question as to the severance or joinder of charges.]⁸

(4) He may order the prosecution—

(a) to supply the court and the defendant or, if there is more than one, each of them with a statement (a 'case statement') of the following—

(i)   the principal facts of the prosecution case;

(ii) the witnesses who will speak to those facts;

(iii) any exhibits relevant to those facts;

(iv) any proposition of law on which the prosecution proposes to rely; and

(v)   the consequences in relation to any of the counts in the indictment that appear to the prosecution to flow from the matters stated in pursuance of sub-paragraphs (i) to (iv) above;

(b) to prepare their evidence and other explanatory material in such a form as appears to him to be likely to aid comprehension by [a]⁹ jury and to supply it in that form to the court and to the defendant or, if there is more than one, to each of them;

(c) to give the court and the defendant or, if there is more than one, each of them notice of documents the truth of the contents of which ought in the prosecution's view to be admitted and of any other matters which in their view ought to be agreed;

(d) to make any amendments of any case statement supplied in pursuance of an order under paragraph (a) above that appear to the court to be appropriate, having regard to objections made by the defendant or, if there is more than one, by any of them.

(5) Where—

(a) a judge has ordered the prosecution to supply a case statement; and

(b) the prosecution have complied with the order,

he may order the defendant or, if there is more than one, each of them—

(i)   [...]¹⁰

(ii) to give the court and the prosecution notice of any objections that he has to the case statement;

(iii) [...]¹¹

(iv) to give the court and the prosecution a notice stating the extent to which he agrees with the prosecution as to documents and other matters to which a notice under subsection (4)(c) above relates and the reason for any disagreement.

(6) [Criminal Procedure¹²] Rules may provide that except to the extent that disclosure is required—

---

⁶ Repealed by Criminal Justice Act 1988.   ⁷ Inserted by Criminal Justice Act 1993.
⁸ Inserted by Criminal Justice Act 2003.   ⁹ Amended by Criminal Justice Act 2003.
¹⁰ Repealed by Criminal Justice Act 2003.   ¹¹ Repealed by Criminal Justice Act 2003.
¹² Amended by SI 2004/2035.

(a) by [section 5(7) of the Criminal Procedure and Investigations Act 1996][13] (alibi); or

(b) by [such rules made by virtue of][14] section 81 of the Police and Criminal Evidence Act 1984 (expert evidence), a summary required by virtue of subsection (5) above need not disclose who will give evidence.

(7) A judge making an order under subsection (5) above shall warn the defendant or, if there is more than one, all of them of the possible consequence under section 10[...][15] below of not complying with it.

(8) If it appears to a judge that reasons given in pursuance of subsection (5)(iv) above are inadequate, he shall so inform the person giving them, and may require him to give further or better reasons.

(9) An order under this section may specify the time within which any specified requirement contained in it is to be complied with, but [Criminal Procedure][16] Rules may make provision as to the minimum or maximum time that may be specified for compliance.

(10) An order or ruling made [under this section][17] shall have effect during the trial, unless it appears to the judge, on application made to him during the trial, that the interests of justice require him to vary or discharge it.

(11) An appeal shall lie to the Court of Appeal from any order or ruling of a judge under subsection (3)(b)[, (c) or (d)][18] above, [from the refusal by a judge of an application to which section 45 of the Criminal Justice Act 2003 applies or from an order of a judge under section 43 or 44 of that Act which is made on the determination of such an application,][19] but only with the leave of the judge or of the Court of Appeal.

(12) Subject to rules of court made under section 53(1) of the Supreme Court Act 1981 (power by rules to distribute business of Court of Appeal between its civil and criminal divisions), the jurisdiction of the Court of Appeal under subsection (11) above shall be exercised by the criminal division of the court; and the reference in that subsection to the Court of Appeal shall be construed as a reference to that division.

(13) The judge may continue a preparatory hearing notwithstanding that leave to appeal has been granted under subsection (11) above, but [the preparatory hearing shall not be concluded][20] until after the appeal has been determined or abandoned.

(14) On the termination of the hearing of an appeal, the Court of Appeal may confirm, reverse or vary the decision appealed against.

---

[13] Amended by Criminal Procedure and Investigations Act 1996.
[14] Amended by SI 2004/2035.
[15] Repealed by Criminal Procedure and Investigations Act 1996.
[16] Amended by SI 2004/2035.
[17] Amended by Criminal Procedure and Investigations Act 1996.
[18] Amended by Criminal Justice Act 2003.
[19] Amended by Criminal Justice Act 2003.
[20] Amended by Criminal Justice Act 2003.

B. CRIMINAL PROCEDURE AND INVESTIGATIONS ACT 1996

Part III

Introduction

Introduction.

28.— (1) This Part applies in relation to an offence if—

  (a) [on or after the appointed day the accused is sent for trial for the offence concerned,][21]
  (b) proceedings for the trial on the charge concerned are transferred to the Crown Court on or after the appointed day, or
  (c) a bill of indictment relating to the offence is preferred on or after the appointed day under the authority of section 2(2)(b) of the Administration of Justice (Miscellaneous Provisions) Act 1933 (bill preferred by direction of Court of Appeal, or by direction or with consent of a judge).

(2) References in subsection (1) to the appointed day are to such day as is appointed for the purposes of this section by the Secretary of State by order.

(3) If an order under this section so provides, this Part applies only in relation to the Crown Court sitting at a place or places specified in the order.

(4) References in this Part to the prosecutor are to any person acting as prosecutor, whether an individual or a body.

Preparatory Hearings

Power to order preparatory hearing.

29.— (1) Where it appears to a judge of the Crown Court that an indictment reveals a case of such complexity, [a case of such seriousness][22] or a case whose trial is likely to be of such length, that substantial benefits are likely to accrue from a hearing—

  (a) before the [time when the][23] jury are sworn, and
  (b) for any of the purposes mentioned in subsection (2), he may order that such a hearing (in this Part referred to as a preparatory hearing) shall be held.

[(1A) A judge of the Crown Court may also order that a preparatory hearing shall be held if an application to which section 45 of the Criminal Justice Act 2003 applies (application for trial without jury) is made.][24]

[(1B) An order that a preparatory hearing shall be held must be made by a judge of the Crown Court in every case which (whether or not it falls within subsection (1) or (1A)) is a case in which at least one of the offences charged by the indictment against at least one of the persons charged is a terrorism offence.

(1C) An order that a preparatory hearing shall be held must also be made by a judge of the Crown court in every case which (whether or not it falls within subsection (1) or (1A)) is a case in which—

---

[21] Amended by Criminal Justice Act 2003.
[22] Inserted by Criminal Justice Act 2003.
[23] Amended by Criminal Justice Act 2003.
[24] Inserted by the Criminal Justice Act 2003.

(a) at least one of the offences charged by the indictment against at least one of the persons charged is an offence carrying a maximum of at least 10 years' imprisonment; and

(b) it appears to the judge that evidence on the indictment reveals that conduct in respect of which that offence is charged had a terrorist connection.][25]

(2) The purposes are those of—

[(a) identifying issues which are likely to be material to the determinations and findings which are likely to be required during the trial, (b) if there is to be a jury, assisting their comprehension of those issues and expediting the proceedings before them, (c) determining an application to which section 45 of the Criminal Justice Act 2003 applies,][26]

(d) assisting the judge's management of the trial.

[(e) considering questions as to the severance or joinder of charges.][27]

[(3) In a case in which it appears to a judge of the Crown Court that evidence on an indictment reveals a case of fraud of such seriousness or complexity as is mentioned in section 7 of the Criminal Justice Act 1987 (preparatory hearings in cases of serious or complex fraud)—

(a) the judge may make an order for a preparatory hearing under this section only if he is required to do so by subsection (1B) or (1C);

(b) before making an order in pursuance of either of those subsections, he must determine whether to make an order for a preparatory hearing under that section; and

(c) he is not required by either of those subsections to make an order for a preparatory hearing under this section if he determines that an order should be made for a preparatory hearing under that section;

and, in a case in which an order is made for a preparatory hearing under that section, requirements imposed by those subsections apply only if that order ceases to have effect.][28]

(4) [An order that a preparatory hearing shall be held may be made—][29]

(a) on the application of the prosecutor,

(b) on the application of the accused or, if there is more than one, any of them, or

(c) of the judge's own motion.

[(5) The reference in subsection (1)(a) to the time when the jury are sworn includes the time when the jury would be sworn but for the making of an order under Part 7 of the Criminal Justice Act 2003.][30]

[(6) In this section 'terrorism offence' means—

(a) an offence under section 11 or 12 of the Terrorism Act 2000 (c 11) (offences relating to proscribed organisations);

(b) an offence under any of sections 15 to 18 of that Act (offences relating to terrorist property);

(c) an offence under section 38B of that Act (failure to disclose information about acts of terrorism);

(d) an offence under section 54 of that Act (weapons training);

---

[25] Inserted by Terrorism Act 2006. [26] Inserted by Criminal Justice Act 2003.
[27] Inserted by Criminal Justice Act 2003. [28] Amended by Terrorism Act 2006.
[29] Amended by Terrorism Act 2006. [30] Inserted by Criminal Justice Act 2003.

(e) an offence under any of sections 56 to 59 of that Act (directing terrorism, possessing things and collecting information for the purposes of terrorism and inciting terrorism outside the United Kingdom);

(f) an offence in respect of which there is jurisdiction by virtue of section 62 of that Act (extra-territorial jurisdiction in respect of certain offences committed outside the United Kingdom for the purposes of terrorism etc);

(g) an offence under Part 1 of the Terrorism Act 2006 (miscellaneous terrorist related offences);

(h) conspiring or attempting to commit a terrorism offence;

(i) incitement to commit a terrorism offence.

(7) For the purposes of this section an offence carries a maximum of at least 10 years' imprisonment if—

(a) it is punishable, on conviction on indictment, with imprisonment; and

(b) the maximum term of imprisonment that may be imposed on conviction on indictment of that offence is 10 years or more or is imprisonment for life.

(8) For the purposes of this section conduct has a terrorist connection if it is or takes place in the course of an act of terrorism or is for the purposes of terrorism.

(9) In subsection (8) 'terrorism' has the same meaning as in the Terrorism Act 2000 (see section 1 of that Act).][31]

Start of trial and arraignment.

30. If a judge orders a preparatory hearing—

(a) the trial shall start with that hearing, and

(b) arraignment shall take place at the start of that hearing, unless it has taken place before then.

The preparatory hearing.

31.— (1) At the preparatory hearing the judge may exercise any of the powers specified in this section.

(2) The judge may adjourn a preparatory hearing from time to time.

(3) He may make a ruling as to—

(a) any question as to the admissibility of evidence

(b) any other question of law relating to the case.

[(c) any question as to the severance or joinder of charges.][32]

(4) He may order the prosecutor—

(a) to give the court and the accused or, if there is more than one, each of them a written statement (a case statement) of the matters falling within subsection (5)

(b) to prepare the prosecution evidence and any explanatory material in such a form as appears to the judge to be likely to aid comprehension by [a][33] jury and to give it in that form to the court and to the accused or, if there is more than one, to each of them

(c) to give the court and the accused or, if there is more than one, each of them written notice of documents the truth of the contents of which ought in the

---

[31] Inserted by Terrorism Act 2006.   [32] Inserted by Criminal Justice Act 2003.
[33] Amended by Criminal Justice Act 2003.

prosecutor's view to be admitted and of any other matters which in his view ought to be agreed

(d) to make any amendments of any case statement given in pursuance of an order under paragraph (a) that appear to the judge to be appropriate, having regard to objections made by the accused or, if there is more than one, by any of them.

(5) The matters referred to in subsection (4)(a) are—

(a) the principal facts of the case for the prosecution

(b) the witnesses who will speak to those facts

(c) any exhibits relevant to those facts

(d) any proposition of law on which the prosecutor proposes to rely

(e) the consequences in relation to any of the counts in the indictment that appear to the prosecutor to flow from the matters falling within paragraphs (a) to (d).

(6) Where a judge has ordered the prosecutor to give a case statement and the prosecutor has complied with the order, the judge may order the accused or, if there is more than one, each of them—

[…][34]

(b) to give the court and the prosecutor written notice of any objections that he has to the case statement

[…][35]

(7) Where a judge has ordered the prosecutor to give notice under subsection (4)(c) and the prosecutor has complied with the order, the judge may order the accused or, if there is more than one, each of them to give the court and the prosecutor a written notice stating—

(a) the extent to which he agrees with the prosecutor as to documents and other matters to which the notice under subsection (4)(c) relates, and

(b) the reason for any disagreement.

(8) A judge making an order under subsection (6) or (7) shall warn the accused or, if there is more than one, each of them of the possible consequence under section 34 of not complying with it.

(9) If it appears to a judge that reasons given in pursuance of subsection (7) are inadequate, he shall so inform the person giving them and may require him to give further or better reasons.

(10) An order under this section may specify the time within which any specified requirement contained in it is to be complied with.

(11) An order or ruling made under this section shall have effect throughout the trial, unless it appears to the judge on application made to him that the interests of justice require him to vary or discharge it.

Orders before preparatory hearing.

32.— (1) This section applies where—

(a) a judge orders a preparatory hearing, and

(b) he decides that any order which could be made under section 31(4) to (7) at the hearing should be made before the hearing.

(2) In such a case—

---

[34] Repealed by Criminal Justice Act 2003.   [35] Repealed by Criminal Justice Act 2003.

(a) he may make any such order before the hearing (or at the hearing), and

(b) section 31(4) to (11) shall apply accordingly.

[Criminal Procedure Rules.]³⁶

33.— (1) [Criminal Procedure]³⁷ Rules may provide that except to the extent that disclosure is required—

(a) by rules under section 81 of the Police and Criminal Evidence Act 1984 (expert evidence), or

(b) by section 5(7) of this Act, anything required to be given by an accused in pursuance of a requirement imposed under section 31 need not disclose who will give evidence.

(2) [Criminal Procedure]³⁸ Rules may make provision as to the minimum or maximum time that may be specified under section 31(10).

Later stages of trial.

34.— (1) Any party may depart from the case he disclosed in pursuance of a requirement imposed under section 31.

(2) Where—

(a) a party departs from the case he disclosed in pursuance of a requirement imposed under section 31, or

(b) a party fails to comply with such a requirement, the judge or, with the leave of the judge, any other party may make such comment as appears to the judge or the other party (as the case may be) to be appropriate and the jury [or, in the case of a trial without a jury, the judge]³⁹ may draw such inference as appears proper.

(3) In [doing anything under subsection (2) or in deciding whether to do anything under it]⁴⁰ the judge shall have regard—

(a) to the extent of the departure or failure, and

(b) to whether there is any justification for it.

(4) [Except as provided by this section, in the case of a trial with a jury]⁴¹ no part—

(a) of a statement given under section 31(6)(a), or

(b) of any other information relating to the case for the accused or, if there is more than one, the case for any of them, which was given in pursuance of a requirement imposed under section 31, may be disclosed at a stage in the trial after the jury have been sworn without the consent of the accused concerned.

Appeals

Appeals to Court of Appeal.

35.— (1) An appeal shall lie to the Court of Appeal from any ruling of a judge under section 31(3) [from the refusal by a judge of an application to which section 45 of the Criminal Justice Act 2003 applies or from an order of a judge under section 43

---

³⁶ Amended by Courts Act 2003.   ³⁷ Amended by Courts Act 2003.
³⁸ Amended by Courts Act 2003.   ³⁹ Inserted by Criminal Justice Act 2003.
⁴⁰ Amended by Criminal Justice Act 2003.
⁴¹ Amended by Criminal Justice Act 2003.

or 44 of that Act which is made on the determination of such an application,]42 but only with the leave of the judge or of the Court of Appeal.

(2) The judge may continue a preparatory hearing notwithstanding that leave to appeal has been granted under subsection (1), [the preparatory hearing shall not be concluded]43 until after the appeal has been determined or abandoned.

(3) On the termination of the hearing of an appeal, the Court of Appeal may confirm, reverse or vary the decision appealed against.

(4) Subject to rules of court made under section 53(1) of the Supreme Court Act 1981 (power by rules to distribute business of Court of Appeal between its civil and criminal divisions) —

    (a) the jurisdiction of the Court of Appeal under subsection (1) above shall be exercised by the criminal division of the court

    (b) references in this Part to the Court of Appeal shall be construed as references to that division.

Appeals to House of Lords.

36.— (1) ...

    (2) The judge may continue a preparatory hearing notwithstanding that leave to appeal has been granted under Part II of the Criminal Appeal Act 1968, but [the preparatory hearing shall not be concluded]44 until after the appeal has been determined or abandoned.

Reporting restrictions

Restrictions on reporting.

37.— (1) Except as provided by this section—

    (a) no written report of proceedings falling within subsection (2) shall be published in [the United Kingdom]45

    (b) no report of proceedings falling within subsection (2) shall be included in a relevant programme for reception in [the United Kingdom.]46

    (2) The following proceedings fall within this subsection—

    (a) a preparatory hearing

    (b) an application for leave to appeal in relation to such a hearing

    (c) an appeal in relation to such a hearing.

    (3) The judge dealing with a preparatory hearing may order that subsection (1) shall not apply, or shall not apply to a specified extent, to a report of—

    (a) the preparatory hearing, or

    (b) an application to the judge for leave to appeal to the Court of Appeal under section 35(1) in relation to the preparatory hearing.

---

42 Inserted by Criminal Justice Act 2003.   43 Inserted by Criminal Justice Act 2003.
44 Inserted by Criminal justice Act 2003.   45 Amended by Criminal Justice Act 2003.
46 Amended by Criminal Justice Act 2003.

(4) The Court of Appeal may order that subsection (1) shall not apply, or shall not apply to a specified extent, to a report of—

(a) an appeal to the Court of Appeal under section 35(1) in relation to a preparatory hearing,

(b) an application to that Court for leave to appeal to it under section 35(1) in relation to a preparatory hearing, or

(c) an application to that Court for leave to appeal to the House of Lords under Part II of the Criminal Appeal Act 1968 in relation to a preparatory hearing.

(5) The House of Lords may order that subsection (1) shall not apply, or shall not apply to a specified extent, to a report of—

(a) an appeal to that House under Part II of the Criminal Appeal Act 1968 in relation to a preparatory hearing, or

(b) an application to that House for leave to appeal to it under Part II of the Criminal Appeal Act 1968 in relation to a preparatory hearing.

(6) Where there is only one accused and he objects to the making of an order under subsection (3), (4) or (5) the judge or the Court of Appeal or the House of Lords shall make the order if (and only if) satisfied after hearing the representations of the accused that it is in the interests of justice to do so and if the order is made it shall not apply to the extent that a report deals with any such objection or representations.

(7) Where there are two or more accused and one or more of them objects to the making of an order under subsection (3), (4) or (5) the judge or the Court of Appeal or the House of Lords shall make the order if (and only if) satisfied after hearing the representations of each of the accused that it is in the interests of justice to do so and if the order is made it shall not apply to the extent that a report deals with any such objection or representations.

(8) Subsection (1) does not apply to—

(a) the publication of a report of a preparatory hearing,

(b) the publication of a report of an appeal in relation to a preparatory hearing or of an application for leave to appeal in relation to such a hearing,

(c) the inclusion in a relevant programme of a report of a preparatory hearing, or

(d) the inclusion in a relevant programme of a report of an appeal in relation to a preparatory hearing or of an application for leave to appeal in relation to such a hearing, at the conclusion of the trial of the accused or of the last of the accused to be tried.

(9) Subsection (1) does not apply to a report which contains only one or more of the following matters—

(a) the identity of the court and the name of the judge

(b) the names, ages, home addresses and occupations of the accused and witnesses

(c) the offence or offences, or a summary of them, with which the accused is or are charged

(d) the names of counsel and solicitors in the proceedings

(e) where the proceedings are adjourned, the date and place to which they are adjourned

(f) any arrangements as to bail

[(g) whether a right to representation funded by the Legal Services Commission as part of the Criminal Defence Service was granted to the accused or any of the accused.]⁴⁷

(10) The addresses that may be published or included in a relevant programme under subsection (9) are addresses—

(a) at any relevant time, and

(b) at the time of their publication or inclusion in a relevant programme
    and 'relevant time' here means a time when events giving rise to the charges to which the proceedings relate occurred.

(11) Nothing in this section affects any prohibition or restriction imposed by virtue of any other enactment on a publication or on matter included in a programme.

(12) In this section—

(a) 'publish', in relation to a report, means publish the report, either by itself or as part of a newspaper or periodical, for distribution to the public

(b) expressions cognate with 'publish' shall be construed accordingly

(c) 'relevant programme' means a programme included in a programme service, within the meaning of the Broadcasting Act 1990.

Offences in connection with reporting.

38.— (1) If a report is published or included in a relevant programme in contravention of section 37 each of the following persons is guilty of an offence—

(a) in the case of a publication of a written report as part of a newspaper or periodical, any proprietor, editor or publisher of the newspaper or periodical

(b) in the case of a publication of a written report otherwise than as part of a newspaper or periodical, the person who publishes it

(c) in the case of the inclusion of a report in a relevant programme, any body corporate which is engaged in providing the service in which the programme is included and any person having functions in relation to the programme corresponding to those of an editor of a newspaper.

(2) A person guilty of an offence under this section is liable on summary conviction to a fine of an amount not exceeding level 5 on the standard scale.

(3) Proceedings for an offence under this section shall not be instituted in England and Wales otherwise than by or with the consent of the Attorney General.

[(3A) Proceedings for an offence under this section shall not be instituted in Northern Ireland otherwise than by or with the consent of the Attorney General for Northern Ireland.]⁴⁸

(4) Subsection (12) of section 37 applies for the purposes of this section as it applies for the purposes of that.

---

⁴⁷ Inserted by Access to Justice Act 1999. ⁴⁸ Inserted by Criminal Justice Act 2003.

APPENDIX 9

Sample Indictments

A. FRAUD BY FALSE REPRESENTATION

Statement of Offence

FRAUD, contrary to section 1 of the Fraud Act 2006.

Particulars of Offence

JOHN SMITH, on the... day of..., 20 ..., dishonestly made a false representation, in that he... , and intended by making the representation to make a gain for himself or another or to cause loss to another or to expose another to a risk of loss.

B. FRAUD BY FAILING TO DISCLOSE INFORMATION

Statement of Offence

FRAUD, contrary to section 1 of the Fraud Act 2006.

Particulars of Offence

JOHN SMITH, on the... day of..., 20 ..., dishonestly failed to disclose to another person, namely, David Jones, information which he was under a legal duty to disclose, namely,..., and intended by failing to disclose the information to make gain for himself or another or to cause loss to another or to expose another to a risk of loss.

C. FRAUD BY ABUSE OF POSITION

Statement of Offence

FRAUD, contrary to section 1 of the Fraud Act 2006.

Particulars of Offence

JOHN SMITH, on the... day of..., 20 ..., occupying a position, namely,..., in which he was expected to safeguard, or not to act against, the financial interests of David Jones dishonestly abused that position by... and intended by means of the abuse of that position to make a gain for himself or another or to cause loss to another or to expose another to a risk of loss.

D. POSSESSION OR CONTROL OF ARTICLES FOR USE IN FRAUDS

Statement of Offence

POSSESSION OF AN ARTICLE FOR USE IN FRAUD, contrary to section 6(1) of the Fraud Act 2006.

Particulars of Offence

JOHN SMITH, on the... day of..., 20 ..., had in his possession or under his control an article, namely,..., for use in the course of or in connection with fraud.

E. MAKING OR SUPPLYING ARTICLES FOR USE IN FRAUDS

Statement of Offence

MAKING OR SUPPLYING AN ARTICLE FOR USE IN FRAUD, contrary to section 7(1) of the Fraud Act 2006.

Particulars of Offence

JOHN SMITH, on the... day of..., 20 ..., made [adapted] [supplied] [offered to supply] an article, namely,..., [knowing that it was designed or adapted for use in the course of or in connection with fraud] OR [intending it to be used to commit or assist in the commission of fraud].

F. OBTAINING SERVICES DISHONESTLY

Statement of Offence

OBTAINING SERVICES DISHONESTLY, contrary to section 11(1) of the Fraud Act 2006.

Particulars of Offence

JOHN SMITH, on the... day of..., 20 ..., obtained a service, namely,..., for himself [another] by a dishonest act, namely,..., and the service was made available on the basis that payment had been [was being] [would be] made for [in respect of] it and he obtained it without any payment having been made for [in respect of] it, and when he obtained it he knew that it was being made available on the basis described above [might be made available on the basis described above] but he intended that payment would not be made [would not be made in full].

G. PARTICIPATING IN FRAUDULENT BUSINESS CARRIED ON BY A SOLE TRADER

Statement of Offence

PARTICIPATING IN FRAUDULENT BUSINESS CARRIED ON BY A SOLE TRADER, contrary to section 9(1) of the Fraud Act 2006.

Particulars of Offence

JOHN SMITH, a person outside the reach of section 458 of the Companies Act 1985 and Article 451 of the Companies (Northern Ireland) Order 1986, between the 1st November 2007 and 23rd January 2008 was knowingly a party to the carrying on of a business, namely..., which was carried on with intent to defraud creditors of any person [for a fraudulent purpose, namely...].

Index

Gain
  common element of various
    offences, 2.15–2.17
  false accounting, 8.21–8.23
  intention, 2.25–2.27
Gambling swindles, 3.74
Going equipped, 4.08–4.11
Ghosh test
  common element of various
    offences, 2.04–2.10
  criticisms of new law, 8.13
  fraudulent trading by sole trader, 5.41
  human rights, 8.14

Half-truths, 2.42
Human rights
  limitations on use of conspiracy, 3.50
  retention of common law conspiracy,
    1.33
  tax evasion, 8.49
  theft under retained law, 8.14–8.16

Inchoate offences
  articles for use in fraud
    making or supplying, 4.34–4.37
    possession, 4.15–4.33
    scope, 4.12–4.14
  attempts
    false representation, 2.29
    general requirements, 4.02–4.07
  going equipped, 4.08–4.11
  overview, 4.01
Indictments, App.9
Insider dealing, 1.44
Intellectual property
  conspiracy to defraud, 3.70
  retention of existing law, 1.44, 8.58
Intention
  common element of various
    offences, 2.13–2.14
  defined, 2.23–2.27
  false representation, 2.46–2.49
  fraudulent trading by sole trader, 5.52
  obtaining services dishonestly, 6.29–6.32
  statutory conspiracy, 3.09–3.11
  theft under retained law, 8.08–8.09

Jurisdiction
  classification of offences, 7.01
  conspiracy to defraud, 7.03
  relevant events, 7.02
Jury trials, 9.50–9.54

Knowledge
  failure to disclose information, 2.62–2.63
  fraudulent trading by sole trader, 5.42–5.51
  statutory conspiracy, 3.17–3.18

Loans, 3.88–3.89
'Long firm frauds', 3.73
Loss
  appropriation under retained law of
    theft, 8.03
  common element of various
    offences, 2.15–2.17
  false accounting, 8.21–8.23
  intention, 2.25–2.27

Market practices
  failure to disclose information, 2.57
  retention of existing law, 1.44, 8.58
Maximum penalties, 7.18–7.19
Mens rea
  false accounting, 8.21
  false representation, 1.26–1.27, 2.28
  possession of articles for fraud, 4.22–4.25
  statutory conspiracy
    abuse of position, 3.26–3.27
    failure to disclose
      information, 3.22–3.25
    false representation, 3.20–3.21
    intention, 3.09–3.11
    knowledge, 3.17–3.18
    recklessness, 3.14–3.16
    strict liability, 3.12–3.13
  theft under retained law, 8.08–8.09
Misrepresentation. *see* False representation
Money laundering
  conspiracy, 8.39–8.43
  principal offences, 8.31–8.38
Money transfers, 3.88–3.89

New offences
  articles for use in fraud, 1.29
  business fraud, 5.01–5.04
  confidential information, 2.21–2.22
  dishonestly obtaining services, 1.26–1.27
  fraudulent trading by sole trader, 1.30–1.31
  scope, 1.22–1.27

Obtaining services dishonestly
  distinguishing elements, 6.03–6.07
  essential ingredients
    dishonesty, 6.22–6.24
    intention not to pay, 6.29–6.32
    key summary, 6.33
    'services', 6.25–6.28
  established principles
    continuous offences, 6.47
    key summary, 6.48–6.50
    'services', 6.35–6.43
    services obtained by another, 6.44
    unlawful services, 6.45–6.46
  general requirements, 6.01
  inadequacies of previous offence, 6.08–6.12

Lightning Source UK Ltd.
Milton Keynes UK
UKHW02f1027200318

319728UK00003B/283/P